The Only Ticket
Off the Island

The Only
TICKET
Off the Island

Gare Joyce

AUGUST 1990
THE DANFORTH

LESTER
&ORPEN
DENNYS
PUBLISHERS

FIRST EDITION

Canadian Cataloguing in Publication Data

Joyce, Gare
  The only ticket off the island

ISBN 0-88619-324-9 (bound) ISBN 0-88619-326-5 (pbk.)

1. Baseball - Dominican Republic. 2. Baseball - Social aspects - Dominican Republic. 3. Toronto Blue Jays (Baseball Team). I. Title.

GV863.29.D65J68 1990   796.357'097293   C90-093280-5

Cover design by Pam Pfohl

Printed and bound in Canada for

Lester & Orpen Dennys Limited
78 Sullivan Street
Toronto, Canada
M5T 1C1

Dedication

To Sydney and Ellen (wife and child)
For patience and tolerance
and
To Rita and Toby (mother and father)
For support and enthusiasm

Contents

Author's Note

My conversations with the Dominican people, ballplayers and others, were usually in Spanish, combined with a smattering of English. I have translated fairly freely where needed. What appears in quotation marks here reflects as accurately as possible what was said.

Most of the events described in this book took place from November '88 through January '89. Some scenes are set earlier. This book is bound, therefore, to be overtaken somewhat by events—players are traded from team to team, some make gains, a few take losses, and others retire. For instance, José De León is a much more respected pitcher today than he was in November '88. All I can suggest is that you take yourself back to that winter, sit in the stands, and watch what happens.

G.J.

Acknowledgements

This book began by being impossible. Many people told me so. Let me begin by thanking the naysayers—you know who you are—because the Irish in me thrives on adversity. With the help of close friends this book became merely improbable. The aid of a few heavyweights made it only unlikely. Others pitched in, and *The Only Ticket Off the Island* progressed: doubtful, shaky, chancy, possible, likely, probable, real, and finally, on the shelves. Where the people whose names follow fit in the big picture, only they can tell. Thanks to all.

My agent, David Johnston, for grace under pressure; Paul Williams, who first assigned me to the Dominican; Epy Guerrero, who has always been a gracious host; Manolo the Santo Domingo cab-driver, for guidance; Roosevelt Comarazamy; Susan Haldane, who aided with research; Heinz Avigdor and Tracie Tighe, for readings; Davids—Hayes and Lees respectively—for sage counsel; Dr. Joe Visicale, for medical attention; the Second Cup, for coffee; teachers along the way, including Carol Allen, Joan Donaldson, Paul Nowack, and Messrs. Rempel, Demuth, and Kofsky; Sydney and Ellen and my parents, for everything.

ix

x

And finally, special mention for the staff at Lester & Orpen Dennys, who have been helpful throughout, and for my editor, Kirsten Hanson, who has endured all my writerly eccentricity.

G.J.
March 1990

Introduction

Long ago, when the British and the Americans ventured to the islands in the Caribbean, they brought with them the bat-and-ball games favoured in their homelands. The native people of the islands quickly adopted these games as their own. On the islands where the British suffered the heat with stiff upper lips, cricket developed into the sport of choice. So it remains in Jamaica, Barbados, Trinidad, and other regions in the British West Indies. On the islands where the Americans excercised influence, islands such as Cuba, Puerto Rico, and the Dominican Republic, baseball became a national passion. While it is true that these islands have never joined the colonist nations in the front ranks of global affairs, the islanders have managed to threaten the traditional powers on the cricket pitches and the baseball diamonds.

Recently, there was news of a shocking event in cricket—the British managed to defeat a West Indian side in a test match. This was considered an enormous upset. The British hadn't beaten the Caribbean stars in years. The West Indian teams were at the game's vanguard. Cricket had been a staid game that had not changed for generations, but the West Indians promptly reinvented it, adding to the game sensational athleticism and

1

inimitable style. The West Indians' domination of cricket has long overshadowed the fact that it was the Brits who brought the game to the tropics in the first place.

Since the '50s, Cuba, Puerto Rico, and the Dominican Republic have had a significant impact on major-league baseball. In the grand old game, these island nations have not yet equalled the B.W.I.s' domination in cricket; but if the Americans succumb to hubris and assume that the game will always be their own, they might find themselves, like the British, celebrating those rare victories over the islanders. In the '80s the Dominican Republic moved to the forefront of major-league baseball, providing a disproportionate number of star players. Dozens of big leaguers (no less than seven starting shortstops) came out of San Pedro de Macorís alone. If New York City were as prolific a producer of baseball talent, New Yorkers would fill virtually every spot on every roster in the major leagues. The Dominican Republic's impact on baseball is, I believe, a phenomenon without parallel in sport.

Then again, baseball's impact on the Dominican Republic is a phenomenon without equal in that nation of six million people. Baseball, like sugar-cane, seems well suited to conditions there. It requires only flat, not necessarily fertile land, and warm weather. The Dominicans have those in abundance. The players require only time to devote to the practice of the game; in a nation where every other young male is unemployed, many play the game all day long to forget the bleakness of their lives away from the diamond.

Baseball is so well suited to this nation that it has no competition for the public's interest. The sports fans in the U.S. divide their attentions between baseball, football, basketball, and a variety of other games, depending on the time of year and personal tastes. In the D.R., however, baseball is a year-round game and the people care for it alone among sports.

Professional ballplayers out-number all other celebrities combined in the Dominican. This is not to suggest that the country is without musical stars, infamous politicians, talentless starlets, shyster tycoons, and other tiresome sorts who crowd North

American tabloid pages. This one-to-one ratio of *peloteros*-to-celebrities merely reflects the unprecedented numbers of Dominicans in the major leagues these days, not to mention dozens of minor leaguers who might break through in the next few years.

When Jackie Robinson broke the major league's colour barrier in 1948, it was a landmark accompanied by controversy and fanfare. The emergence of the Latin players was less celebrated, and the arrival of Dominican players seems to have been accomplished under the cover of night.

The Dominican Republic will never hold a monopoly on baseball; it will just have to share the game with the U.S.A., with its Latin neighbours, with Japan, and even with Canada. But make no mistake: study a game of baseball in the Dominican Republic and you will learn about its people and the nation.

CHAPTER ONE

Just Another Day at the Park

On a Friday night in Santo Domingo, a garbage fire beyond Estadio Quisqueya's left-field fence blackens the hazy twilight before an eight o'clock game. In the capital garbage piles up in gutters and vacant lots and fires burn on every corner. The government service can remove only a third of the city's trash, so the citizens set waste to burn. In the parking lot behind the left-field wall, a fire will always be burning, or at least smouldering. Car exhaust hangs in the air like a leaden mist. Santo Domingo suffers such air pollution that houses on busy streets must be washed every fortnight to remove the grime. The concrete walls of Estadio Quisqueya are charcoal black from the exhaust. When the smoke and smog waft through the stadium, the effect is like the dry-ice fog at a rock concert: when the clouds lift the players look like apparitions.

Steps from the back-lot inferno, braving the bad air, young men work the stadium scoreboard, putting up, letter by letter, the names of tonight's opponents: Licey and Escogido. Though Escogido will have last ups, both Los Tigres de Licey and Los Leones de Escogido are "home" teams. Both ballclubs play out of Estadio Quisqueya, and the stadium hosts a game nearly every night of the winter. When these teams square off, it is like a New

5

York Subway Series game—though here it is a routine event, not an occasion. In this six-team league, Licey and Escogido meet about twice a week. The citizens of Santo Domingo are evenly divided on the subject of their favourite team, and nobody claims non-allegiance.

At the moment, neither ballclub appears inclined to play or practise. The stadium crew has rolled the batting cage out to home plate and the protective screen out to the mound for batting practice, but no batters stand in the box. The coaches who would be throwing b.p. sit in the dugouts and smoke cigarettes. The players huddle around the cage, talking, doing a pinch, and spitting or downing *mani*—peanuts rolled in paper— given them by the twelve-year-olds who work as vendors. Even the television cameras, twenty-year-old relics from CBS turned down by high-school journalism programs, are untended on top of the dugouts.

Though it hardly looks it, this is the big time in the Dominican: the nation's capital, the nation's pastime, and the nation's sports heroes. In a country that knows much about despair and mediocrity, joy and excellence are limited almost exclusively to its baseball diamonds. And tonight's match-up features the two most fervently followed teams and the most storied rivalry in the Dominican winter league. Licey, the common people's team, wears blue and white. Escogido, clad in red and white, is the team of General Rafael Leonidas Trujillo Molina, the late dictator. Though Trujillo was assassinated en route to a liaison with his mistress almost three decades ago, many Dominicans believe he is still looking over their shoulders. Or perhaps looking down on them from the stadium's presidential box. His influence remains ubiquitous. Indeed this stadium was built by his administration as a show-case for his favourite sport and his favourite team.

But even baseball's demigods, be they favoured in the streets or in the president's house, cannot escape the vagaries of life on this demi-island. Los Tigres and Los Leones are not idle out of bone laziness. Rather they are reduced to killing time by an environmental inconvenience: there are no lights at the stadium. There is no electricity at all. In the capital and through-out the country, brownouts and blackouts are inescapable daily (sometimes day-long) annoyances for both the common folk and the sporting gentry. Games are often delayed, suspended, or postponed, just as everyday life is often delayed, suspended, and postponed. These electrical woes are not brought on by antiquated transformers or wind-blown power lines; indeed, the government borrowed hundreds of millions of dollars to improve the nation's utilities and to construct new hydro-electrical stations. But the government invested in stations it could not complete, or could not maintain. On this island, tortured on both small and grand scales, the power authority is in every way as inconsistent and unpredictable as the authorities in power.

In the stands, in the twilight, the talk of the day is not limited to the field of play. Indeed, much of the conversation revolves around the sentencing of Jorge Blanco, former president of the Dominican Republic, to twenty years in prison and a fine of $17 million U.S. Blanco was convicted of embezzlement, though charges of bald cheek could surely have been laid. His government issued $20 million U.S. to companies linked with administration cronies—all this just in Blanco's last two weeks in office. The Dominican people view the conviction with a sense of vindication—that a criminal who robbed them shall be punished. Nevertheless they are not cynical so much as realistic about their government—they know that just as the judge was banging down the gavel, other officials were being bought, other deals were being cooked. At his inauguration, President Joaquín Balaguer promised a purging of his top ranks. But even at this heady moment Balaguer, a legally blind octogenarian, said nothing of a clean-up beginning at the lowest ranks. The blind *presidente* can see clearly that this country's government, indeed the way of life in the Dominican, is destined for corruption and inefficiency.

Phil Regan, Escogido's manager, stands on the steps of the team's dugout and looks out on the ever-darkening field. He hitches up his pants but shows no emotion, neither anger nor amusement, neither disgust nor distress. At fifty-one and hankering for an opportunity to pilot a major-league club, Regan is a long way from his home in Grand Rapids, Michigan; but he says that he's content "to go with the flow, do my best and not make any noise". An American player asks Regan if he thinks they'll get the game in. Regan shrugs. "Hey man, it's the Dominican," he says. He repeats this line every day. The young American player isn't quite sure what message the manager wants to get across. But Regan and others with tenure on the island know that if there is a pattern to events in the D.R., it escapes the American ken.

Seconds later a youngster from the stadium crew approaches Regan and advises him "*luces* ... five minutes". Not convinced that there will be light so soon, Regan grins. Outsiders often take such estimations too literally. Regan and other initiates in the winter league know that Dominicans frequently and arbitrarily rewrite the rules of time and space, and that their assurances of a solution five minutes away usually herald oncoming disaster. Regan just assumes that his team will have no batting and fielding practice. He figures the game will be delayed but still played.

In the Licey dugout across the diamond, Silvestre Campusano doesn't worry about the proceedings, play or not. An outfielder with Los Tigres and the Toronto Blue Jays organization, Campusano sits on the bench. His brown eyes are set far apart—he could look around two corners at the same time. If he looked his age, twenty-two years, Campusano would seem more shifty than mischievous.

For this talented kid—once described as the best prospect in all of the minor leagues—the off-season has been divided between play and pine, much like the regular season in Toronto. Campusano has played for Licey since October '85, back when the team had a strong, although not exclusive, affiliation with the Blue Jays. But since then the Los Angeles Dodgers have filled a majority of spots on Los Tigres' roster. This includes manager Joe Ferguson, general manager Ralph Avila, young shining lights such as pitcher Ramón Martínez, and old, faded prospects such as infielder Mariano Duncan. It's a lonely clubhouse for Campusano, lonelier still when he's playing part time and struggling.

Campusano is not pouting or complaining that circumstance has conspired against him. He does not pass off his hardship to a Dodgers' directive to play their own. If he were less experienced he might do this. José González, the Dodgers' outfielder, has been in a funk during the winter league. González made a marginal contribution to L.A.'s World Series triumph and he believes that entitles him to star treatment with Licey. But Campusano is honest and takes all the blame for his predicament. When I ask him what's going on, he says simply, "I'm not playing good and I'm not playing a lot."

A plump, attaché-case-toting American walks into the Licey dugout and asks Campusano, "Who is *su agente*?" Campusano laughs and says that he's represented by Mario Guerrero and Associates, the gents who draw up papers for Tony Fernández, among others. "You come with us," the American says insistently, handing Campusano his card. "We're a good organization." The agent adds, reaching for any sort of selling point, that in his backyard in Florida he grows fruit indigenous to the Dominican. Smelling something ripe that isn't fruit, Campusano laughs and says that when he's in spring training he'll come over to eat some. Then, without a handshake or fond adieu, Campusano takes off like a base runner given the green light.

Just then half of the stadium lights flicker on and the confines of Estadio Quisqueya are bathed in light. Within thirty seconds, the lights shut down again. "Goddamn," says the American agent. "It takes another twenty minutes before they can fire them up again." The blanket of darkness doesn't prevent the agent from making his appointed rounds. He hits on the youngest charges, minor leaguers all, some not out of their teens. He does not waste the time of established big leaguers. He is, though he'd never admit it, a small fish in the shark tank of agentry. He leaves the dugout, pulls out a fistful of business cards, and looks for likely clients among the bodies huddled around the cage.

Among the big leaguers standing around the cage, one especially can use some wizardly agentry. If Dámaso García feels like an outsider among the ranks of high-priced talent, it is because he is a major leaguer by only the most charitable definition. Going into the 1989 regular season he has played in only seven big-league games in the last two campaigns. His last full year, the 1986 season with Toronto, was the worst in his career, statistically and aesthetically. In 1988, after being released by the

Atlanta Braves, García signed with the Los Angeles Dodgers'
Triple A ballclub in Albuquerque. But now, between seasons, he
is without a contract. Los Angeles has expressed a little interest,
García claims, and so have a few other clubs. But obviously they
have not expressed enough interest to justify a major-league contract, or even a contract for the minors. García's only hope for
staying in baseball at this point is to be given a tryout in spring
training, a tryout without guarantees. He stands on the fringe of
baseball, a step away from being out of the game.

This afternoon García arrived at the ballpark shortly before
four, when there was daylight and a light rain. This early arrival
was not an expression of serious intent. It was so that García
would not have to shoehorn himself into the batting-practice
rotation once Licey began to warm up. He came early to ensure
his privacy and convenience. As he walked out to the diamond,
he was followed by a bunch of ten- and twelve-year-olds, some
with shirts, others half-clad, some with shoes, others barefoot.
They did not ask for autographs, a bat, a batting glove, or
anything like that. They pulled out the batting cage for him and
then they went to the outfield to shag balls for one of the island's
heroes. Dámaso showed up for a bit of a run, a few swings in the
cage, and some modest, none-too-taxing fielding practice.

García will not stay around to play in or even watch tonight's
game. Although his playing rights still belong to Licey he
hasn't played in the winter league in five years. And never
could García's interest in baseball be described as all-consuming.
When players ask him if he's going to stick around to watch the
big rivalry, García says he's going home to the family, that he'll
be back tomorrow. As he heads up the tunnel to the clubhouse
he shakes the hand of Silvano Quezada, Licey's pitching coach
and the man who showed up early to throw batting practice to
García.

When García is safely out of earshot I ask Quezada to assess
García's chances, and he's surprisingly candid. "Dámasito can
help somebody," says Quezada, a veteran of more than thirty
winter-league seasons as a player, and now a coach. "García can
play in the majors. He has tools, ability. But he has to want it,
in his mind, in his heart. Right now I don't know. I watch him

work but he doesn't come every day. It's not the most important thing in his life. If it was he'd play in the majors this year. But if it isn't that important, then he's not serious—he's just not letting go. That's all."

A man behind the screen behind home plate takes particular interest in Campusano and García. Epy Guerrero, the Jays' director of player development in Latin America, signed both men (García signed with the New York Yankees in '75, during Guerrero's period of employment there, Campusano with the Jays in '83). Epy Guerrero, older brother of Mario, is not on an assignment at the stadium tonight. The Jays' bodies in attendance—Licey's starting pitcher Juan Guzmán, first baseman Luis Reyna, and bench warmer Campusano, Escogido's second baseman Nelson Liriano, and fleet centre fielder Junior Felix—are known quantities. The scout doesn't need to monitor their progress.

Epy Guerrero comes to the ballpark just out of habit. At Estadio Quisqueya he can witness his handiwork. He has groomed many players, suffered through their problems, readied them for play in the winter league and the big leagues. Watching them is, along with a paycheque from his employers, his reward.

Another of Guerrero's discoveries is sitting in the executive box above the crowd. George Bell, Jorge to the natives, is taking in the game and waiting for an opportunity, once the power returns, to do radio and television plugs for his charity golf tournament to benefit an orphanage in his hometown of San Pedro de Macorís. Bell is also here to watch his younger brother Juan, or Tito as he prefers. George starred for Licey five years ago and today Juan is emulating his brother, both in style on the field and in temperament away from the fray.

In the dark dugout Pepe Lucas provides the only light, that at the end of his Marlboro. He looks blankly forward. For more years than he'd care to discuss, Lucas played in day games in the searing Caribbean heat and suffered through blackouts, rainouts, and all manner of delays. For every inning he played, he has probably spent an hour waiting somewhere—hotel lobbies, bus depots, airports, benches, locker rooms. Just as his smoke burns down to the filter, the lights flicker on at last.

As soon as the power returns, the radio and television crews scramble into position. Not coincidentally many of them are the same men and women who write for the local dailies. They use microphones with forty- or fifty-foot cords. Some even work from portable phones. They walk about the infield looking to flag down possible interview subjects. They hijack their subjects, introducing them to the listening audience with no more prior notice than a tap on the shoulder.

Ballplayers, coaches, and managers generally do not evade these interrogators, but neither do they seek them out. Yet one large man wanders the infield, from microphone to microphone, from one camera crew to another, with an insatiable hunger for attention from the media. Rico Carty is a player from days past, from the '60s and '70s, and he's intent on telling and retelling his story. Today's heroes and their bosses shake his massive hand and greet him enthusiastically. The kids grew up worshipping Carty and his contemporaries, the Alou brothers and Juan Marichal; the older regulars at the ballpark played beside the first generation of Dominican big leaguers. At every winter-league game one of yesterday's heroes will put in an appearance and tonight Carty has the honours.

The lights are on and the fans, late as always, are still pouring into the stands at 8:10. The game is late, but most are. The sound system emits a scratchy cacophony that is the stadium's recording of the national anthem. The players in the field put their caps over their hearts. Those in the dugout come to the top step and do the same. The fans are, for the only time this night, silent. Even the ballpark urchins bring a halt to their hucksterism. Everyone is turned to the flag-pole. But incongruously, or at least incongruously to the outsider, no flag hangs in the stillness. The tricolour cannot be flown after sunset. So the ballplayers stand in their grim patriotism, facing the fire behind the billboard ads for Bermudez rum. Guillermo, the gnome-like fifty-year-old batboy stands on the mound alongside Escogido's starting pitcher José De León and punctuates the song with punches in the crescendo and conducts the more lyrical parts with a maestro's wave of his thirty-year-old glove.

It's any day at the ballpark. Within this ballgame, within the dance in the dark beforehand, within this sometimes absurd tableau, many elements and personalities making up this sport in this alien land are evident. Scouts who are celebrities, one who has much material support, another who operates what's almost a family baseball business. An American manager trying to use the winter league as a stepping stone to a big-league position. An agent pitching his services like a door-to-door encyclopedia salesman. Young prospects, some who will soon be millionaires. Other prospects who will find expectations too burdensome and will never realize their immense potential. An older ballplayer struggling to recapture the game of his youth. A strange set of habitués and hangers-on. Journalists who start their day's activities in a bar with the approval of their bosses. A Dominican hero, vilified in Canada and the United States, a beloved and charitable champion in his homeland. A former big leaguer who imagines the spotlight still shines on him. A coach who in seventy-some years has seen the nation and the game change, often not for the better.

It's also any day outside the ballpark, any day in a city of 1.7 million, any day in this country of 6 million. The majority of citizens take home no more than $100 a month. Beyond the centre-field fence, out where the fire burns, is a wasteland, a tough, squalid neighbourhood representing all that's awful and sad in the Dominican Republic. Out near the front gate of the stadium lie the government-built basketball courts for youth leagues. But now the rims and backboards have been torn down, glass and garbage cover the courts and all that survives are the arching poured-concrete supports. They rise up like brackets, which is fitting, because *baloncesto* and all sports other than baseball belong in parentheses here. On and around the courts, in the dirt and in little lean-tos, the homeless sleep. They walk, stagger, limp, or crawl to the front gates of the stadium, to beg there, or worse. A white face is always greeted with the refrain, "Me hongry, peso, peso." Those who at least have a place to go and a peso to get there wait by the sidewalk flagging down cars with a roll of the wrist and a half-opened hand. It's a Dominican variation of hitch-hiking with a promise of small payment and the only way of getting around in a city with an inefficient and over-crowded transit system.

While the stadium's hinterlands typify the grim, depressing sameness of the worst of a poor nation, baseball provides a colourful variety that is the best the country can offer.

Inside the stadium a nearly peaceful, nearly happy setting awaits the good citizens of Santo Domingo. Oh, the soldiers frisk the ticket holders at a weapons check, but they operate it more like a hat check. Guns and machetes from sugar-field workers who have trekked into the city are passed over a table and the militiamen hand over a chit. After the game, the weapons and hardware are reclaimed by their owners. The violence of Santo Domingo's mean streets is checked at the door and peace is declared until the final out.

Those on the field embody all the hope this country has to offer. You can go to any game in the Dominican and witness a rich mosaic. No doubt, it's a mosaic with a few tiles missing, and some are loosely glued. But as Phil Regan advises and warns: Hey, it's the Dominican. And, for now at least, the lights are on.

CHAPTER TWO

Mining for Diamonds

The ball flies around the horn and the infielders take grounders. The pitcher rolls the wrist on his glove hand and motions for the curveball. Two outfielders exchange throws. The third *jardinero* throws to a barefoot twelve-year-old who stands in foul territory and puts all of his ninety pounds into every throw. The top of the line-up takes cuts and stretches in the on-deck circle. The umpire dusts the plate. The devoted fan scarcely needs this scene sketched out.

These on-field rituals are as old as grass and as universal as the game itself, yet a Dominican pre-game throw-around differs in subtle ways from the American custom. Stateside the pre-game is a walk-through in execution; the island version is a frolic. A *merengue* band plays high up in the roofed section and provides an appropriate sound-track for a winter-league warm-up. Throws snap. Infielders exaggerate their footwork, dancing towards balls. When given double-play balls, shortstops kick up their heels, evading phantom runners at second. First basemen take throws with feigned boredom, as if only the most difficult chance would rouse them. Perhaps flair, hot-doggery say some, and something so ephemeral as a joy in the game elevate the familar routine. For the elite players, major leaguers or those near, the pre-game is an unpressured opportunity to flash skills, showing their best to the scouts behind the plate and friends in the stands.

Los Leones go through the last of their pre-game tosses around the infield. After pitcher José De León's last warm-up throw, Wilfredo Tejada, the other half of the Escogido battery, fires the ball down to Nelson Liriano, who covers at second. The leader of the infield and the best player on the team this season, Liriano catches the ball directly over the bag and holds it there for a couple of seconds in case a scout looking for a catcher or a would-be base stealer missed Tejada's throw. Miguel Santana and Rafael Belliard, the top of Los Tigres' batting order, take their cuts in the on-deck circle, but all the while they talk with fans and friends in the front rows.

Tonight Escogido, sixth in the six-team circuit, starts its ace, De León, a man regarded as the best of the veteran Dominican pitchers active in the winter league. De León has earned a reputation for having "great stuff"—his big-league career average is about one strike-out per inning pitched. If his ability to fan batters flattered him, his win-loss record certainly did not. One year he lost nineteen games with Pittsburgh; the Pirates did not use him after he racked up Number Nineteen, sparing him the indignity of losing twenty, a benchmark of badness. After frustrating stints in Pittsburgh and Chicago, De León was obtained by the St. Louis Cardinals and their canny manager, Whitey Herzog. Though he has pitched effectively if not spectacularly for St. Louis, De León still puzzles the insiders. He has been labelled an underachiever, a project that more than a few managers would be loath to undertake. In this category, he joins what is perceived to be an inordinately large group of his countrymen.

The umpire yells "PLAY BALL." This arbiter in a blue shirt is an American who, like the American players here, is spending a winter away from home to hone his game. From the first pitch, a fastball on the outside low corner for a strike, De León looks to be in fine form. Tonight he has his great stuff.

Even on those nights when his is not the stuff of dreams, De León, like all hurlers, is in paradise here at Estadio Quisqueya, while all the batters are in a spacious hell. For any foolish strongboy who dares hit to deadaway centre, the green backdrop stands 411 feet from home plate and rises more than twenty feet. Flies that so much as reach the warning track out there receive ooohs and ahhs. Few fans or players can remember a ball hit over that wall. For those who jerk the ball down the line, the foul poles are 335 feet distant. But even the pull-hitters face frustration—again the high fences knock down and keep in play many balls that would be in the tenth row of an average-sized yard. Another advantage for pitchers is the lighting. Estadio Quisqueya is not as well lit as most minor-league ballparks, and batters find it difficult to pick up the ball in the gloamin'. And so this game starts out as many do down here: with pitchers overpowering.

On a two-and-two count, Miguel Santana, reputed to be the fastest player in the Dominican, one-bounces the ball back to De León. The pitcher makes a difficult pivot and fires a fastball to Hector de la Cruz at first to retire the speedy centre fielder. Next Rafael Belliard, a diminutive slap-hitter and property of Pittsburgh, tops the ball back to De León. This one-bouncer is a more routine play, an easier out, 1–3. And to end this opening stanza, Luis Reyna, a farmhand with the Blue Jays, swings at the first pitch, popping up the ball and fouling out to third base. The inning could scarcely have been easier. De León has cruised through on ten pitches.

Licey starts Juan Guzmán, a swarthy, hard-throwing right-hander who pitched last year in Double A for the Blue Jays. Though Guzmán would be the headliner for a couple of other clubs down here, he is not the starring pitcher for Licey. Ramón Martínez, a skinny twenty-one-year-old who has already put in quality time with the Dodgers in their pennant drive is the leading man for the blues.

While Licey goes through their equally exuberant warm-up, while Guzmán gets in his last tosses, Liriano stretches and loosens up in the on-deck circle. He gives a conspiratorial wink to his younger brother Martin who is sitting in the third row behind the Escogido dugout. Martin knows that these things run in cycles. He's confident that one day it will be him instead of Nelson on the field, that he'll be waving to Nelson from the dugout. Martin, a second baseman like his older brother, is about to sign with Oakland. Another of the Liriano brothers, Charlie, is playing in the Cleveland organization and with some distinction.

In the seats behind the plate, beneath a hole-riddled net that is supposed to catch foul balls, Epy Guerrero watches Nelson Liriano intently. Guerrero's business cards, at least the English-language ones, read "Epifano Guerrero, Director of Player Development (Latin America), Toronto Blue Jays". Guerrero watches Liriano with an admiration that only a scout can feel—as if this young major leaguer were not only his discovery but also the fruit of his labour. Guerrero doesn't come to the park as often as he used to. He believes it's not the best way for him to spend his time. Press, fans, and agents demand his time and distract him from the business at hand. He doesn't get much scouting done at the games. The level of competition is so uneven that it's difficult to evaluate players. Besides, he has his contacts on each of the teams and they can report to him any notable developments. He prefers to watch games on television, but a game between Licey and Escogido can still get him, and virtually anybody else connected with the game in the Dominican, out to the ballpark early.

Before the game, in the idle darkness, I talked with Guerrero and Liriano about the latter's first days at the Blue Jays' training site in the Dominican, called El Complejo Epy.

"First, look where he is today," Guerrero said. "He's going to play every day in the big leagues this year. He's improving all the time. He's a good kid, first-class attitude. He's still filling out, 5'10", 175 pounds. Muscular. Five pounds more than last year, all muscle. He might even hit for a little power." Liriano let loose a little nervous laugh and flexed his right arm as if he were a longshoreman.

"But six years ago when I signed him he was maybe 5'7", 140 or 145 pounds," Guerrero continued. "Skinny kid. Fast but needed more pounds. When he came in, there were other guys with more talent, flashy guys, but none of them worked like Liriano. I'm really happy for him." Liriano has won a special place in the scout's heart because his work ethic provides an excellent example for Epy's young prospects. Though Guerrero's scouting has been well publicized, player development, that other portion of his title, is the lesser known but ultimately more important of his duties.

"After the tryout Epy went to my parents and told them that he wanted to sign me," Nelson said. "He said he could give me a $4,000 bonus. I had to go. It's easy, don't have to think about it. My father is a policeman. My mother is a nurse. Four thousand dollars is a lot of money so I had to go. And I thought about it like all the other guys. This is $4,000 now, there's a lot more later on. Epy even has the incentives—so much for making Double A, Triple A, and the majors. Right away I want to sign and go." Other players have echoed Liriano's sentiment: Tony Fernández, for one. After signing a three-year contract worth $4.5 million, Fernández said that the deal was less exciting than that first contract, one that paid him a signing bonus of $3,000.

First signings, for Liriano, Fernández, and all the others, are accompanied by cautionary advice. "When I signed Epy warned me, 'Go in with open eyes, look straight ahead, don't let anything bother you.'" Liriano said. "He told me there would be big players, fast players, guys who would throw hard. In Puerto Plata we had some fast guys, a couple of big pitchers, one guy that threw hard. But when I got to El Complejo, *all* the pitchers were big. *Everybody* threw really hard. *Everybody* ran fast."

Liriano comes to the plate to lead off the game for Escogido. Though Guerrero has seen a score of his players go to the major leagues, he says he experiences a sense of anticipation each time he sees one of his signees in action. At this moment he cannot be distracted by press, fans, or agents. He is focused on Liriano's at-bat. At moments such as this, it is not only a talented player at the plate, but with him, vicariously, the scout. Every time a native player comes to the plate or fires a pitch or fields a ball in a winter-league game, Guerrero or one of his scouting peers sits up and takes special notice.

It happens every day, the tryouts and, for the chosen, the signings. For some it is the first step on their way to the major leagues. For the vast majority it means nothing more than a summer's employment in the Dominican rookie league. All the native sons in this game between the Lions and Tigers have thrived in the tryout and signing process. All the Dominican players Liriano sees from the batter's box, all of his friends in the dug-out, all of them have suffered through the indignities and hardships of the first pro camp. By the time they reach the winter leagues, El Torneo de Beisbol Dominicano, they are men of different temperament and changing fortunes. Yet the entry into pro ball, this rite of passage of trying out and signing, does not vary. Like Liriano, they tried out with success, perhaps unexpected. Like Liriano, they went to camp "with open eyes", only to have them opened wider.

*

With its green-brown waters and an air of fecal pungence, Río Ogoma marks the eastern border of San Pedro de Macorís, a city of 60,000 about fifty miles east of the capital. From the high point of the bridge spanning the Ogoma, one can see only four landmarks that break through the green calm of the palm-tree tops: the light towers of Estadio Tetelo Vargas, the steeple of the church by the town square, and, on the easternmost and westernmost perimeters of the city, the smoke-stacks of the sugar mills. Crossing this gateway into the city one can see other sights—a beached freighter in the river mouth, shacks along the banks of the Ogoma—but it is these four sites that stand out. In the skyline of San Pedro, a city that has turned out dozens of major leaguers, baseball has taken its rightful place, as an industry second only to sugar, and as a spiritual pursuit almost on a par with the Catholic church.

On weekdays and Saturdays, early in the morning, the luckier citizens of San Pedro—Macorístas, as they are known—head to those mills or board buses en route to sugar-cane plantations outside of town. On Sundays many head to church. But the true meeting place, one that combines employment and spirituality, one that both pays and uplifts, is the baseball stadium. At the stadium any line between work and worship is erased.

Estadio Tetelo Vargas bears the name of a man who walked tall in the community, a man whom the elders of San Pedro still revere. Tetelo Vargas was perhaps the greatest of all Dominican players, a hero in the Negro Leagues. (That the "s" in his surname has fallen off the stadium's façade indicates only the passage of time and not any damage to his reputation.)

On weeknights and late Sunday afternoons during the winter, Estadio Tetelo Vargas is home to Estrellas Orientales—the Eastern Stars—de San Pedro de Macorís. Their uniforms are green and their logo is, like the Oakland Athletics, an elephant. In an effort to show their loyalty to their team, Macorístas young and old wear hats that feature this not-so-fearsome elephant wielding a bat in the grip of his trunk.

Outside the stadium is an amusement park for the young. In the many times I've passed it, the park has never been open. It would likely do little business even if it were put into operation. This park could offer precious little amusement to the young Macorístas. The Ferris wheel—it rises no higher than a low liner—cannot compete with climbing the light standards for entertainment. The merry-go-round, with its tiny horses and pint-sized motorcycles, is only a few feet away from the highway, where half-exhausted nags and souped-up scooters compete with trucks and buses. Youngsters find their rides on the back bumpers of buses far more exciting than any of the dilapidated rides here. But the source of the most excitement in these parts is *beisbol*. A visitor to San Pedro might assume that the kids play the game in the street so that one day they might play at Tetelo Vargas Stadium. That is not exactly the case. They can play there every day of the year.

Within the confines of *el estadio*, on the field where Los Estrellas will play tonight, twenty boys ranging in age from eight to seventeen are playing and practising the city's game, industry, and religion. Imagine Yankee Stadium or the SkyDome being opened to kids without supervision. It would be absolute chaos. Yet Estadio Tetelo Vargas is never locked. The authorities know the kids would find a way in anyway. And their morning gatherings are quite orderly, if not quiet. The preferred piece of real estate isn't dominated by the older kids. A bunch of ten-year-olds have the plate and the mound. At the plate they half swing a bat only slightly smaller than themselves. Each cut lifts their feet off the ground and corkscrews them into the hallowed turf.

The older kids have the left side of the diamond, third and short. From behind the plate and slightly up the third baseline, one of them is hitting grounders to others lined up to accept chances. While the younger kids are wild with the glories of their mock game, the older kids practise with grim intensity. Several of the boys in their late teens have signed contracts with big-league organizations and work out during the week with other prospects. This is a Saturday, ostensibly their day off, and they are working out on their own time, trying to win any edge they can on their competition.

Alfredo Antonio Arias de Curet takes balls at shortstop, although he might be better suited to the outfield or the bas-ketball court. He has a high-waisted, long-armed, short-bodied physique. This is accentuated by disjointed attire: he sports an Atlanta Braves cap, a Miami Dolphins tearaway football jer-sey (Dan Marino's lucky number 13), red baseball pants, and well-worn black spikes. All but the spikes are products of textile sweatshops in San Pedro.

Arias does not have a contract, so he's working out at his leisure. Arias may have a lot of leisure, because he's hardly a stand-out prospect. On sharply hit balls his glove seems to react faster than his feet, and on a couple of tough chances when he bobbles the ball, he slams his glove as if it has betrayed him. If he were to place the blame properly, he would be throwing down on his spikes. Arias is a plodder, but it would be tough to be nimble with his size twelves. For all his practice and sweat and hours and dogged determination, nothing can make the feet of Alfredo Antonio Arias de Curet move any faster.

Though playing ability does not distinguish Arias, his tongue certainly does. In this whirl of bats swinging, balls flying and bouncing, kids yapping, there is a voice, clear rather than loud, calling "I got it", and "mine, mine, mine" in clearest English. This, of course, causes problems. Inevitably, players collide with him because their ears are as yet unfamilar with the international language of baseball. When players fail to yield to Arias and bump with him, they give him dirty looks. A custodian watching this from the stands says to me, "The kid is crazy, speaking English."

With ballplayers I'm always drawn to the crazies. On rare occasions they are set apart by genius or something that passes for it. Otherwise, well, the view is always good from the clouds. When the older boys conclude their practice, they are chased away by the ground crew waiting to drag the base paths and chalk the foul lines. I walk down on to the field. Arias approaches me before I can approach him.

"You speak English, yes?" he asks.

Yes, I say. We then exchange handshakes and names.

"You are a scout, yes?" he asks.

No, I tell him, just a writer.

"You are from the United States, yes?" he asks.

No, I say, from Canada. Toronto.

His reaction is surprise and smiles. "There is a, how you say, tryout next week. The Blue Jays. At Parque La Vega, near the university. You will go there, yes? I am going there. Shortstop. I will be a shortstop. What do you do for the Blue Jays?"

I repeat that I am a writer, unaffiliated with the Jays. But I add that I have written about them in the past.

"You know George Bell. Epy Guerrero. Tony Fernández."

I tell him that I have talked with them on occasion.

"You know powerful people that can help me," he says summoning up optimism that is without foundation. "They can help me. I have wanted always to be a ballplayer. I know my English will help. It is true, yes?"

At this point I feel obligated to interject a little feet-on-the-ground realism. I tell Alfredo that Bell and Fernández, even with their pull, could not influence their organization to sign him. I say that I know Guerrero but there's nothing I could say or do that would advance his cause. I tell him that Señor Guerrero makes his judgements on ability, not on facility with another language. But I say that a knowledge of English will help him at some point down the line. It may—and at this point I re-engage his optimism—it may be useful if, after a career in the game, he wants to get into coaching or the like.

"I would like to coach, yes, after the major leagues," Arias says. "This is something I would like to do. To be *jefe*, boss."

I ask Alfredo if I can go with him to a tryout. He says this will be fine and he invites me to his home.

"I am one of the lucky ones," Alfredo Arias says. He walks along the waterfront near the Hotel San Pedro. This is his neighbourhood, the Barrio Mirámar. "Many people do not have food. Hungry, yes. My family has food. My father works hard in construction. He drives a cement truck. Yes, I think this is the best place in this country to live. San Pedro. I like it very much, yes."

This waterfront section of Barrio Mirámar is a relief from some of the impoverished neighbourhoods, those dusty frame boxes around Estadio Tetelo Vargas or the leaning water-logged shacks along the Ogoma, for instance. The houses closest to the beach road are well constructed and well protected. A few garages house BMWs and other luxury cars. And while residents in other neighbourhoods think themselves lucky if there is a market or running water nearby, attractive restaurants that double as discos dot the main drag in the Barrio Mirámar. The air is clean, not fouled with car exhaust or sewage fumes as it is in other parts of the city. When Alfredo Arias says that he considers himself lucky, it is an astute assessment.

The Arias household is not on a preferred street in Barrio Mirámar. The house has no view of the beach. It stands at the corner of two dirt roads five blocks away from the road along the seashore. The Arias parents and their nine children live in this four-room, tin-roofed, cinder-block structure. They have a bathroom, running water, a phone, electricity, a fifteen-year-old television, and a beat-up stereo. Wrought-iron security bars decorate the front window. "We have a good life," says Alfredo. "My father works very hard. My mother cannot work because there are children. But we work to make money. We help."

Señor Arias has parked his cement truck outside. He is not as tall as his son Alfredo, but he is broader through the chest. He wears square, horn-rimmed glasses and talks in something like a croak-and-growl.

"What do you do for the Blue Jays?" Miguel Arias asks me when I tell him I am from Toronto. His questioning follows the same pattern as his son's.

Miguel Arias tends to wax philosophical on many subjects. As breadwinner for eleven people, he clearly feels entitled to offer opinions as he pleases, and when he talks in his home, he holds the floor. His children dutifully sit or stand around him, remaining in rapt silence, apparently transfixed.

"This is our city's game. Our nation's game. Johnny has signed with a team, an American team...."

Here Miguel Arias's memory fails him, but Johnny, as tall but not as out-going as Alfredo, jumps in. "Minnesota," he says.

"Yes, Minnesota," the father says. "And I know he will succeed and look after us when he can. I know that all my sons will go to the scouts and try out. Alfredo will do well. This is an opportunity for them and they must try this before anything else. My sons are strong. Strong bodies. And they have strong minds. They will do well because I have taught them discipline."

I tell Miguel Arias that many baseball scouts prefer to work with sixteen-year-olds or seventeen-year-olds. At that age, they learn and develop good work habits more readily than older players. Scouts prefer to reach them too early rather than too late.

Miguel Arias nods and closes his eyes. "My boys will do what their bosses will say. I will have it no other way."

Like Alfredo, Johnny is all arms and legs. I ask him how the Minnesota organization has been to work with. He shrugs. I tell him that Minnesota has had a reputation for taking players who are "*gordo, despacio, y blanco*" (fat, slow, and white), and he says that he doesn't have any friends who signed with the team. Johnny speaks no English. He says that he will learn English when he gets to the majors.

"He thinks this will be very easy," Alfredo says. "He does not know this is very hard."

When I ask Johnny about his signing, it is clear he does not know much: where he will play next year; when or if he is to report to spring training; how he would get to Florida to report;

how to get in touch with Minnesota's scout down here. Johnny explains that he has to work out by himself, that Minnesota does not have a baseball complex or a group of young players who work out together. Johnny gets a friend or Alfredo or one of the other brothers to catch for him. He does not run or work out on a program. "I know what to do," he says. "I do it."

Johnny's somewhat sketchy regimen does not faze his father. Miguel Arias smiles all the way through. "You see, this is God's will," Miguel Arias says as he draws a deep breath and as the assembled family looks towards him expectantly for another parable. "It is God's will that San Pedro and the Dominican should have so many ballplayers. He has given us this game." Miguel Arias goes on to say that the sport is a God-given dispensation in a city that so lacks hope.

Alfredo Arias sits on the couch, stares at his father and hangs on his every word.

"I got a call from *People* magazine," Epifano Guerrero says. He wears a Blue Jays golf shirt. He is driving his van along the highway that lines the Dominican's south coast. He makes this trip out to San Pedro at least once a week. He stages about half a dozen tryouts in San Pedro and, he says, thirty or forty in a year throughout the country. "*People* magazine. They want to do a story on me. They're sending a photographer."

You'll be on the page beside Madonna, I say. He keeps looking at traffic. The remark draws no reaction whatsoever. For all I know he may be wondering who this Madonna scouts for.

"I got a guy coming from the *Boston Globe*. He says I've found more major leaguers than any other scout." Guerrero continues to rhyme off requests for interviews and to quote at length praise that newshounds have lavished on him.

Few scouts have merited inclusion in the pages of *People*, and rarer still is the scout who would regard an audience with the fourth estate as anything but an annoyance. Most times a scout's work is trumpeted in an organization's boardrooms and unrecognized anywhere beyond. And scouts are a quiet breed, skeptical appraisers of horseflesh. It is a job they choose and their work entails much time spent alone. Life in the background suits most scouts just fine. Sociable men choose managing and coaching. Scouts are, generally, loners.

Guerrero is the exception, a scout who not only attracts attention but also enjoys it. In fact, Guerrero openly courts celebrity. Every long-time scout has tales of prospects found, but Guerrero's stories of his discoveries have evolved into legends, legends that epitomize traits most desired in a good scout.

The burro story, for instance, a favourite of Jays' scout Wayne Morgan, illustrates an ethic of preparedness. On Morgan's first visit to the Dominican, Guerrero asked him if he would like to go along on a road trip. One of Guerrero's far-flung correspondents had sent a promising report about a youngster up in the hills. Morgan was eager to accompany the superscout. When Guerrero said that he would have to pick up his burro for the trip, Morgan took this as a metaphoric reference to the remoteness and ruggedness of their destination. However, when the pair reached El Complejo, Guerrero indeed loaded a burro onto the back of the truck. After a few hours of driving across fields and washed-out roads, Guerrero and the car-sick Morgan reached an isolated settlement in the Dominican Alps. There they tracked down their prospect and tested him. After he graded out well, the pair decided he was worth signing. The youngster said he couldn't sign without his father's approval. Guerrero went to the truck, unloaded the burro, and rode up the side of the mountain. When he returned from the trek with the kid's father, the contract was signed. To celebrate the signing the Jays' new prospect then climbed a tree and came down with a coconut.

The Nicaragua story, Guerrero's signing of Brant Alyea Jr., is a testament to the bravery required of a scout who works in Latin America. Guerrero, whose domain is all of Latin America, not just the Dominican, went behind the lines in Nicaragua to sign this prospect, the illegitimate son of Brant Alyea. Even with all the hostilities between Sandinista and Contra forces, Guerrero was afraid that another organization might get to the kid first. Once he signed Alyea, Guerrero played the story for all its worth, posing for photos in his battle fatigues, armed with a machine gun.

Another story in Guerrero's scouting mythos is his discovery of George Bell, a tale of initiative and timing. Back in 1980, Guerrero was in San Pedro to pay off a bird-dog, a part-time scout. On his way home he was passing Estadio Tetelo Vargas, and he couldn't resist taking a peek inside, even though it was midday and the winter-league teams would not be taking the field until some time later. Once there, however, Guerrero saw a kid taking batting practice, cranking out 400-foot homers. Guerrero made some preliminary inquiries—his name was Bell, signed by the Phillies, not playing in the winter league because of a bad back. As it happened, Philadelphia did not want him to play in the winter league because they had not placed him on their protected list, the forty-man roster. The Phils didn't want other ballclubs to get a look at him. Guerrero recommended to the Jays that they pluck him in the draft. When one of the execs mentioned that this fellow was reputed to have a bad back, Guerrero retorted: "If he's hurt, I don't know what he's going to do when he's healthy." Bell developed into one of the most fearsome hitters in the game and was the American League Most Valuable Player in '87.

While the major-league brass cannot punish a snooping scout for ambition and nosiness, legislators have attempted to curtail or, at least, delay the signing of Dominican kids; one of Guerrero's better-known signings brought about age restrictions for signing Latin players.

Though prospects in the U.S. aren't eligible for the draft until their high-school class graduates, Latin American kids were free to negotiate, not encumbered by either a draft or age restrictions. This changed when Epy Guerrero signed Jimy Kelly, a shortstop. Kelly was a talented infielder, hotly pursued by several clubs— hotly pursued even though he was not yet fourteen years old. It had long been common practice for scouts in Latin America to sign boys in their mid-teens. But the prepubescent Kelly became the youngest player ever to sign with a big-league organization. Thereafter the major leagues established what is known as the Jimy Kelly Rule: players from outside the United States must prove that they've reached their sixteenth birthday before signing up. Guerrero claims that he didn't want to sign Kelly so early but was forced to because the youngster would have been lost to another organization if the Jays' scout dragged his feet. "These guys want to play the game," Epy says, "but they want to change the rules when they lose. Now the players are like women. Until they're sixteen you look but you cannot touch. But if they're going to change the rules [at least] I got Kelly first. He's eighteen years old now, four years pro, a year in Double A and on the forty-man roster. For sure a major leaguer." Though Kelly has already played for the Jays in spring training exhibition play, his graduation to the big club is hardly as automatic as Guerrero describes. I've heard a few minor leaguers express doubt that Kelly will ever hit well enough to play for Toronto; nevertheless, even if he doesn't play a single game in the majors, his signing will be a landmark in Latin American baseball if only for the termination of child labour.

One man who is keeping Kelly down on the farm is Tony Fernández. Guerrero's signing of this All-Star shortstop is one marked less by a rapacious lust for young talent and more by compassion and canny judgement. Fernández lived on Calle N in an impoverished barrio behind the right-field fence at Estadio Tetelo Vargas. Young Fernández was one of the boys who came out to play ball in the afternoons at the stadium. At night he would stay around the ballpark to fill any number of duties: ground crew, gofer, ballboy, anything. Fernández was familar with a good number of the players in the winter league and from these he received his nickname Cabeza, an unflattering reference to his oversized cranium, which looked the more disproportionate atop his undersized torso. Though Fernández had baseball talent and a precocious understanding of the game, he suffered from bone chips in a knee, an affliction severe enough to scare off many scouts. Guerrero took a flier on Cabeza and brought him to Santo Domingo for an operation that would have been far beyond the Fernández family's budget. When Fernández recovered, Guerrero signed him. The shortstop took off through the organization as if taking vengeance for the cruel taunts of his youth. Guerrero's payment of Fernández's medical bills was not solely an act of charity. It was both an act of compassion and a calculated risk; every day Epy sees children afflicted with diseases and conditions, kids who aren't prospects, kids he can't help. But if Fernández never achieved greatness on the field, Guerrero's risk would have paid off in a life without pain for Cabeza.

Guerrero's stories portray the exotica, the derring-do, the undercover surveillance, the gall, and the compassion that are part of Guerrero's occupation. The names of the players in the tales are less important than the enterprise of the scout. Guerrero likes to dwell on these stories. A burro going up the side of the mountain. Gunfire overhead in pursuit of young player. Seeing a future All-Star through a stadium peephole. Beating ballclubs to a precocious thirteen-year-old. Finding a kid nearly crippled by bad knees and giving him a life as a millionaire shortstop. Yet moments of such splendid serendipity are rare. Most of the signings result from routine tryouts or, even less glamorously, from the recommendation of bird-dogs and contacts. While Epy's productivity is unique, his methodology resembles that of most scouts in Latin America.

Epy Guerrero has signed three All-Stars (and scalped a fourth from another organization) when most career scouts are fortunate to sign one. In twenty years of scouting, he has signed, or, as in the case of Bell, played a pivotal role in the acquisition of a couple of dozen major leaguers.

For a good scout, life and work are seamless. Duty is not a burden but a weightless pleasure. For Guerrero this is true. "There's nothing I like to do more than find ballplayers," he says. "My family is always first but nothing makes me as happy as scouting." The line is indistinct: he did, after all, not only raise his oldest son Epifano, but he also signed him. After young Epifano, or Sandy as he prefers, spent a couple of years in the low minors in the Blue Jays organization, Epy decided that his son would fare better in another organization, and avoid charges of nepotism. Sandy, along with younger brother Mike, signed with the Brewers. "We had to let Sandy go," Epy says. "Mike and Sandy are gonna be good players, major leaguers for sure, but I don't want anybody asking questions about how they got there. And for me there are no questions. Some players would complain that they're not moving [up in the organization] so fast 'cause the Jays want Epy's sons there. It was difficult for all of us," says the father and the scout.

On days when his back acts up, he dreads the drive out to San Pedro or La Romana. He does not look forward to trips around the Caribbean basin and time away from his family. But assessing the potential of young men, the essence of his work, exhilarates him like a first love.

As his van pulls up to La Vega park, I ask if it's easy to pick out a talented player. "It's the easiest thing," he says, "no problem." Most American scouts I've talked to portray their business as a demanding science, requiring both skill and a sixth sense, but Epy and other Dominican talent hunters view their work as a simple, empirical pursuit. Ralph Avila, the Dodgers' scouting director in the Dominican, draws a vivid analogy: "Picking out the talented player is like trying to find a ten-carat diamond in a donkey's asshole. They're hard to find, but when you have one you know it."

Where grass grows on the field at Parque La Vega it reaches your knees and looks as though it has never been mowed by anything that doesn't have four legs and horns. But most of the diamond is dirt, dust really, and it is littered with husks from sugar-cane. The kids lift stalks off the boxcars and strip them down so they can suck on the centres. If a major-league park were left so unattended perhaps chaws of tobacco and cigarette butts would make up a similar carpeting from foul line-to-foul line. During the rainy season the kids play on something sweet and brown and muddy, sort of like melted chocolate. They go home with uniforms filthy but fragrant. Over the left-field fence is a railyard. Railroad cars loaded with sugar shuffle through or wait to be towed to one of the refineries. The air is hot, dry, and sickly sweet.

Forty-five boys have shown up to get a look from the Blue Jays. The boys, whose ages range from fourteen to something less than forty all claim to be sixteen or, perhaps if the claim is too implausible, seventeen. Some are stars in their youth leagues, others are kids who would be the leftovers in a neighbourhood pick-up game. Likewise some are dressed in near professional uniforms while others wear the only sneakers and shorts they own and the best gloves they can borrow.

Epy directs the players to run a lap and then break into positions. Some of the boys are clearly nervous. Others have been through it all before. The most assured and practised are the flotsam and jetsam from the other tryouts. "The ones that have been at other tryouts know what goes on," Guerrero tells me as the players launch out into their lap. "The only trouble is that if they've been at other tryouts, then they're only here 'cause they're not so good." They wash up at ballparks every Saturday, or close to it.

The novices take off like harriers, as if this were an audition for the Dominican Olympic track team. The more practised conserve their energy. Alfredo Arias is one of the first finishers. He does not appear nervous. He says he's feeling "pretty good", that he's going to make "fantastic play, yes". His calm, however, breaks when he makes an excited request. "I must talk to Epy," he says. "Can you ask him if I can talk?"

I advise him that perhaps I can do that after the tryout. I say this knowing full well that Guerrero will leave quickly. All the boys will want to talk with him, as if it could do them any good. One of the more dreadful of Guerrero's responsibilities is the ending of boys' dreams. Boys come to Epy after the tryouts and claim that they have had a bad day. They say they can do better and beg for another chance. They tell Epy that their future rides on signing with a club and tell him about their problems at home. They speak of unspeakable despair.

After Tomás Santana, Guerrero's assistant and a bird-dog in San Pedro, takes the players' names, Epy lines up the boys to time them for a sixty-yard dash, the scouts' standard measure of foot speed. One boy, a kid in the green pants of Estrellas Orientales, knocks off a 6.7, a decent if not sensational time for a prospect and the best of the day. Alfredo Arias plods along in 7.4. By the conclusion, Epy Guerrero knows that he will not discover diamonds at today's tryout.

The players break off into groups at positions. There are only two catchers, four pitchers, a couple of first basemen. Virtually all the rest have lined up behind second and short.

"People always want to know why San Pedro has so many shortstops," Guerrero says as he watches Santana hit grounders to the boys. "San Pedro has a lot of kids that don't eat so well. They're not physically big. They get mature late. But they're always out there throwing hard. Good arm but too small to hit for power—shortstop, second base, that's all they can play. You need size to pitch or power to play the other positions. The kids fight to play short and second 'cause they know they're not going anywhere at the other positions."

He takes a better look at the kids. "We're gonna give Green Pants a look, maybe a couple of others." Arias fumbles an easy ball but scoops it up to make a nice throw. He grabs his hamstring and complains that it is sore and then misses a turn in the rotation before returning. It seems unlikely that he will be contending, however. Arias is the second tallest of the boys in the infield. The tallest is a kid in an Oriole hat. He stands 6' 3" but wouldn't weigh 160 pounds if he stepped on the scales carrying a bucket of balls. He says he's sixteen and he is one of the few who is telling the truth. He has softer hands than Arias but is also cursed with no speed. Too many of the other players here are not big, not fast, and not young.

After an hour and a short conference with Epy, Santana asks three boys to go out to the infield for a few more balls: Green Pants, the Oriole, and Arias. The latter is the most surprising selection among the three asked to stay after class. He was tanglefooted on the toughest chances. Others ran down more difficult chances, ran better times, plainly showed more. A scout must draw on first impressions when it comes to character or attitude, and Arias must have looked as if he were dogging it a bit, complaining about injury in what was his chance of a lifetime.

Guerrero watches them take a couple of balls each. "Bring them to El Complejo on Monday," Guerrero says. His mind was made up even before he called out their names. "Let's get a look at them." This is standard practice for Guerrero. Only in the remotest parts of the island will he sign a player on the spot. Whenever and wherever practical he will wait until a prospect has worked out at his camp before risking one red *centavo*.

Alfredo Arias does not get a chance to speak to Epy. The master scout has already left by the time Santana finishes with the three players in the field, before the others can start to plead for a second chance. When Arias comes off the field he looks at me with disappointment. He is not disheartened because of his play but rather with Epy being incommunicado. But when Santana tells Arias and Green Pants and the Oriole to pack their bags and meet him outside of Estadio Tetelo Vargas on Monday, Alfredo's outlook brightens.

On the Monday morning following the tryout Tomás Santana meets the Oriole, Green Pants, and Arias on the main drag in San Pedro, not far from Estadio Tetelo Vargas. He will accompany them to El Complejo Epy. They board a rickety school bus, so crowded that they must stand all the way from San Pedro to Santo Domingo. The Oriole and Arias are a couple of sizes too large for this vehicle so they must hunch over to avoid banging their heads against the roof. This hour-long ride costs five pesos, about one Canadian dollar, a sum that many Macorístas can't afford. The sides of the roads are lined with people who can't pay the fare.

The youngsters are silent throughout the ride. The commuters fill every seat and are tightly packed in the aisle as well. The three are jammed together, standing, each facing in a different direction. The bus interior is like a sauna. Open windows do nothing but allow in more hot air. Like their fellow travellers, Green Pants, the Oriole, and Arias are soaked in sweat. But even if the ride were more comfortable, they probably would stay quiet, out of nervous excitement or paralysing intimidation. When at last Santana and his recruits reach the capital, they embark on an odyssey involving five more buses and many more centavos until they reach the north-west end of town. From there it is one last bus past the village of Punta, out to El Complejo.

In two hours, the Oriole has said not a word. Green Pants too has said barely anything. Santana has only directed them bus to bus and handed them fares. Even the outgoing and flakey Arias has said little.

When they board the final bus Arias at last breaks the silence and asks, "How long will we be here?" In English. Santana gives him a puzzled look. Arias repeats the question, this time in Spanish, and Santana replies that it will be two or three days.

"I want to talk to Epy," Arias tells Santana. Again in English, and again he pauses before repeating himself in Spanish. The Oriole and Green Pants look on, worried that the cheek of their fellow prospect may reflect poorly on them. Santana, by now pissed off about the trip and the questions, tells Arias that he can talk to Epy, no problem—an assurance so perfunctory that it can be no assurance at all.

The bus lets them off at a road sign that reads EL COMPLEJO EPYY (*sic*), and DEPORTES SI, DROUGAS NO (*sic*—sports yes, drugs no). The sign is decorated with a bat, a ball, and a glove, though nothing else within sight suggests anything to do with baseball. This is farm country, and the terrain seems too uneven and rolling to be home to a ball diamond. The four start walking up the quarter-mile gravel path to El Complejo. It is overgrown, unpaved, almost too tough for a four-wheel-drive vehicle. At dawn a few players who commute by bus from the capital walk up this path and at day's end they drag themselves back out to the main road to flag a ride. A few villagers from Punta also make their way up this path, either to do chores or to watch the future stars. By repetition, they are blind to the scenery. The path off the highway passes a neighbour's farmhouse and then a rocky field where skinny cows graze slowly, and search out shade under the palms. Then comes a decline of roller-coaster steepness. At the foot of the hill, through the thick brush, runs a yard-wide stream. Though it is dry and shallow now, the river has left a shroud of mud over the bridge spanning it. During the wet season, or even after a good day's rain in what is supposed to be the dry season, the stream builds to a torrent and campers wouldn't walk across the bridge so much as wade across it. The regulars don't pay any mind to the steep hills or the treacherous footing. For first-timers, it is different. The Oriole, Green Pants, and Arias look for a diamond or a residence. Half-way up the path they feel as if they have already gone through a workout just to get to the camp—and they haven't even arrived yet.

The media and the team's front office call it "The Blue Jays Complex". As major-league baseball has become a billion-dollar business, the words "Blue Jays Complex" no doubt conjure up a vision of well-appointed athletic excellence. After all, the Toronto Blue Jays, one of the more profitable corporate wings of this bountiful collective, can easily afford the investment in capital resources, especially in a country that produces so many ballplayers, and where a dollar goes very far indeed. But this title, "Complex", misleads terribly. Team officials are always warned that the site will not meet their expectations, yet they are still shocked when they see El Complejo Epy for the first time. One television reporter from Toronto, on arriving at El Complejo, offered his profane assessment of the Blue Jays' centre in the Dominican Republic. "This ain't a baseball complex," he said. "This is the heart of fuckin' darkness."

But, to be fair, such a comparison is not altogether accurate. Visitors do not find skulls mounted on sticks or come face to face with worshipping savages. It's only the near-unreachable location, and the jungle setting, that are reminiscent of *Heart of Darkness*. Otherwise it is a Latin pastoral, lush growth bathed in light, a setting more out of Gabriel García Márquez than Joseph Conrad. It is a place of fables. Here young men strive to make the impossible real, and each presumes that his will be the happy ending. It is a magical place where the residents and regulars live a fantasy.

At the crest of the last hill is a clearing: El Complejo. By the time they have made that final climb, Santana looks haggard and the three youngsters apprehensive. The road forks at the top. The diamond is to the right and north, the dormitory and mess hall to the left and south.

Santana takes them to the left, to the dormitory, so that they can take bunks and change into their sweats and spikes. With undue optimism, Arias asks if there are uniforms. "Not yet," says Santana. "If you get signed, we'll get you something." Santana wants these kids to understand that this is not a place for hand-outs and charity.

The mess hall is a roofed but open-sided area with tile floors and picnic tables. Linke, the cook, the only year-round resident at El Complejo, smokes a Marlboro, sits at the table and watches cats and dogs and chickens fight over table scraps. The cook waves to Santana but does not acknowledge the boys. Under the brown dome of Linke's bald scalp is a face that is sun-wizened like a raisin. Linke leads a solitary existence. He is the only year-round resident of El Complejo and, without family, he spends weekends and holidays alone there. During the weekday mornings he prepares food for the players and listens to a transistor radio. He also watches youngsters from Punta play on the Little League diamond across from the mess hall. On this ground, riddled with sharp stones and still-steaming cowchips, the young boys play. Few of these eight-, nine-, and ten-year-olds have gloves, and the cover is usually falling off the game ball. The boys come wearing the same clothes everyday, walking two or three miles each way to and from Punta. Some don't have shoes. Sitting at a picnic table in the mess hall, Linke umpires the games from a distance, spitting out smoky calls of balls and strikes.

The two dormitory rooms are primitive compared to even the raunchiest of minor-league accommodation. Then again, they are sumptuous by the standards of housing in Punta. The dorms are not equipped with electric lights. The only conveniences are overhead fans, necessary particularly during the summer league, and a small portable black-and-white television, the only form of entertainment at El Complejo. The rooms are grim and crowded with beds for twenty players. The boys have to walk sideways between them. Santana shows Arias his bed. Sitting in the soft centre of a well-used mattress where Arias will lay his weary body tonight is a chicken waiting for its egg to hatch.

Once changed into their outfits, the same that they wore at the tryout, the three go with Santana over to the main diamond. To get to the diamond they walk through muddy savannah lands. When the three hopefuls arrive at the diamond they see what is an everyday battle at El Complejo Epy: the old-timers, the nineteen-year-olds who have at least spent one season with the Blue Jays' minor-league ballclubs in the U.S., square off against the kids.

These two teams play Monday through Friday, every week of the off-season, from September until the end of March. They have weekends and Christmas off. Today, as usual, the more experienced line-up, one sprinkled with "name" players who have played as high as Double A, kicks butt. The squad of veterans is bolstered by Sandy and Mike Guerrero, second base and shortstop respectively. Though Epy's sons are the property of the Milwaukee organization and by strict definition trespassers at their father's own property, and interlopers among his recruits, the brass in Toronto and Milwaukee understand filial considerations and sanction their presence. A few of the prospects on this squad will work next year with Dominican winter-league clubs and are a couple of years away from their shot at the Jays' forty-man roster. If these players seem a long way off, consider the new kids, losers once again. They have been signed with the Jays for a year or less, have never left the island and, in a few cases, have seen action in only a handful of professional games. Yet even they are not the neophytes at the Complex.

Steps away and down from the diamond, on a neighbouring patch of grass groomed into an uneven practice infield, two seventeen-year-olds vie for the honour of being thrashed on the main diamond. They are professional shortstops who have yet to play with or against a professional team, in a professional game, in any game under lights, or with more than a single umpire. Like the Oriole, Green Pants, and Arias, they were born and raised in San Pedro de Macorís. The two on the lower infield were not signed for their developed baseball talents. They have few. They are just able bodies, little more. They were signed at one of the many tryouts. They are just a single step further along than the Oriole, Green Pants, and Arias.

Watching from on high, Epy Guerrero sits on a fold-out chair in a newly built section of the stands behind the backstop of the main diamond. This area is shaded, and reserved for Guerrero and his special guests. From here Guerrero barks directions and encouragement. When he speaks all go silent and his words seem to echo off the mountains miles behind the left-field fence. When angered, he sounds like the voice of doom. The players quake before him for his is the ultimate judgement: he decides who stays, and who ships out. His presence in the box ensures that proceedings will be orderly and spirited. He usually sits there alone and youngsters fetch him water, pop, or cold beer from an ice bucket kept in the dugout. Townsfolk from Punta come out to watch the games but they must stay in the unshaded seats. The youngsters who come out line the walls in foul territory. They run down *pelotas* fouled away, even those fouled left into the snake-filled wet lands. Few balls are lost. Those who try to abscond with baseballs face the wrath of Epy. No matter how dense the brush, they can be sure that Epy will spot them and forever banish them from El Complejo, which provides just about the only entertainment in these parts.

Guerrero turns his attention away from the game and looks at the two boys practising on the lower infield. One boy, the taller, is a ripple of muscle. He wears sweats and spikes but no shirt. His is a boxer's torso. The other is shorter, 5'6", short-legged, and as thin as a rumour. "I signed these kids here," he says. "Look. Good bodies. Strong arms. With a little bit of coaching, this kid could be something. They're gonna put everything into this. This is the best chance they've got."

When I ask what he paid them in signing bonuses, Guerrero wavers. "More money than they've ever seen in their life," he says. "I don't remember exactly. A couple of thousand. I could have signed them for less but I always look at how much their family needs. An extra thousand doesn't hurt the Blue Jays but you don't know how much that is down here."

Guerrero portrays himself as a wellspring of generosity, and the agent of unbounded opportunity. But for Guerrero's bald claims, the money that these kids exact is not as much as meal money and green fees for major leaguers. The cost of maintaining these players all winter—each receives fifty dollars a month in salary and up to a dollar a day in travel money—might amount to the weekly wage of a security guard at Toronto's SkyDome.

"I've got the boys from San Pedro," Santana yells to Epy from the foot of the tower.

"Wait until the game is over and then we'll run them," Guerrero says.

Santana takes the three over to the infield. If they know the pair working out there, they do not let on out of nervousness.

His bat swinging like the arm of a metronome, Melvin Perez, the trainer, hits grounders at the rate of five a minute to the two young Macorístas. The drill is only for fielding the balls, not for throwing. Once one of the Macorístas handles the ball, he takes a posture as if to throw to first or second and then freezes, holding the ball. Then he lobs the ball to Melvin's assistant, a barefoot twelve-year-old from Punta, who catches the ball and underhands it to the drillmaster. On routine chances, when the ball bounces cleanly, a player is able to punch the pocket of his glove before scooping up the ball. On the difficult chances, he will bellyflop after balls spinning wildly or bouncing off pebbles in the grass just out of reach. Melvin hits the balls with what seem to be identical strokes, always with the same expression and giving no warning of what will come. The bounces and speeds and directions of the grounders vary widely. He follows no pattern in slashing out chances. He is as eminently arbitrary as the fates of the game.

Here are three generations of prospects: the two in the field, representing the current stream of kids who pour through; the twelve-year-old, surely the future; and Melvin, once a prospect, now a prospector. The players who work at El Complejo today have a story about Melvin. They say that he was a great player, certain to make the major leagues until he broke his wrist in Double A. They say that after that he was never the same. It is an instructive story, the moral being that nothing is less certain in baseball than the certainty of talent, that the best talents of one generation sometimes end up hitting grounders to the next.

But even the most wobbly, spin-crazy grounder bounces more true than this story. Melvin Perez is not the unhappy man that this story suggests. In the early '70s, he hopped around the minors as an infielder in the Padres and Pirates organizations, but probably never had the goods to be a regular big leaguer. After giving up the chase in the States, Perez returned to the Dominican and played in the winter league and various semi-pro summer leagues until his fortieth birthday. He left the game as a player in '81. "A good run," he calls it, "a good career." Epy ended Melvin's hiatus three years later, bringing him in as a full-time instructor. He says that he's happy in this job and he seems ideally suited to it.

He throws batting practice indefatiguably. He breaks down less frequently and requires less oiling than any machine that could do the job. At seventy-five dollars a week he gives Epy good value. To a new generation of players he passes on knowledge of the game, knowledge that he was never able to use in the big leagues.

The only time Melvin takes a break from this regimen is for instruction. Though every player expects that his own eccentric genius, self-taught, never-coached, will lift him from El Complejo to the majors, Melvin demands of all the players an orthodoxy of form. He is a teacher of fundamentals and a stickler for details. When a kid with a rifle arm makes an exceptional play, Melvin doesn't look at the ball or the throw, but rather watches the boy's footwork. Even on a ball fielded cleanly, or spectacularly, he will tear a strip off a boy who has violated one of the sacred rules—waiting too long on a ball that should be charged, bending at the back and not at the knees, throwing across the body rather than squaring up, and so on.

Epy Guerrero descends from the tower and walks over to Melvin. The eyes of *los nuevos torpederos* widen. In a spasm of nervousness the boxer jabs at a grounder hit directly at him, knocking it down, punishing it instead of fielding it.

"*Coño!*" Guerrero exclaims, shaking his head as if the boy is beyond hope. Melvin motions with palms down and tells the kid to relax. The boxer looks looks puzzled and, with the boss watching, frazzled. Relaxing now is tougher than any chance he'll see. The survivors of El Complejo have all developed a knack for remaining calm under extreme duress. Melvin—and 100,000 grounders—cauterizes their nerves. Playing in the major leagues before a potentially hostile crowd of 50,000 is not nearly as daunting as playing at El Complejo in front of Guerrero. If you screw up in the majors, you're sent to the minors. If you screw up at El Complejo, you're sent back to the barrio.

"These two are going to be good, you watch," Guerrero reassures me. He folds his arms and watches them field balls. He points to the ballboy helping Melvin. "I tell you, one day this kid's going to be out there too. He's gonna be wearing blue."

On the next throw in, the ballboy flubs the ball and it rolls into the bush behind him. Though they have yet to breathe hard from labour, Arias, Green Pants, and the Oriole, struck stiff and silent like statues, are awash in nervous sweat. They're next.

The economy in the Dominican Republic falls into three categories: natural resources, agriculture, and labour-intensive low-tech production. While not soaked in oil like Mexico or Venezuela, the Dominican Republic does have natural mineral wealth. The gold mines in Bani are among the largest in the western hemisphere, and the government has financed much of its debt by selling off rights to nickel deposits. But the majority of the working populace finds employment in the latter two sectors, back-breaking agriculture and the drudgery of factory work.

The dominant images of agriculture in the Dominican Republic are the high, dense fields of sugar-cane and workers flailing away with scythes. On this side of the island, sugar represents the bulk of agricultural export. Sugar does not need fertile soil. In fact, cane will grow in land where many other crops would fail. It demands only diligent harvesting.

In Dominican cities, factories are shooting up nearly as quickly as cane stalks. Half the Fortune 500 have set up shop in the Dominican, manufacturing everything from light bulbs to computer circuit boards. The world has come to the country not for Dominican expertise or efficiency—the world wouldn't go around the corner for that—but for non-union labour at Third-World rates. Consider the manufacture of jeans. The big companies import cotton fabric for jeans into the country; in sweat shops, local workers do the majority of the cutting and stitching; the near-finished product is then shipped to Puerto Rico where the buttons are sewn on (this last bit of business enables the manufacturers to stitch in labels that read "Made in the U.S.A.").

Fans of baseball are sorely tempted to categorize Dominican ballplayers as "Natural Resources". But for all Miguel Arias's claims that "God touches us with baseball", there can be little sustained argument that the quality and quantity of ballplayers, and particularly shortstops, are heaven sent. The two young men whom Melvin drills are good examples. Despite Guerrero's enthusiasms, they would fare poorly in high-school competition in the United States and Canada. At best they would be the most marginal of prospects, not draft-worthy. As resources, as talents, they seem anything *but* "naturals". And yet all the players on the main diamond this day, even those who have made it to the States, have worked on the practice infield. So too have major leaguers such as Nelson Liriano. And many have fared worse than these two Macorístas today.

Among scouts, one school of thought steadfastly holds that no player is "naturally" talented. On one occasion a scout took me to task for calling a player "a natural". "Nothing you see out there is natural," the scout said. "Announcers will say a guy is 'a natural' or that he did something 'instinctively'. But nothing you see out there is something that is happening for the first time. No player is born knowing how to play the game at the major-league level. If a player has done something in a game—even if it looks like a miracle play—you can bet he's done it a thousand times in practice. As the old saying goes, baseball's not a game you play, it's a game you practise."

If Epy Guerrero and the other top scouts in the Dominican perceived their jobs as strip-miners of raw talent, Dominicans would have a small presence in the major leagues today. Such is not the case. The status of the game in Dominican society, the structure of this camp and the work ethic of the players suggest that Guerrero and his peers borrow from the farm and the factory.

The approach taken to business at El Complejo Epy is similar to that of the sugar fields and the Dominican jeans factories: it is low-tech and labour-intensive and the corporate owners consider this end of their business more favourably situated in the Dominican because of the low costs of manpower. The facilities at the Blue Jays' would be considered insufficient for even the most deprived U.S. high-school baseball program, but what the players here give that their North American peers cannot is a working dedication to the game. The winter regimen of Epy's charges is a good example. In what is the off-season and resting period for North American players, a forty-hour work week would be a soft interlude at El Complejo. The day on the diamond begins at eight o'clock with running, stretching, and throwing drills under the watchful eye of Ignacio Javier and Melvin Perez. The players then take infield and batting practice. At ten, when the inter-squad game begins, the greenest players head to the lesser infield to continue intense workouts. The game on the main diamond may be anywhere from nine to fourteen innings long. The score has no bearing on the length of the game. The availablity of live pitching alone determines its duration. When the game concludes, they work out once again until four. After dinner they go to the poorly equipped weight room beside the mess hall to build strength, or go to the nets to hit as long as the light lasts. The players have the weekends off, but usually they go home where they practise and play in pick-up games. "One of the problems for the kids going to the minors is getting used to playing and practising so little," Epy Guerrero says. Indeed under even the most hard-driving manager, Dominican players in the minors will be on the diamond just a fraction of their customary time. At El Complejo, *beisbol* is more than a low-tech, labour-intensive industry. It is a low-tech, labour-intensive passion.

It's worth noting that the Dominicans have been less successful as pitchers and outfielders than as middle infielders, particularly shortstops. In the industry of baseball, in the production of ballplayers, shortstop is the labour-intensive position. Many thousands of hours go into the cultivation and maturation of a single shortstop, regardless of whether he's a major-league talent destined for the All-Star Game or just a middling middle infielder who never escapes the low minors.

"It's the most difficult position," Guerrero says. "It takes a lifetime to learn and maybe some guys never do. A kid has to be out there every day, learning to get a jump on the ball, learning to play the hitters, learning the right techniques." The key concept is "learning". A shortstop's split-second reactions are learned rather than instinctive. I am reminded of a conversation with Tony Fernández, a player who seems to fans to be the game's most instinctive shortstop, one whose feel for the game seems not just natural but preternatural. He complained that fans think that everything he does is natural. "They see what you do on the field and imagine that is all there is," Fernández said. "People don't know the thousands of hours of playing and *thinking* about the position."

They were thousands of hours spent under the watchful eye of Guerrero and his assistants, thousands of hours like those being spent by the players at El Complejo today. "We take the rough parts off," Guerrero says in massive understatement.

Ignacio Javier, another of Epy's assistants, the one who works with the players who have already made the States, tells me that the intensity of practices and games varies day to gruelling day: "You can't go 100 per cent all the time. It's like working in a factory. Some days you just show up and put in the hours. Most of the time they're going 80 per cent. If we play a game against another organization, then 90 or 100 per cent. That's like payday. I don't mind. If they're going so hard all the time, they get disappointed when things don't happen fast."

When I say to Epy that the players must think the camp is an unpleasant place and an unexciting lifestyle, he laughs. "Think what they have left behind." It's true. A sports psychologist once told me that great athletes use the game as a substitute for something missing in their lives, be it love at home, acceptance by peers, or whatever. When one walks the streets of San Pedro and sees the unemployed, the homeless, the hungry, it is easy to see that if this country is rich in anything it is rich in a sense of deprivation. That being the case, no wonder it is a cornucopia of shortstops. Young men use work on the diamond to fill the voids in their lives, and shortstop is the one place in the game where work and work alone wins out.

"Another Cabeza," Epy Guerrero says as he watches a prospect taking infield grounders. That Guerrero is comparing a youngster to Tony Fernández is not news. Each time I have talked to Guerrero he has touted one young prospect as "another Cabeza". Of all the players that he has signed when they were youngsters, Guerrero is proudest of Fernández. Each time Guerrero names another kid as the inheritor of the rather insulting nickname, he knows the comparison is a reach. The touted have yet to make the majors, or even much of an impression in the minors.

"One day they will say that Tony Fernández is the greatest of all Dominican ballplayers," Guerrero says. "No doubt. He has the heart to play, the head to learn. I have never seen anybody work as hard as him. He's the best shortstop in baseball but he's still learning, still improving, still working harder and harder. I stay in scouting because I want to find another. This kid, I don't know. He could be another Cabeza. Look at him."

At shortstop, the most recent Cabeza strikes an odd figure. He wears his baggy white baseball pants down to his ankles, split open along the seams and outside his socks. The effect makes his short legs look even shorter. By comparison his arms look too long and his hands too large. He has a severe case of what the English call "steptoe", a springing action that makes mere walking look like skipping. He is thin enough to be swept up by a gust of wind. He is unbalanced. His body could have been constructed of spare parts. Atop a bushy, upright growth of hair, a Houston Astros hat is perched, lop-sided.

The hat is a tip-off. Houston. An odd team to back on an island of fans of the Jays and the Dodgers. But he does not wear this hat as an homage to his favourite team. It is, rather, like a coat of arms. This boy has All-Star bloodlines. His name is Domingo Cedeño and he is a cousin of César Cedeño, the first great star signed by Epy Guerrero.

"Gillick loves this kid," Guerrero says. Young Cedeño goes after a ground ball and his footwork, an impeccably precise blur, swift, slashing, but controlled, has Melvin nodding in approval. As if pushed along by a tailwind, he runs down a ball hit up the middle. He fetches it without breaking stride, then throws it sidearm and across his body, the type of play that Alfredo Griffin is noted for. But rather than a limp toss, Cedeño has the ball over to first with as much pepper as Alfredo Arias would if he had time to set and fire. A big-league play. "I think Cedeño's gonna be in high A this year," Guerrero enthuses. "Last year he led the Dominican summer league in triples and doubles. He steals bases, can run with anybody. Fields good. Surprising power. A good arm, not the best arm here, but still he's gonna have a major-league arm." Indeed, this, the weakest part of Cedeño's game, is stronger than Arias's throwing, perhaps his solitary asset.

Alfredo Arias takes a turn or two in the rotation at shortstop. If he had any notions of future major-league stardom in that position, after a few turns it must be clear even to Arias that it is not meant to be. Seven boys, among them Cedeño, Epy's sons, and Blue Jays' charges who have yet to leave the island, flash skills that are beyond Arias's realm. Even Green Pants makes a creditable if hardly spectacular showing.

I ask Ignacio Javier about the chances of the three kids from San Pedro. I'm fishing for the inside dirt on Alfredo Arias's chances. To me, only Green Pants would seem to be worthy of even a glance. Javier has a different opinion.

"It's not always the best player, the guy you sign," he says. "If you're picking a team to play here today, then the first guy you take is Green Pants. But they knew that when they talked to him in San Pedro. Easy. But he's older, more mature. He's fast, but he isn't going to get faster. He's not going to grow. He's already about as good as he's going to be."

Javier likes something he sees in Arias. What it is he can't say. I'm relieved that Javier might recommend Arias to Epy. "Arias has a quick bat," says Javier. "The Oriole too. They're young. The Oriole is really skinny. What's he going to be like when he puts on weight? Is he going to have power? You can't say for sure but that's what your job is—to take a good guess."

"I don't think the Oriole is sixteen," Epy says. "I'd like to have another look at him in six months, a year. Arias, I don't know. Can't run, not a good glove but a good arm. Not much of a prospect really." Epy leaves it at that. His words are a ringing indictment that would shatter the young men if they were within earshot.

Cedeño fields a last ball and comes to the dugout for some water. There I ask him where he hopes to play this coming year. "The States," he says. "The minors. Somewhere, not here, I don't know." When I ask him if he ever saw his cousin play, he displays respect but is anything but worshipful. "I saw him many times. I liked him as a player. He was an All-Star so he was a good player. And he's still going to try to play this year. But my time is soon, a few years. I am not César. I'm a shortstop, a different player, a major leaguer one day."

He holds Green Pants, the Oriole, and Arias in low regard, in understated contempt. "They try out," he tells me. "They come every day. Maybe one out of twenty stays. Some guys have no chance at all, but they come. I don't know why. We always give them a test, jokes. It's always the same."

Cedeño is not threatened by any of the newcomers. None of them is another Cabeza.

After putting the players through a few wind sprints, Ignacio Javier declares the practice is over. It's late afternoon. The sun is barely above the mountains that rise behind left field. Players walk slowly by the pastures and back to the kitchen and showers. While Linke heats up the chicken and rice and slices the vegetables for dinner, a few of the players go to the weight room. The three most recent arrivals follow.

The ringleader is a fellow named Berroa. Besides his loud mouth and fairly strong physique, Berroa is most memorable for a boast, a claim. He tells the other players that he is the cousin of Geronimo Berroa, once a prospect in the Jays organization, who was recently salvaged from the scrap heap by the Atlanta Braves. His bragging point is not so much skill and ability but that he, like Domingo Cedeño, is a legacy. To a man, the players at El Complejo dispute his claim. He has never been visited by this famous "cousin" and he shows none of the material advantages—flashy clothes, a Walkman or boom box, jewellery—that go with being related to a major leaguer. Epy never asks Berroa about this famed relation or even mentions Geronimo Berroa; with Cedeño, with a true legacy, Epy tells stories about César and, when not comparing him to Tony Fernández, mentions how Domingo resembles César. Nothing with Berroa. To a man, they mock him, but, also to a man, never to his face.

Berroa strips off his ratty Blue Jays T-shirt. "You new guys, you got to do this," Berroa says. He gets down on the bench with about 150 pounds and does a few reps.

Obediently, although without enthusiasm, the Oriole gets on the bench. Berroa helps him up with the barbell. Even before

Berroa releases the full load, the Oriole's wings are quivering. The weight comes crashing down on his chest.

"You got it," he says, "bring it up now, bring it up slowly." The veterans are laughing now. The Oriole is straining but he cannot move the barbell an inch. Tomorrow he will be throwing the ball with an arm he cannot straighten and swinging a bat with shoulders knotted in pain. Green Pants and Arias are not laughing. The initiations at El Complejo are cruel, and the players don't wait to find out which newcomer will be signed. If one of the initiates has a bad day tomorrow, it may mean a veteran's job saved.

Epy Guerrero descends the wrought-iron, circular stairs down from the secluded second storey of his wing of the building. He has poured himself a beer and is bringing me a cold one. In this part of the grounds El Complejo begins to live up to the visitors' expectations: though not plush, it is at least decent.

With Ignacio Javier we cool out after another hot if not arduous day on the diamond and sit around a picnic table in this conference room, a gallery of photos, clippings, and trophies.

"It's a tough life being a scout but if you love the game you do it," Epy says. "When I was growing up in Santo Domingo, our family owned a store. We were middle class—not rich, not poor. We had a house, not that big. We always ate. I played ball but I wasn't meant to go to the majors. I didn't get the breaks."

The photographs and newspaper clippings that hang from the walls of the meeting room at El Complejo encapsulate Epy Guerrero's life history. The photos from his playing days are mostly eight-by-ten glossies, fast yellowing, in plain black frames. In one of these, a young Epy in the flannel uniform of the Lara ballclub is accepting a trophy from a group of men in business suits. "You see this," he says pointing to a corner torn off, taped back on but spoiled by a precise round hole in the loins of one of the businessmen. "That's a bullet-hole. This was hanging in my house for years and during the revolution back in '65 a bullet came in the window and went right through the picture. It missed me." And it did miss him, in the flesh and in the photo. He was star-crossed in a limited way: he has always loved the game, probably more than his brother Mario, and yet it was Mario who made the bigs and stuck around for parts of eight seasons. Epy never got a look. Though signed with the Astros, he never played a big-league game. Indeed, even in the Dominican winter league, he had a brief and hardly memorable career—three games, two at bats, and no hits, a lifetime .000 batting average with Licey during the 1967–68 winter-league season. This personal Hall of Fame celebrates some of Guerrero's limited on-field accomplishments, but primarily it illuminates the vicarious thrills he has known as a scout.

In one large shot, Tony Fernández makes the double-play pivot from second base and jumps to avoid the slide of a charging base runner. It is signed with many thanks to Epy. There are other shots, stand-ups with big-league players like Lloyd Moseby and Jesse Barfield and others with players he has signed like Nelson Liriano and Campusano. There is a photo of George Bell in full swing. The most recent shots are poster-sized colour enlargements.

Though he did not advance beyond the minors with the Astros, Guerrero met Pat Gillick and Bob Engle in the Houston organization. Like Guerrero, Gillick and Engle would never know on-field stardom, but would become heavy-hitters in the boardrooms around the league.

"This is Pat and me with the Astros," Guerrero says, pointing to one photo of the two friends in the Astros' old, loud uniforms. "Back then I knew this was a smart man. I knew he was going to do something later on."

I ask Guerrero if he ever thought about working with another organization. With his connections and facilities and scouting instincts, he surely must be marketable as more teams are investing and showing interest in the Dominican. Guerrero is adamant that he would stay if not with the Blue Jays then in tow with Gillick. "When Pat is with the Astros," he says. "I'm with the Astros. When he's with the Yankees, I go there. And he's with the Blue Jays, so I work for him there. We go together. I don't think he's going anywhere, so I'm staying with the Jays."

When I suggest to Epy that a few Dominican players are not content with the Blue Jays' management, he explains what may cause dissent. "The Dominican player thinks that he has to be better than the American just to be equal," Guerrero says. He then raises his hands and makes two fists. "You have two ballplayers, one American, one Dominican. Equal. Do everything the same. Which one plays more? Which one moves faster in the organization? If there's one position open, who plays, the Dominican kid or the American? It's the American every time. No matter what the organization, that's true. Some kids have a problem with that. They see American kids who don't deserve it moving up, and they're not playing. It's been that way for a long time. Maybe that's not bad. We sign a kid and we can promise him a chance. Maybe it's not a fair chance, but it's a chance. If he thinks that he has to be that much better just to be equal to an American player who's not so good, then maybe that just makes the Dominican kid work harder." He says this now with some resignation. But no wordstorm or sea of ink can change the practices in the minors. What outsiders might call discrimination, the young Dominican ballplayers just see as realities.

Alfredo Arias is making his way out of the showers and, on the way back to the dorm, steps over a uniform strewn on the floor.

"Hey, what are you doing?" Berroa demands and grabs Arias by the arm. "You knocked my stuff on the floor. What are you doing? You're a tough guy. Tough guy." Berroa loosens his grip on Arias and then shoves his hand in Arias's narrow chest. "You want to start, tough guy?"

By now naked bodies and sweaty ballplayers are gathered around watching the incident. Linke is busy in the kitchen. Javier and Perez are drinking coffee in the mess hall. They hear something but think it is just the usual din.

Arias bends down and picks Berroa's clothes off the wet floor. "These are very nice," he says in Spanish, brushing them off and folding them. "I'm sorry, I didn't mean to do this. I won't do it again."

Arias has avoided confrontation more artfully than he has ever fielded a ground ball. When I ask him about it later, he shows a knowledge beyond his years. "He is not harmful," Arias says. "He does not want a fight. He wants to see if I will fight. He wants me to be thrown out of the camp. To see if, how do you say, I make problems. They will do this to all new players."

He shrugs and summons up his best phrase-book English. "I must be skilful."

Tomás Santana has good news. The best news. On Wednesday night he goes to the Arias home in San Pedro. Miguel Arias invites him in. Santana has phoned ahead.

Miguel Arias offers the messenger a drink. Santana declines. He will keep this as dispassionate and brief as possible.

Santana tells Arias that Epy Guerrero wants to sign Alfredo to a contract. He says that Guerrero is prepared to offer an amount equal to $2,000. Miguel Arias pauses. He smiles but is not yet convinced that this is the best his son can garner. "Alfredo is in good condition," he says. "A good athlete. He can speak English. Studied it. This must be worth something."

Santana knows this is a done deal. He tells Miguel Arias that Alfredo's English is handy but it doesn't make him a major leaguer. He explains that Guerrero wants to make a pitcher of Alfredo. Guerrero is willing to give the kid a chance. Santana is candid. He tells Miguel Arias that his son is a longshot. Santana explains that Alfredo will make some money playing at El Complejo.

It is over in less than half an hour. Again Miguel Arias offers Santana a drink. Again Santana declines. The Arias family walks into the street to bid *adiós* to Santana. When he is gone, Miguel Arias pours himself a rum and turns on the stereo. It emits a *merengue* distorted into a loud dissonance.

This is the most momentous occasion of Alfredo Arias's life. He has taken the first step. In absentia.

On this, the third and final day of Arias's audition, the game between the old hands and the young bucks is winding up. The novice pitcher for the perennial losers has reached the hundred-pitch maximum limit and Ignacio Javier motions for him to come out.

On the sidelines, a left-handed pitcher chews gum nervously and waits for a call in. Decked out an Astros uniform—but no legacy he—the kid has shown up Monday through Friday for two weeks now. Throughout the proceedings he has run laps, stretched, thrown only when someone else has needed a warm-up. Mostly, he has sat on the outfield wall and watched others get their shots. He is unsigned, wanting only a tryout.

Javier waves him into the game. Without a warm-up he has to go live after only three throws to the catcher. After two pitches it's plain to players, instructors, and spectators that the boy has no fastball and, like a lot of young southpaws, has fallen in love with his curveball. This is a dangerous affection, especially when the curveball rides in waist high. This is batting practice in a game situation.

Batter after batter rips the kid. Line shots to all fields. One ball is hit four hundred feet into the left-field power alley, high enough to knock down coconuts.

"He tries out," Guerrero says, by now laughing. "But he don't sign."

Meanwhile, on the other diamond, Melvin still cranks out the grounders and the shortstops water the infield with sweat falling off their brows. They will run with the teams after the game, work in a few drills. After another 100,000 or so grounders they may be ready to play in the intramurals.

At the dinner table, Guerrero calls over Green Pants and the Oriole. He tells them to pack their bags, that he can't offer them a contract. He hands them ten pesos, about a buck-and-a-half, for the bus ride back to San Pedro.

Guerrero then calls over Arias. "Congratulations," Guerrero says, "We signed you last night at your parents'. We're going to make you pitcher."

Arias responds in excited but clear English. "Thank you, this is good. I am going to do my best, yes. You will see. You will not be disappointed in me."

"*Hablas español*," Guerrero says, impatiently. "Don't confuse me. You want to speak English, go speak it to the players, they need it." Arias smiles, thanks Guerrero again, this time in Spanish, and then goes back for seconds. He's been a professional for a day and hasn't even known it. He always thought it would feel different, the biggest chance, the biggest day of his life.

Late at night, the only electric light that burns out at Epy's complex is a forty-watt bulb in Linke's solitary room. In the players' dormitory, where fifteen beds are crowded together in the darkness, the future Blue Jays players sit on the beds and a dozen youngsters from Punta sit on the floor. The kids come from the village every night and the players allow them into the dorm so long as they keep quiet, so long as they know their place.

From his bed against the wall furthest from the huddled viewers, Alfredo Arias can barely see the grey, fuzzy glow of the television. As the newest camper, Arias has the least favoured bunk. Arias too cheers. All part of being skilful.

On the screen, sugar-field workers are singing, hacking away with their scythes at the fields of cane. It is a commercial for rum and it celebrates the traditional values of the fields. This is nostalgia. It would be nostalgia, that is, if anything had changed in this national industry in the last hundred years. Another commercial comes on, this for a beer, and featured prominently are bikinied beauties lounging on the deck of a yacht piloted by playboys. No doubt a few of the players have this idyllic vision of their future. For a few, it may come true.

On the screen Nelson Liriano is coming to bat. The announcer mentions that this at bat is brought to you by Cerveza Presidente, "the better beer". After a long day of the mind-bending monotony of the drills, the frustrations on field, here late at night in a complex with no lights, these young men, rough diamonds, watch one of their number who has been cut and polished. By day they work on the facets of their game; by night they steel their resolve watching others shine.

*

Before the game against Licey, Liriano told me what he believes he has to do to stay in the majors and get the best out of his game.

"I know what I need to play in the big leagues. You see what the big leaguers do and what they do different than the minor-league guys. You work it like a job. It's easy to work when you know the game [better]. That's what the complex was, a place to learn the game. If you think you know the game when you go there, you find out how much you don't know. It's easy when you start to see the money."

I asked him if Guerrero's assessment of him were true, that his work habits and not his ability have taken him to the majors. He nodded in qualified agreement and said, "You have to have some ability." I asked him if he ever thought about the complex.

"I used to think about those first days when I was young," said this man of all of twenty-five. "It was hard at El Complejo. Tough. I was at El Complejo for four months before I went to the minor leagues. After the season I went back there. You have to do these things to be a ballplayer. Playing the game all year long, eight hours a day. Lots of time away from your family. Lots of time in different places. Lots of time working on the game. I used to think about how hard it was back there when I was in the minors. El Complejo was a sacrifice that I had to make. You go in thinking that you'll do what it takes, but you never know what it takes. And you never know if you have what it takes."

Liriano leads off the Escogido half of the first and grounds weakly to third, and Belliard makes a routine throw to set him down. Junior Noboa, Escogido's diminutive third baseman, swings at the next pitch and drops the ball into centre field. With that however the rally stalls. First, Junior Felix, the touted speedster owned by the Blue Jays, strikes out on four pitches. Then Geronimo Berroa, who may or may not be the cousin of the loudmouth at El Complejo, crushes the ball deep to centre field only to have Miguel Santana run it down. With cheers from the fans in blue and a sigh from those in red, Licey's side runs back to the dugout. Liriano and his teammates grab their gloves and caps and take the field once again.

CHAPTER THREE

Regan, Avila, and the Contract God

LICEY	0	0 0 0
ESCOGIDO	0	0 1 0

Though the end of the regular-season schedule is a month and a half away, this is a critical game for Escogido and manager Phil Regan. Nearly every Escogido game this season has been a nail-biter. During this ulcer-inducing period, Los Leones have fumbled away too many for Regan's and the fans' liking. Many of the *fanaticos* believe in a conspiracy theory, believe that games in the Dominican winter league are cooked, rigged like wrestling matches, to guarantee tight finishes. Even insiders, sportswriters, ex-players, and officials have no other workable theory to explain the unusually high number of games decided in the late innings and the relative paucity of blowouts in a league of such unequal distribution of talent and such wide-ranging skills.

Even on a night such as this, with his best hurler, De León, on the mound, the silver-haired manager can get no relief from jangling nerves. Before the game he was describing the team's plight to reporters: "Our defence holds up in games, but all season long we've had to scrape for runs. Our pitching has been solid, but it has to be. We get hits but we don't bunch them together."

In the top of the second, De León is doing his part. He mows down Domingo Michel, the barrel-chested, thick-legged out-fielder. The next batter, Doug Jennings, a kid from the Oakland Athletics' bench and Licey's right fielder, pops out to first. Two out. Mariano Duncan fists a soft liner to José Vizcaíno. Inning over.

In the stands behind home plate a section of the best seats is reserved for dignitaries, team officials, and major-league scouts. Ralph Avila, the Dodgers' head man in the Dominican, is seated in front of Pablo Cruz, his counterpart with the Pirates. When Regan, standing on the dugout steps, looks over to Avila and expresses concern—it's going to be more of the same tonight, just another heart-stopper—Avila and a few others are laughing. Meanwhile a man in the back row, an American not affiliated with a big-league club, is sending a kid on an errand. He wants names and addresses of the young minor leaguers at the end of Licey's bench. And phone numbers if they have telephones.

Regan, Avila, and this fellow in the back row work daily with Dominican ballplayers. Each brings to his work a different perspective. Regan, an American and a former big leaguer, sympathizes most of the time for the Dominicans. Avila is a college-educated Cuban, an Hispanic but still an outsider in this nation; he is less patient with the locals, but then again he has worked on the island for twenty years. As for the fellow in the back row, he'll tell young players that he can lead them to the promised land with just their signatures.

*

"You run, you slide, *cabeza, si, cabeza primo*, head first, I give you peso," says John Davis, one of the import pitchers for Escogido, a tall Yanqui drooling Red Man out of the side of his mouth. In a rainy interlude before a game against Los Estrellas of San Pedro de Macorís, he talks to one of Estadio Quisqueya's peanut vendors, a barefoot ten-year-old with a shirt that doesn't come within four inches of the top of his pants. The pitcher tries to persuade the *manicero* to make a fool of himself during a rained-out batting-practice session. The pitcher wants to see this ballyard buffoonery perfected by Rick Dempsey a few years back: sliding around a slick tarpaulin, throwing more water than a water-skier slaloming.

Dempsey performed to entertain big-league crowds during rain-outs, but the Escogido pitcher has more selfish designs, his own personal amusement.

"Peso, peso, peso, peso," the kid says, quoting the going rate for self-respect at sixteen cents U.S.

"Yeah, yeah, I'll give you a peso," the Yanqui says. He then points at his teammates. "And he'll give you one and he'll give you a peso—lots of pesos. Now you go and slide. Head first."

Once the ground crew is safely distracted, the kid goes out to home plate and pantomimes a few warm-up cuts with a phantom bat. Then, with a sense of theatre and an aura of authenticity that's grounded in the many games he has watched, the kid stands in as if to face José De León. His first swing is an invisible line drive up the middle. The boy runs in furious short strides up the first-base line and celebrates his safe arrival with a head-first slide. The pitcher yells "Safe" and orders the peanut salesman to go to second. Not content just to sprint around, the kid acts out the old cat-and-mouse game, the imaginary hurler throws over to first base twice. The first time the kid makes it back standing up, but the second has him sprawling. Then the peanut boy takes off for second, half-tripping over the tarp. He caps his successful steal with a hook-slide into second. On the next pitch he steals third with a perfect pop-up slide. Finally, he sprints home, crashing into the plate in belly-flopping saturated glory.

The pitcher then pulls the sopping, panting kid aside and tells him to race against the kid who was doing the translation. Ready-set-go, and they're off in a race for the right-field wall, or so the peanut gallery in the dugout surmises. Yet when the vendors get the wall, they touch it and begin to race back to the dugout. With a late charge the base runner pulls away. "Look at him," the pitcher says. "He's gassed." The kid asks him for the peso. The pitcher ignores him and heads into the tunnel and up to the clubhouse to goof off some more. The peanut vendor doesn't cry, but a good night has suddenly turned bad.

An old-fashioned "baseball man", as one of the number would call himself, Phil Regan doesn't encourage or laugh at this sideshow stuff. As manager of Escogido, his job is getting the best out of the thirty bodies on his roster, reading the players and pulling the strings. To this former big-league pitcher, nicknamed the Vulture, the rain-delay cabaret was never that funny in the first place and after four seasons down here—seeing so many poor neighbourhoods, so many rail-thin beggar kids—it seems mean-spirited.

Forty games into the winter-league season, Regan has felt less like a bird of prey and on occasion more like a carcass in the badlands. The defending Dominican Winter-League and Caribbean World Series champion, Regan's team started 0–7 and 5–15 and has yet this season to break into the top four in the league, the select circle for playoff competition. Usually, the public, not to mention the owner, expects the manager to deliver a winning team shortly after he's sized for his uniform. Such slow starts often result in a flurry of flight booking and cancelled hotel reservations. Regan surely would have been fired were it not for last year's glories.

I talk with Regan at a time when his team has won ten of its last fourteen games, affording him as much security as the job allows. "If you can manage down here, you can manage anywhere," Regan says. "In the majors you have to fill out the line-up, make a few moves, put on a few plays that everybody knows. You have to win, but with talented players you've got a good shot. And in the majors you don't have to worry before the game or after the game. The guys are paid well enough to look after themselves.

"In the minor leagues, winning isn't everything, player development is," he continues. "You're a teacher first. Your job is to take kids and prepare them so they can help the big-league club. If you win, it's a bonus.

"But down here, it's a tough job," Regan adds, as the rain thins out to mist and the field crew contemplates rolling the tarp. "You've got to win. There's pressure from the fans and front office to win. And you're working with kids who range from rookie ball up to the majors. They come from all sorts of organizations, so it's not as if there's a team report on some player. I have to wait and see what they can do. You're managing in the dark.

"Other places you're managing—you might be second-guessed, but you're the boss. Down here, the owners do the talking. Last year I had Juan Samuel from the Phillies and Julio Franco [then of Cleveland, now a Texas Ranger], two outstanding hitters and players, stars down here. So I've got some punch in the middle of the line-up. I bat Samuel third and Franco fourth. I know that I'm getting some offence out of those spots. But the owner pulls me aside and tells me that he doesn't want them batting together in the line-up. I ask him why. Any other manager would want those guys there in the order. He says to me that the fans think these guys are such good hitters that each time they come up the fans expect at least one of them to get a hit. The owner says that's too much pressure for them and he wants me to separate them. Hey, it's the Dominican. What can you do?"

Regan has worked winters in the Dominican for four years so far and it provides a refreshing counterpoint to his regular-season job as a special-assignment and advance scout for the Los Angeles Dodgers. Before coming down to the Dominican in late fall of '88, he followed the teams of the National League, eyeballing upcoming opponents for Lasorda's boys and filing the comprehensive reports. His scouting of the Mets and the Athletics was instrumental in the Dodgers' World Series victory.

Though his scouting is important work, it is draining and impersonal. Through it all, Regan says, a few times during the regular season, when he lugs his Juggs gun (the radar device used to time pitches) to the park, when he analyses a rookie batter's stance, he misses being in uniform and working with young players. When Regan once voiced his discontent, the Dodger executive, Fred Claire, told him he could have both, filing reports in the summer, filling out line-up cards in the winter in the Dominican.

"It's hard to say that anything is better than winning a World Series ring," the Vulture says. "The Dodgers have always been very good to me. But the work I do down here in the winter is really more rewarding than the scouting. To put the uniform on and to work with the players—you can see the effects, the progress. Scouting reports are used, but when you're filing them you never get to see your club put them to use."

The manager's load in the Dominican sometimes wearies Regan—bus rides every other day, dealing with officials and players who only speak Spanish—"You have to play mind-reader with some kids. The coaches try to help but even they don't know what a kid is thinking." Of late, Regan has been bothered by the way one of his young kids has been working out. Not a star, not a starter, not even a kid who gets in the blowouts or runaways. A kid right on the end of the thirty-man roster of Los Leones de Escogido. "He doesn't look sharp," says Regan to his third-base coach Eduardo Dennis. "I don't know if he's dogging it, if he's sick, if he's got family problems or something. I just remember that at the start of the season that kid looked pretty sharp, now he looks run down."

Dennis agrees. When he gets a chance, he'll talk with the kid. Players move in and out of the dugout as the crew rolls the tarp and drops sawdust on the mound.

"Are we gonna do infield, Phil?" asks one of the players.

"Yeah, we're gonna do it," Regan says and then raises his voice to holler. "Come on, get off your asses and get on out there. Let's get on with it." He gets the players on to the field, braving the wetness. If he were up in the clubhouse and not on the bench, the players wouldn't be taking infield, he says. "That's one of the things about the players down here," Regan says. "Americans or Dominicans, I guess. You've got to get on them to do the small things. They would just keep putting things off until it was too late."

The players take the field and a couple of the Dominican kids look indignant. "Do they feel like things are against them?" I ask. Regan says that after four years down here he has become "more sensitive" to the Latin players' situation. "Look at it from a Dominican kid's perspective and you'll see a lot of things look like they are against them. When the Dominican kid goes to the States, he's on his own in another culture. The club just puts him there and says, 'Find an apartment, work things out and be at the ballpark at four.' If the kid complains or has trouble, he's either a trouble-maker or stupid. Now when the

Dominican kid comes back home, he sees how the clubs here treat the Americans. The Americans get a free room in a five-star hotel, a ride to the ballpark, better pay than all the rest. The clubs go out of their way to accommodate the Americans and they're usually whining about how they're treated anyway. And in this league American minor leaguers are making twice as much as Dominican major leaguers. It doesn't make sense, and it contributes to the us-versus-them thing."

I ask Regan if four years of experience have helped him better read the Dominican players. A look of incredulity crosses the Vulture's placid face. "It's just when you think you know what a player will do that he'll do something that surprises you. And if you're relying on logic when you're working with them, there's a good chance that you're doing it all wrong.

"Last year I sat and rested one of my players, a major-league guy who makes $800,000 or so," Regan says. "I just wanted to sit him down, give him the day off 'cause he was struggling at the plate. Anyway, I posted the line-up on the dugout wall. This guy comes by and looks at it and heads up the tunnel to the dugout. I figure he's going to go in there and play cards with his buddies.

"I go up to the team's offices and there's this player sitting across the desk from the owner. He's told the owner that either he plays now or he's going home. I thought it was a joke. Anyway, the owner just gets up and tells me that it's up to the two of us to sort it out. He was no help at all, but he can't win. He can't tell the manager what to do in the situation but he sure wasn't going to offend a national hero and have it blown up in the press. It was a tough situation but I just looked at the kid and told him, 'Look, I want you on my team. We need you to win. You'll play another night, but you're not starting this game. But if you walk out of here tonight, don't come back. You won't play for me again.'

"Well, the storybook ending. Doesn't the kid I put in get hurt. I pinch-hit this guy who was sulking in the office and he gets the game-winning hit." Regan laughs. It seems that managing in the Dominican is nothing but a series of surprises. Just a few days before, Manny Lee, the Jays infielder and second baseman with Azucareros del Este, the Sugarmen from La Romana, was among the league batting leaders, hitting over .300. Then without notice, he didn't show up for a game. It has been three days and he has not notified his team of his whereabouts or intentions. "That's just the way it is down here," says a coach with Los Azucareros. "You have a league All-Star playing for you but there's no guarantee that he's back tomorrow." Lee's disappearance was so routine that the newspapers didn't even mention it.

"I don't know if I'm ever going to get a handle on the Dominican players," Regan says. He mentions Mario Soto, the former All-Star pitcher with the Cincinnati Reds. Soto was one of Regan's chief projects this winter. After the pitcher had a series of arm problems, the Reds released Soto. The Dodgers quickly signed the right-hander and assigned him to the Triple A ballclub in Albuquerque where he pitched for the second half of the '88 season.

"Pretty well every day I went out to the Dodger complex to work with Mario," Regan says. "After a few weeks I figure he's making real good progress. He's a talent and a smart pitcher. After a month, I say to Mario that I think that we've done all we can do working out at the complex, throwing on the side. I tell him that I want him to pitch for Escogido. I want to see what he can do against live hitters, against a few major leaguers, so I can get an idea of where he is coming back. It seemed like a reasonable thing to ask him. I thought it would be a good opportunity. An American guy would be jumping at it.

"But Mario said no way. He told me that he wouldn't pitch in the Dominican league until he made a comeback in the majors. That seemed backwards to me—you use this league to get ready for the majors, not the other way around. He said to me that he did not want the Dominican fans to see him when he was anything less than his best.

"I tried to understand but I said, look at what goes with playing in the majors—it can be millions of dollars, the fame, everything. He said that he wanted the fans to remember the Mario Soto who was one of baseball's best pitchers. He said he didn't want to hurt his reputation.

"So I made him a proposition. I told him that I would go to the press and tell them to write up stories about how he was making a comeback, stories about how the fans should understand that he was working in games down here to get ready for the majors. I told him I'd tell the reporters not to expect the Mario Soto of '81 or '82 when he was one of the best pitchers in the game, but a guy trying to pitch his way back to the majors.

"That did it. He was adamant. He would not pitch for Escogido this winter. Period. I figure that it's over, but two days later I pick up the morning paper and see a story: Mario Soto has made an offer to *buy* the Escogido ballclub for six million pesos [about $ 1 million U.S.]. I don't know if his wanting to buy the club had anything to do with what I had said to him, but I came away thinking about the pride this guy had. He was more concerned about how the Dominican people thought of him than he was about making a million bucks and playing more in the majors. Now I can't understand that really, but I bet if you had a bunch of Dominican ballplayers sitting around, it wouldn't faze them. They'd probably do the same thing in the same situation."

Regan looks out on the field and sees the peso-less peanut vendor in near collapse. The manager knows that the youngsters here will suffer nearly any indignity for a just cause, in this case a peso. Later, when they need not run for the amusement of others, when the poor become rich but the boys not yet men, they will interpret anything that is not of their design as an insufferable slight.

After the game a player comes up to Regan to talk in private. He has overheard Regan talking to Dennis before the game about the kid who looks run-down.

"Phil, the kid comes from a town twenty minutes past Santiago. He has to take the bus or hitch-hike down to the games in the day and back out there after."

The kid's problem is not lost on Regan. The trip to Santiago is the most daunting in the Dominican. It's a three-hour haul from Santo Domingo. To make a comparable trip on home ground Regan would have to commute by bus or thumb from his home in Grand Rapids, Michigan to Chicago—every day, there and back.

"So if we're playing out in La Romana, he's got three, three and a half hours here, ninety minutes with the team to La Romana, five hours or so at the park, ninety minutes to the capital and then, if he's lucky enough to get rides, three and a half or four hours home."

"Why didn't he say anything?" Regan asks.

"He didn't want to make any problems," the player says. "He wants to play."

"I'll talk to the kid. And I'll talk to the owner to see if we can get the kid some more money. If only he had said something."

It's a strange story, this silent suffering, but the player is by no means alone. A few nights before I was talking with Sam Joseph, a trainer in the Angels organization who's working with Azucareros del Este. Sam told me a story on a similar theme. He has a young Dominican kid for an assistant, learning the art and science of taping ankles and icing arms. For a week or so the young assistant didn't talk very much and Sam assumed that the kid was mad at him. When Sam asked a clubhouse attendant if he knew what was eating the kid, the attendant told Sam that the boy's brother had died of a drug overdose, probably a suicide, a few days before. The assistant missed his brother's funeral because he didn't want to ask for a day off; he didn't want to jeopardize his job. That's how it is for the young kids, would-be players and trainers. The outsiders can only guess at what goes unsaid.

Before he climbs into the showers, I ask Regan what he has learned from all his time down here. He looks to the ceiling and rolls his eyes back, then stretches a two-syllable word out across four or five seconds. "*Paaa*tience," he says. This he learns from the young players the team bus picks up on the side of the road. This he learns from the kid who hitch-hikes in from past Santiago every day and staggers in to games as if sleep-walking. This he uses when dealing with headstrong millionaires who won't suffer a day off in front of the home fans. And this he probably has to use when he watches John Davis, that ugly American pitcher who for his own amusement makes the peanut vendor run and jump himself into exhaustion.

Phil Regan, a patient man, hardly a vulture, climbs into the shower and flips it on full blast. No hot water.

Campo Las Palmas, the Los Angeles Dodgers' baseball complex, contrasts as sharply with El Complejo Epy as First World does with Third. Construction for this training ground and home of L.A.'s aspirants to the majors was completed on March 21, 1987 at a cost of about a quarter-million U.S. dollars. That may sound like an insignificant sum in light of two-million-dollar salaries, but in this region a quarter-million dollars goes a long way. For that sum, the Dodgers put up the equivalent of a five-star hotel. Indeed the only difference between this Dominican Dodgertown and the Ritz is that these plush residences are surrounded by baseball diamonds, not golf courses. However, the location gets no stars at all. The Dodgers' complex is out past military installations and sugar fields a few miles north and east of San Pedro de Macorís. The Dodgers' rationale for this location is founded on proximity to raw materials. "If you're gonna build a shoe factory, you put it where the leather is," says Ralph Avila, the innkeeper at Campo Las Palmas. "If you're gonna make ballplayers, you put a diamond where the bodies are."

Ralph Avila's office is in the Walter O'Malley Headquarters, just across the courtyard from the Tommy Lasorda Dining-Room. Avila has mounted on the walls photographs of Dominican stars who have worn Dodger blue: pitcher Alejandro Peña; pinch-hitter-supreme Manny Mota; infielders Rafael Landestoy and Mariano Duncan. These photographs hang above a four-drawer filing cabinet loaded with every scouting report on every young prospect on whom Avila has cast an eye since the Dodgers assigned him to the Dominican in 1970.

"I've never thrown anything away," Avila says as he leads a tour of the grounds. "I still have the reports I made when I was a region scout in the States. Rick Rhoden—how old is he, thirty-eight or something—I still have the reports that I filed on him when he was a fifteen-year-old sophomore in high school. I was the one that told the Dodgers to draft Rhoden and he's still around.

"All my work on the island, in all of the Caribbean, is in that filing cabinet. I don't really think about it that way. I look on the walls and see the champion teams, World Series teams, and when

I see a Pedro Guerrero up there, a Mota, Peña, no matter who it is, I know I've done my job."

Ralph Avila is a greying, distinguished, slightly owlish man and his enthusiasms are quiet and restrained. One might have guessed he is not a native Dominican. He doesn't go for much of the local back-slapping and loudness. He is not unfriendly, just a little distant at first. Avila was born in Cuba and spent many years in the States, in Florida, where he graduated from college with a degree in physical education.

In the scouting fraternity on the island, Ralph Avila is second only to Epy Guerrero in seniority. Epy's discovery of César Cedeño predates by a couple of years Avila's dispatch to the island. And Epy is certainly a more charismatic figure than Avila. The Jays' scout revels in drawing attention to himself, while Avila prefers a more peaceful existence. But as most baseball executives will admit, Ralph Avila is an even more powerful figure in Dominican baseball than the better-known Guerrero. Though the Blue Jays have been the most successful organization in signing and developing Dominican players during the '80s, there is overwhelming evidence that the L.A. Dodgers will supplant them in the coming decade.

Avila sits at his desk in a well-appointed, airy office, with ornate tile work and pastel blue walls. "Epy has had success doing things his way," Avila says. "We're having success doing things our way. The Dodgers are a class organization and they're not afraid to spend if you have to spend to win. The money they've invested here at the Dodger complex will get paid back to them over and over. The money they spend sending down their people—Joe Ferguson with Licey, Phil Regan with Escogido, lots of others coaching the winter-league teams— they'll get it all back. Our kids get the best instruction from major-league coaches. The organization gets the best reports from major-league scouts."

A shout from outside. The phone for Señor Avila. Though these are attractive grounds and the organization has attempted to recreate the wonderful atmosphere of its Dodgertown spring training complex in Florida, certain inconveniences are unavoidable, namely the phone. The Dodger complex is, like El

Complejo Epy, off the beaten track, isolated so that nosy scouts from other clubs can't spy on Dodger talent. That means that all telephone communications are done by radio link-up.

When Avila returns, he bemoans the fact that the phone service has not reached this hinterland. "Bad government, that's all," he says. And it's true that the administration of the Dominican does not run nearly as efficiently as the Dodgers. "We had a Japanese group down here a few weeks back. They want to set up a baseball complex like ours in La Romana. Can you imagine— baseball people from Japan where everything runs perfect, here in the Dominican?"

As a proud Cuban, Avila sounds unsympathetic towards the Dominican people and their government. The Dodgers, he explains, have tried to work with the administration but that proved sheer folly. "About a year back, I tried to set up a program with the government to train coaches and managers," Avila says. "The Dominican turns out a lot of ballplayers but, except for the pros, the coaching is bad. So the government sent me about twenty guys who coached teams in cities and towns from all over. We gave them nice rooms here in the complex. We told them that we were going to feed them, look after them. Uniforms, laundry, food, everything. Just let the Dodgers do it. It was going to take maybe three or four months of training and then we'd bring them back for a few weeks every year so they could keep learning.

"So then I said there was just one condition. While you're in the Dodger complex you have to follow Dodger rules. You stay on the grounds during the week, go home on the weekends. You can't drink while you're here and you can't bring women into the complex. That did it. Fifteen guys walked out right away. Another four lasted a week but never came back from the weekend. I thought the one guy might work out, but after a month, he was gone.

"These guys didn't want to make any of the sacrifices you have to make to be a good coach or a good scout and that's what I see out there. The coaching in the towns is terrible compared to the States. It makes it tougher to tell about boys in games because they're just coached wrong. You don't look at what he's doing, you've got to think what he could do."

Avila walks out to the main diamond where he watches a few boys working out under the direction of a coach. These players are dressed in neat, fitting Dodger practice uniforms, so I'm surprised when Avila tells me that they are unsigned and have only arrived at the camp in the morning.

"I like to have a kid at camp for two or three or four weeks before signing him," Avila says. "That gives the boy a chance to show me he can play and it gives me a chance to figure out if he's going to be a problem. If he's going to have trouble getting along with us, something will happen in that time for sure. While he's here he gets a physical, gets food, a few English lessons, everything. Even the kids we don't sign get something—some shirts, maybe some old spikes or an old glove. When they go back to their town they can say that they got a fair shot and that the Dodgers are a good organization. It's public relations, but in this business public relations count. You never know if that kid who you don't sign has a brother who can really play. So you don't piss anybody off."

Avila says that baseball in the Dominican will remain the same but that the business of baseball on the island will probably change considerably in the next decade. "It's a matter of time before the major leagues have a draft for Latin America, the Dominican included," he says. "That would change everything completely. Now it's a free market. You see a kid, you can sign him. It pays off those who do their homework—find a kid first, hustle, sign him. You got to have scouts all over, all the time. Most clubs don't want to do that, so they'll vote to have a draft— that way a scout or two can go around the country, gather the same information on the same kids, make it more even."

Avila bristles at the idea that a draft for Latins would render the Dodger complex here redundant. "We've already paid it off with the kids we have coming out of the system," Avila says. "Look at Oferman, Vizcaíno, and Ramón Martínez. Here are three kids in the Dodger system who would probably be the best minor-league talent in any other organization. They all came from this complex. If not one other boy came out of here, we've still done a helluva lot for the organization."

Avila overstates his case with the broad claim about the three Dodger prospects. Nonetheless, it's true that no other organization has three young players so coveted in its system; and certainly no organization has two from the island so heralded as Oferman, a star in the Pioneer League last summer and now an eighteen-year-old *wunderkind* with La Romana in the winter league, and Martínez, who had a cup of coffee with L.A. as a twenty-year-old and overpowered major-league hitters.

"If there is a draft, clubs should still have complexes like this," Avila says. "The Dominican kid should be playing all year. All the players up to the majors should be playing all year. The American kid can always find pretty good facilities no matter where he is. But the Dominican kid in the minors, he might be from a mountain town or some other place with no good diamonds, so the complex is important to him.

"The other thing is the visas. U.S. Immigration limits how many foreign kids—Dominicans, Venezuelans, even Canadians—you can have playing in the States. It doesn't give the young first-year Dominican kid the same opportunity to play that a first-year American has. So the Dominican summer league is always going to be important and to do that right, you should have a complex, a place for the team to play, practise, and live together.

"The draft will change things but the Dodgers will still do all right. We spend money down here. A few clubs spend money. Most just sign kids. They don't look for quality, just quantity. They don't spend money to find the best kids—they just figure if they sign a bunch cheap then maybe one or two work out. If that's the way they want to do it, fine. They can't compete with us. We'll still do better with the draft."

According to Avila, it comes down to work, an investment not so much of money as of time. His favourite story is the signing of José Tapia, a pitcher who a few days back was placed on the Dodgers' forty-man roster. "There's a national sports competition every year," Avila explains. "And every town, city, and region has to send a team in, no matter what. You lose a game and you're out. The best teams are always Santiago, San Pedro, and Santo Domingo. Big cities, most kids to pick from. They always win. The teams from the regions are in a lot of trouble. Most scouts just come out to watch the finals or something. The first-round games start at about six in the morning and go all hours. So one day there's a rain delay. The last game of the day doesn't start until three o'clock in the morning. Two of my coaches here at the complex are in the stands. Not only aren't there any other scouts, there isn't a fan in the stands. The only people watching the game are my guys and the umpire. Santiago, a good team, is playing a game against a team of kids from the mountains near the border to Haiti. After the first inning it's 12–0, 19–0 after two. There's a walkover if it's more than a ten-run lead after five innings, but my guys are still there. In the fifth inning—it's about 4:30 in the morning, 35–0, and my guys have to show up an hour and a half later for tomorrow's game—this team from the mountains brings in Tapia. He only gives up a couple of runs to the Santiago third-string guys. My scouts see something, big strong kid with no mechanics. They get his name. Last season he pitched in Double A and now he's on the forty-man roster.

"A draft, money, whatever," Avila says. "When you scout against the Dodgers you're scouting against a guy who's sitting there at a game at 4:30 in the morning, 35–0 and giving up a night's sleep to find a player."

That's the way it is with Avila: Dodgers first, himself a poor second. For the successes of the organization, he points above to management and below to his coaches and scouts. But while a lot of credit must go to his industrious staff, Avila should take a bow for finding not one scout but two who would chart prospects until sun-up.

"Do you want to do it right now? We can go in the dugout and get it over with right now. Come on, let's get it done."

Carrying a black plastic attaché case secured by a three-dial combination lock, a fortyish white Yanqui with lightly greying hair and no perceptible fashion sense walks around the infield during batting practice at San Cristóbal. He is talking to, persuading, coercing, joshing with, and selling to an eighteen-year-old player, a kid in the Detroit organization. If everything breaks right, the kid might shoot up through the thinly talented ranks and might make the Double A ballclub. That's what this American says. The youngster has never had "representation", or so he says when the American asks him. Understanding half what he hears, the outfielder listens to this fast-talker's spiel.

"It's easy, no problem. We can go into the dugout and get it done. You give me your address, phone number if you got one, and I'll make sure that you get all the papers. It'll be all settled. Clean. Easy. I'll look after you. You know there's things I can do so they treat you good. There's ways we can make them give you a fair chance."

The kid nods, acquiesces, and walks to the dugout. The man pulls a ballpoint from the pocket of his sweat-stained blue shirt. The kid scrawls his signature on a few forms. They smile when it is done. The man pats the signee on the back and lets out a *gringo* cry of *"bueno*, all right." When this future star walks back on the field he will be somewhat poorer, somewhat represented.

This fellow on the sidelines is no ex-player. Ex-players have a certain bearing; they are at ease with conversation around the batting cage. This guy doesn't fit. He is dumpy and slightly seedy looking. He gladhands around the infield, has a working knowledge of baseball Spanish and associated profanities, but scouts, veteran organization men, have little time for phony shows of kinship with the players. There is a certain joylessness with which they go about their business. But this guy is effusive.

He is the Contract God. He always brings a few dime-store magic tricks to the ballpark. This time he does a sleight-of-hand disappearing-rag trick. Ballplayers, ballboys, *maniceros*, all watch in wide-eyed, child-like wonder, blind to the plastic container clasped to the underside of his wristwatch. He carries around a few Polaroids of naked women, Dominicans of every age. He tells other American visitors that he has "a friend" who knows how to get Dominican women to undress in hotel rooms for almost nothing.

With an air of superiority he walks about the infield, signing kids, like a baseball *bwana*. "Come on, we can get it done right now," he says to the young players. He hands them his business cards, which announce that his agency represents "TO-MORROW'S CHAMPIONS TODAY". Though he claims today to have signed a couple of briefcasesful of Tomorrow's Champions, at present he does not have any of Today's Champions aboard. He has no major leaguers—"at least, not right now"—but then again, the established talents have latched on with name agents, a club to which the Contract God very obviously does not belong. In fact, he asks that I not reveal his name at all—so I decided to call him simply the Contract God. His explanation for this reticence is that his business is getting other people's names on the bottom of the page, not his. I agree, of course, but I am disturbed. If major-league organizations, and men such as Phil Regan and Ralph Avila, exploit Dominican youngsters at all, they are neither secretive nor apologetic about it. There is no question about the C.G., however. His business is all take and no give, and it demands the same namelessness he affords his "friend" with the nude photographs. Just as he defends his pal's dirty little secret, I will defend the C.G.'s shadowy enterprise.

I ask the Contract God about his percentage of these youngsters' minor-league contracts. In turn, he asks what percentage my agent takes of this book. When I tell him it is 15 per cent, he shakes his head. "My kids can't afford 15 per cent," he says in weak denial. In fact, no matter what his percentage, the Contract God is taking their money for no services rendered; as young minor leaguers, his clients have contracts that are automatically renewed. At this point in their careers, contracts are not negotiated. His cut is like postage and handling.

The Contract God has an encyclopaedic knowledge of the young players in the Dominican. Call up any kid's name and he'll quote that kid's time for the 60 down to the tenth. I point to a player, not one of his, on the sidelines. "7.2," he says and dismisses him as *"un poco"*. If challenged on a kid's speed or ability, the Contract God can produce from his attaché case, say, the thumbnail scouting reports of the Yankees' most recent signees. These are the identical reports filed by the Yankees' man down here and how the Contract God got his stubby little fingers on them is anybody's guess. Complicity with the man down here? Someone bought inside? There's no questioning the authenticity of those reports. There is also, says the C.G., no questioning how this information landed in his lap.

There are still a few minutes before the game begins; time enough for the C.G. He goes to the cage and tells another youngster that he just signed that guy over there, that kid from the Detroit organization. Got a bunch of good players. We're a winning team. He keeps on selling.

At 10 o'clock of a Wednesday morning in November, the Contract God is walking the grounds of Parque Olympico in Santo Domingo. A few major-league teams work their young signees at the park. The level of players working out here is the same as that at El Complejo Epy: recent signees with no pro experience, up to a few prospects with limited experience in Double A. Among the clubs in attendance today is the Pirates and their front man is Pablo Cruz. On this day, Cruz is putting his charges through their paces before an afternoon exhibition game against the Expos' young prospects. And on nearby diamonds major leaguers are working out on their own. Beside the Pirates' diamond two pitchers, Cecilio Guante of the Rangers and José Rijo of the Reds, are throwing and running.

The Contract God talks with Cruz while his players are at various stations on the diamond: outfielders long throwing, pitchers on bullpen mounds, infielders taking ground balls. The Contract God asks Cruz about the best kids he has and the scout is raving about Moises Alou, son of Felipe Alou, part of the ever-expanding Alou clan in pro ball. In spite of the rave-up, though, the C.G. is clearly not content with just one name. He wants to know more names, other talented players. Despite Cruz's enthusiasm for Moises Alou, the Contract God is in a hurry to pass over the youngster, because as the son of a major leaguer Moises is likely being helped by his father in negotiations, or already committed to a name agent. The boy would be too sophisticated to latch on with the first American voice he hears, and the Contract God specializes in unsophisticated clientèle.

All the while the assistant, Benvenido, listens in, offering translation whenever necessary. Though the Contract God does not write down names in a notebook, Benvenido will remember them for him. And when the C.G. gets his hand on a list of Pirates signees—from whatever source—his young assistant will mark asterisks beside the most promising.

The Contract God does not seek to mask his work under a veil of good intentions. His is a speculative business and not especially a service. "At this point it's not like handicapping horses," he says, watching the Pirate futures work out. "It's like a yearling sale. You just have no idea who will do well for you and who'll be a washout."

When I ask him about what he said at the ballpark the other night when he spoke to the kid in the Detroit system, about helping make sure that he gets a fair shot, the Contract God is quick to speak but slow to get to specifics. "There are things I can do," he says. "A few phone calls I can make for the kid. But mostly I can help him with the taxes and immigration. What I do lets them concentrate on baseball. You can't know how hard it is for these kids to look after things like that."

At that point in the C.G.'s discourse an older man passes by and asks if Benvenido is ready. The Contract God says yes. Benvenido goes to the car to get his spikes, bat, and glove out of the trunk and tells his mentor that he will meet him later tonight.

"That's Ben's personal trainer," the Contract God says when he sees my puzzlement. I ask if this is like the personal trainers in Canada and the U.S., the exercise mavens who set up personal workouts for moneyed, health-conscious folks. He is quick to correct me.

"The trainers are like bird-dogs or scouts in the States, but in the Dominican these guys take a more active role," he says. "They find kids, train them, sometimes feed them and give them a place to live. The personal trainer then takes the best kids to tryouts. He gets about $300 for each kid who signs on with a club. The clubs pay him for developing talent and steering the kids towards the club. They have to—in the States the bird-dogs or part-time scouts get a retainer with one specific club. Down here, you work on spec, unsalaried. Without the $300 commissions, there'd be no reason to stay in the game. And if you get ten kids a year, well, you've had a hell of a year."

This explains Tomás Santana's role with Epy Guerrero, Santana's excitement at the signing of Alfredo Arias and his willingness to believe—or make Epy believe—that Green Pants was in fact seventeen instead of twenty-one. Santana was hoping his enthusiasm for Green Pants was infectious. When Arias signed it was money in Santana's pocket.

"This personal trainer can't believe that I'd give him a couple of bucks to work out with Ben," the Contract God says. "I told him that I wanted to try to get Ben a scholarship to a U.S. college, probably a junior college in Florida."

The kid for whom the Contract God will solicit a scholastic free ride is a modestly talented, unusually bookish, computer-adept kid named Benvenido, literally "welcome". The personal trainer is skeptical. It is hard to believe that the black-hearted Contract God would do anything gratis. The trainer's skepticism is well founded. It seems that Benvenido will spend a month providing translation for the Contract God and finding the best buys and most accurate directions. The kid will even pose as just another player at tryouts and games to dope out potential clients for the C.G. In return, the Contract God will make a phone call, probably collect, to a junior-college coach that he knows or, at least, knows of.

The case of Benvenido, a kid aspiring to U.S. college ball rather than the pros, is rarer in the Domincian than a scrupulous politician. According to the C.G., U.S. schools never send their recruiters to the Dominican, even though these same universities have hockey teams manned by Canadians or track teams packed with foreigners. "College [in the U.S.] isn't an option for these kids. They can't turn down the money. Three hundred bucks for an average kid or a grand for something special—it sounds like peanuts to us. But you can't imagine how that money might look to a seventeen- or eighteen-year-old kid from a poor family down here. Besides, a college can't know how a kid will handle the culture shock in going from a barrio to a U.S. campus."

Much of what the C.G. says smacks of racism, insofar as the Dominicans are not given a chance because of discriminatory practices. Unfortunately, his arguments ring true. To make his point, the C.G. sets out a hypothetical situation. "Take two kids of

equal talent. We'll give them a fair bit of talent. Put one of them
in the U.S. and one in the Dominican. Okay, the kid in the U.S. is
a second-round draft choice. He's not that surprised. His coaches
have been telling him for a couple of years that if he works
hard, he's scholarship material and probably a draft choice. The
kid and his family probably know people who've worked in the
game for years and they realize that this kid can command, say,
$80,000 or so for a signing bonus. If the club offers him that,
he won't jump on it. He'll get the advice of coaches. The college
recruiters are talking to him. The kid might get an agent and wait
till the offer is sweetened up. He knows that until he makes the
major leagues that's really the only money he'll see. If the club
doesn't cough up, then the kid can go to college for a couple of
years and go through the draft again. The kid will realize that he's
holding the hammer. The American kid has options and good
advice. If he passes up the pros to play college ball, he can get
the same bonus, maybe better, and get a free college education
as well.

"Now the Dominican kid is a different story completely.
There's no draft, so there isn't a market value you can tag on
him. A scout can offer him a couple of thousand bucks although
he knows that the young Dominican has the same ability as that
second-rounder in the States. The scout tells the kid he has so
long to decide or else he's going to spend the money on another
player. Just gives him a little pressure. The kid has to decide—
sign, or wait. His family doesn't know anything about ball.
And, if it's a poor family, for them two or three thousand bucks
American looks like a lot of money, more money than they've
ever seen at one time in their lives. The only person the kid can
get advice from is the personal trainer and his commission is
fixed at $300 a head. Of course the kid doesn't know that. The
trainer will always do the same thing: tell the kid to sign the first
thing that comes along, sometimes a contract with no signing
bonus at all."

The Contract God must have his reasons, but he has ballparked
his figures somewhat low. Though Arias's bonus was $2,000, and
Tony Fernández's only a thousand more, Dominican ballplayers
have frequently commanded more than what the C.G. quoted.

Besides Liriano's $5,000, other numbers that I've heard include $15,000 for José Oferman, the brightest light in the Dodger system. One minor leaguer told me that a few of the young Dominicans on the Blue Jays were in the $10,000 range.

Though his estimates are off, the bottom line as the Contract God sets it out remains valid: the supply of prospects exceeds the clubs' demand for prospects. This is not to say that clubs don't want the young Dominicans. As always, teams are hungry for talent. It's just that the young Dominicans are starved for opportunity, and baseball, no matter how it is packaged, is seen as the ultimate opportunity. This is a buyer's market.

I ask the Contract God about the possibility of agents stepping in early, signing youngsters before they go to the trainers, or working in tandem with the personal trainers. The C.G., of course, scoffs at any such notion. "The trainers tell the kids that agents just take a percentage of their money and don't do anything for it. And to tell you the truth," he says with surprising candour, "early on, before the kid signs, there isn't a lot I can do."

The Contract God says that he has agreed to represent a couple of kids, small-timers, before they signed. "It's almost a joke," he says. "They're very average, not hot prospects. I'm in no position to shop these kids for a percentage of their signing bonus. It's just not worth my time. I did it just to give these kids a charge. You know, some kids will be bragging, 'I got a contract with the Yankees.' These kids can say, 'Oh yeah, I got an agent.' You've got to remember there's a lot of guys in Double A or Triple A who've never had an agent."

I ask the Contract God if acting, or rather actively acting, on the behalf of players before they sign will violate his relationship with clubs. At present, he is tolerated if not welcomed at most training sites or complexes. Would he be *persona non grata* if he tried to make this a fairer, more competitive market? "No," he says, "I can't change the system by myself." The Contract God clearly has no desire to corrupt this market—cozy for team, personal trainer, and agent, less so for player—with any tinge of fair play or equity.

"You got *un agente*?" the Contract God asks a bulky young man in a Licey uniform. The player's dark and menacing countenance would be enough to scare others off, but this agent to the not-yet-rich-or-famous doesn't know fear when in the hunt for a talent.

"No," he says.

"We can help you. There are things we can do. Where did you play last year?"

"Albuquerque."

"Albuquerque," the Contract God says. "I know Albuquerque real well. Dodgers, right? Well, listen, if you think you're not moving fast enough we can do stuff for you. Believe me, we'll look after you. We're a winning team." The Contract God will not push the sale. This is one for future reference, it might take a couple of days. When the player walks away, the Contract God says to Benvenido, "You can't hard-sell everybody."

Benvenido is grimacing, and for good reason. If his benefactor knew Albuquerque real well, knew the Dodgers real well, or even the winter league real well, he would recognize this fearsome hitter.

"You know that is Domingo Michel," Benvenido says once the outfielder is out of earshot. Domingo Michel was leading the league in average and home runs at the time. "Dodgers. Cousin of Pedro Guerrero. He's stuck in that organization but they don't protect him and nobody drafts him."

The Contract God instantly understands what Benvenido is referring to: Michel is not on the Dodgers' forty-man roster. He was left unprotected at the free-agent draft a few weeks before and not one of the twenty-five other ballclubs figured that he was worth the risk of $50,000 or worth a spot on their twenty-four-man major-league roster—a ringing indictment of a player in his mid-twenties. This, the Contract God knows, is probably as far as Domingo Michel will ever go. "Not in this lifetime will he pull down a major-league wage," the C.G. says later—meaning his is a percentage not worth seeking.

Such glorious and sometimes embarrassing wastes of time notwithstanding, the Contract God will go on about his business, showing off his nudie photos, doing his magic tricks, doling out his business cards and filling young players full of large talk. He will come back to the Dominican winter after winter, taking 15 per cent of a lot of kids' minor-league contracts. Those future signees are on the street now. Many clients will be back there soon.

*

In the home half of the second inning, Geronimo Berroa slams a double deep to centre field. Escogido cannot cash him in, however, and Licey's pitcher Juan Guzmán steams along. Young Vizcaíno blows two attempts to lay down a sacrifice bunt and fouls out to the third baseman. Samuel Sosa, right fielder for Los Leones, lines out to a diving Santana in centre field. And Hector de la Cruz flies out weakly to left field. Phil Regan does not go for theatrics. He walks to the end of the dugout and sits on his hands. This is the way his season has gone: never an easy night and always a sense of imminent disaster.

CHAPTER FOUR

The "Best" Prospect in Baseball

LICEY	00	0 0 0
ESCOGIDO	00	0 2 0

Leading off the third inning for Licey is Henry Rodriguez, the first baseman. De León overpowers him, striking him out with a fastball in on the fists. One out. Rodriguez stomps back to the dugout to a few derisive whistles from the Licey fans behind Los Tigres's dugout. While catcher Gilberto Reyes, the next batter, steps in against De León, Henry Rodriguez tosses his helmet into the rack, retrieves his glove and walks down to the end of the bench farthest from the manager and coaches, farthest from attention. Rodriguez sits beside Silvestre Campusano. Campusano is hunched over, elbow on his knee, chin balanced on the palm of his hand, hat pulled low over his brow. He reacts to nothing taking place on the field.

De León goes to two-and-oh on Reyes before throwing a fastball for a strike.

Rodriguez takes off his batting gloves, looks around distractedly and sulks. Campusano is motionless. No words are exchanged.

Reyes flies out meekly to left fielder Geronimo Berroa. Reyes jogs across the diamond, tosses his batting helmet to the ground in front of the dugout and heads towards the far end. This end of the bench is refuge for Rodriguez and Reyes in a moment of torment and frustration, for Campusano in a season of inactivity and despair.

Tito Bell is the next batter and he is completely overmatched against De León. After a ball on the first pitch, De León runs two strikes on Bell who half-heartedly swings late at a fastball and way out in front on a breaking ball. He then hits what looks like a sand-wedge shot out to short to end the inning. De León is still perfect.

The Licey players take the field again. Rodriguez and Reyes walk up the steps from the heartbreak end of the dugout. Campusano is still camped there. He has been most of this season, a fifth outfielder on a team that rarely uses its fourth.

*

It's a lousy, lousy day to come to the park. It's Sunday, early in the season, and first-place Los Tigres of Licey are scheduled to take on Caimanes del Sur, the weakest team in the loop. It's supposed to be a four o'clock start, but the November rains have waterlogged the field at Estadio Quisqueya. The diamond looks like a patch of Everglades wilderness. Umpires are not needed as much as lifeguards.

Beneath a black sky broken only by lightning, a member of the field crew walks out in bare feet to the most swamp-like regions. Out there, ungrounded and uninsurable, he rolls a six-foot-long sponge in the drink. When he finishes sopping up a couple of gallons, the sponge is about as heavy as he is. When it is at last fully saturated, he carries the sponge to foul territory. There he twists and drains it and returns to the field to repeat the process. He does this dozens of times during the downpour. It's a tribute to Dominican ingenuity that he has made the field almost playable. At the same time, it's a testament to the peculiar

Dominican efficiency that he has transformed foul territory into a water hazard.

The managers and coaches walk around the perimeter of the tarpaulin-covered infield and talk with the umpires about the viability of the day's game. The Licey braintrust is all for sitting out this one. Los Tigres are in first place, so there is no reason to risk injury to their stars. There's no loss of a live gate because the fans have chosen to stay home rather than to take a hot shower. However, the league brass has directed the boys in blue to squeeze in every last date. It's been a bad season for rain-outs, blackouts, and all forms of cancellations. The second half of the season is already fully booked with make-up dates. For the umpires, justifying—or rather, rationalizing—playing this or any soggy session is easy. They tell the managers that conditions are never great and on the make-up date, who knows, the weather might even be worse. The Licey coaches argue with the head umpire and maintain that there should be no game. With a two-hour delay at the start and any number during the game, this will be an awful and long day. After a post-game shower and a beer they will have been at the park at least ten, maybe twelve hours. They make one last appeal for mercy. It's in vain.

While the skies rain and the umps explain and the sponge-keeper drains, I stand in the Licey dugout. There I spot Silvestre Campusano. We shake hands and make small talk. I try to make sport of his situation and say that he's a Blue Jay in the States but a Dodger down here. His face goes blank—for a second he thinks that I've said he's been traded to the Dodgers. In fact, I was just trying to make light of his being one of the few on the club who is not Dodger property. It's never good to joke with a player about getting traded or released. Especially if he is on the periphery, unsettled, and without security.

When the air clears and the misunderstanding is forgotten, Campusano says he's not having a great season down here—playing time for a member of the Jays is hard to find on a club dominated by the Dodgers. I ask if he thinks there'll be a game today. He shrugs. "If there's a game or not it doesn't matter," he says. "I'm not playing." Not playing, just watching the rain fall and the sponge roll. This is a lousy, lousy day to come to the park for Silvestre Campusano. The manager, the umpires, the fans, the players, and God knows, the guy with the sponge, they are all unhappy. But Campusano's discontent is a little different. They're mad. He's sad.

At 5:30, after ninety minutes of deliberation, the umps deem the field ready. Licey takes the field. The players stand ankle deep in puddles and the scratchy anthem echoes around the empty stadium, drowned out a couple of times by thunder.

Silvestre Campusano, hat off and over his heart, looks to the outfield, to the spots occupied by Licey's front line, all property of the Dodgers. He sees in centre field José González, a back-up who played infrequently last season with L.A.; González returned with little personal distinction but nonetheless sporting a World Series ring. In left field Domingo Michel, the player any major-league team could have purchased at the minor-league free-agent draft for a mere $50,000; no team thought he was worth the investment. In right field, Doug Jennings, a young Floridian and a utility player with the Oakland Athletics last season. The A's had to keep Jennings on the big-league roster all year because they acquired him as a free agent; he'll be returned to the minors for seasoning. For Campusano and those who watched him three seasons ago, it would have been difficult to imagine that three young players of middling accomplishment would today be displacing him in the Licey outfield.

Like many Blue Jays fans, I had an opportunity to see Campusano occasionally flash his skills with the big club during the 1988 season, his rookie year in the majors. That he could only flash his skills compelled the Jays to return him to the minors for the proverbial seasoning. Although Campusano had only 142 at bats, playing in only 73 games with the big club, even a casual observer could not miss the lightning bat speed, the superior running ability and an arm that inspired comparisons to Roberto Clemente. The touting of prospects is like advertising, a business of loose talk, part truth, part wishful embellishment. It's an estimation of promise, not a promise of delivery. If Campusano were anything near the equal of Clemente, he would be playing this day for Licey.

I've had the chance to watch Campusano at a few other stops on his odyssey through the minors. This afternoon off for Campusano, be the game played, delayed, or postponed, contrasts sharply with our first meeting, when his name was falling off the lips of every scout in sight.

Back then, in November, 1985, Silvestre Campusano was a year and a half older than Licey's batboy. Campusano was little bigger and only slightly more imposing than the *maniceros* and the young gate-crashers at Estadio Quisqueya. When he entered the stadium through a side entrance for players and employees, he could have been mistaken for a member of the ground crew, a candidate to flog peanuts or roll the tarp rather than a budding major leaguer.

Despite his appearance, his never-shaven face and diminutive stature, Silvestre Campusano was already famous in his homeland, revered by Licey fans and heralded by major-league scouts as one of the brightest talents in the game. Indeed baseball officials and the media embarked on something verging on Campumania, a singing of praise for the youngster based primarily on half a season in Knoxville, Toronto's Double A affiliate. Even big leaguers, usually skeptical of such hype, joined in. "He's the best prospect in all the minors," said Dámaso García. "I heard about him in Toronto, but I can't believe the way he hits. I don't see how he can miss."

The first time I saw Campusano play, his team, Licey, was taking on Escogido. I sat behind the plate, behind the screen with three of baseball's best minds: Tim Thompson, an acerbic, skeptical man whose flat-top hairstyle hinted at his service with the St. Louis Cardinals and his undying allegiance to baseball's best-known brush-cut, Whitey Herzog; Earl Rapp, a veteran scout with the Expos; and Karl Kuehl, a younger but incisive director of player personnel with the Oakland Athletics.

With the exception of Epy Guerrero and a few other charismatic renegades, scouts are protective of their opinions and wary of outsiders. They rarely let their guard down. After all, given their authority, their opinions are elevated to the rank of information, and theirs is an information business. And they are natural skeptics. A prospect isn't a player until he proves beyond any dispute that he is. Platitudes and praise for speculative items do not course from their lips.

Yet before this game, when I approached Thompson, Rapp, and Kuehl and asked them about Campusano, there was no such apprehension. This suggested that the scouting fraternity had reached a consensus, that Campusano was common knowledge and that he had won over his toughest audience.

"He's a blue chipper," Thompson said. "Toronto has got a good one, a major-league type of talent."

"There's no secret about this boy," Rapp added. "Another kid I might not want to talk about, but Campusano, well, everyone knows that this boy can play the game. Just to be playing out there with major leaguers, playing well, at his age and after a half-year in Double A, you've got to have a lot of talent."

Karl Kuehl deconstructed Campusano into component parts for me. "There's five things a ballplayer is graded on," Kuehl said methodically. "Hitting for power, hitting for average, throwing, fielding the position, and running. He rates outstanding in every aspect. If you rate him down a little on hitting for power—it might be the only thing where you might grade him down one notch—then you could grade him up a shade on the arm. He throws better than a lot of boys you'd still rate outstanding."

After this symphony of superlatives, Thompson sounded the cautionary note. "All he has to do is get out there and produce," he said, sounding like a man who too often had seen such sure things go awry.

Though the youngster would have been hard pressed to live up to this billing in the long term, it seemed he was intent on doing just that before we got back to our hotel.

The winter league of '85–'86 featured many more American players and many more big-name Dominican players than subsequent seasons; the quality of the league is tied to the strength of the Dominican peso, and '85–'86 may have been the last good year. Tony Fernández, coming off his first full season with the Toronto Blue Jays, was the designated hitter for Licey; Mariano Duncan, having starred for the division champion Dodgers, was Licey's starting shortstop; and there were others. A measure of the depth of quality was José Uribe, a starting shortstop with the San Francisco Giants but just a utility man with Los Tigres. Tim Thompson said that the level of play in the Dominican league was "between Triple A and the major leagues, although some parts of the league are deeper than others." There were not a few starters and only a handful of players at the end of the bench without some Triple A experience. Sil Campusano was one of this number and the only one starring in the league; he was the starting right fielder for Licey and was not yet nineteen.

The game that Thompson, Rapp, and Kuehl watched was scoreless going into the bottom of the seventh inning. Leading off the home half of the seventh was Campusano. Though Licey had only three hits to that point, Campusano had been on base twice, once reaching on an error, and the other time on a walk. In the seventh, Campusano jumped all over a fastball and lined a shot into left field. When he saw this, Karl Kuehl remarked (somewhat prophetically, as it happened), "He hits everything to left, but when he gets wood on the ball, he smokes it." Campusano then went from first to third on a single that barely reached the outfield grass in right, and scored on a fly to centre. It was the only run of the game and in the the top of the ninth Campusano sealed the win with a running and diving catch of a ball hit deep into the right-field corner. Had it fallen in, it would have been a triple and sent the game into extra innings. Campusano was the star of the night at the plate and in the field.

If producing in the clutch was a criterion for baseball prowess—perhaps a sixth to be added to Kuehl's list—then Campusano was once again outstanding. On this night, like many others back in the summer and early winter of 1985, any day was a good day to come to the ballpark.

In the coaches' office in Licey clubhouse after that game, the team brass talked about the game and Campusano's progress. Luis Pujols was the manager of Los Tigres back then. During his playing days, Pujols was a catcher who could do little more than catch—that is, he couldn't hit, run, or throw much. He was able to scratch out a career with the Astros on the strength of charisma and modesty, and he looked on with envy at gifted youngsters like Sil Campusano.

"Campy's maybe a little like César Cedeño," Pujols said. "Not as good yet as Cedeño was at eighteen—when Cedeño was twenty he was a major-league All-Star and I don't think Campusano is gonna move that fast—but Sil does everything good." When I asked Pujols what he would do if he had Campusano's talent, he only shook his head and laughed; he had no words for such wishful thoughts.

Another fellow in the office told me the story of Epy Guerrero's discovery of Campusano. Nelson Geronimo, a hanger-on with Los Tigres, told me that he recommended that Epy look at this kid from Mano Guayabo. Mano Guayabo was once a town outside of Santo Domingo, north and just west of the city proper. As the city started to swell up, Mano Guayabo became a suburb. It is home to the Bohemia brewery and a number of military installations. Other than that business it was, Geronimo said, "about the poorest place around here". That is, its poverty is virtually beyond the First World comprehension. Geronimo said that at a game in the barrio a kid, a catcher, caught his eye. He passed on word to Epy Guerrero.

When Guerrero found this kid, Silvestre Campusano, and worked him out, the scout couldn't understand why the boy was behind the plate. Too short and thin to take the unrelenting physical beating a catcher must endure, Campusano ran the sixty-yard test in well under seven seconds, very good speed for an outfielder, speed that would be wasted behind the plate. Though Campusano showed a few other assets—a good arm, fast wrists through his batting stroke—it was his speed that convinced Guerrero to sign him.

"Epy signed a lot of poor kids," Nelson Geronimo said, "but Campusano was really poor, just about the poorest. Some kids at El Complejo whose families were really poor, they felt sorry for Campusano."

Not long after that Epy Guerrero walked into the Licey clubhouse. Back then he had the type of sway in this locker-room that Ralph Avila has now, four years later. The Blue Jays farm system had a much more prominent place on the roster of Los Tigres and Guerrero was a more frequent guest in the clubhouse.

He confirmed much of what Geronimo said—although Epy, never one to share the spotlight, contended that Geronimo was "one of the guys who told me about Campusano." This he said when Geronimo was out of earshot. Still, like Geronimo, Epy painted a picture of boy whose beginnings were shockingly deprived.

When players first go to El Complejo, Epy said, they must make several critical adjustments. "They got to play every day, all day, instead of playing on weekends. They have to play the game seriously and they have to listen to coaches. They have to do things they never did before. But Campusano—the biggest change for him, he had to get used to eating every day.

"For the first month or six weeks, Campusano didn't show nothing. Couldn't run, hit, throw, nothing. After that, after some good food and getting looked at by the doctor and everything, the kid started to hit everything. He was the best player at the camp."

Campusano was getting into his street clothes only a few steps away from the door to the coaches' office. "Now look at him," Guerrero said, resisting understatement and modesty. "The best player in the minor leagues, and I signed him.

"Sometimes the poorest kids make the best ballplayers," Guerrero said. "The game is everything for them. When you have nothing the game is everything."

What about the other times? I asked the scout.

"Sometimes the poor kid gets a little money and he gets comfortable. He doesn't want anything else—maybe a car, a nice house or apartment and he's happy. Sometimes once they get the bonus and a year or two in the minors, they don't want anything more. They take a few things from the game and stop.

"I think Campusano is gonna stay hungry," Guerrero said. He then offered a perfunctory proviso. "Nothing's sure with kids nineteen years old, but this is a kid who should make it."

That night in 1985 Campusano impressed fans and scouts in the field. Yet in jeans and a T-shirt he was utterly unassuming. The effect of baseball uniform is unpredictable. It can make a slob look like an athlete, or it can conceal and diminish the physique of an Adonis. With Campusano, he grew inches in his uniform and looked like a man. This star quality on the field did not carry over when the lights went dim and the players returned to the dressing room. He was wiry and trim, but unexceptional.

He was neither brash nor shy but certainly not yet accustomed to the ritual of the post-game interview. He told reporters that his catch in the ninth was not a tough one. He seemed unprepared to talk about the game action. By the time I got to him, he was more interested in talking about what he would do one day rather than what he had just done that evening.

In his complaints and enthusiasms, in his fears and aspirations, he sounded like many Latin-born minor leaguers. There is some truth in the generalization that Latin players in the States have more difficulty with culture shock than with hitting curveballs. Ask them the hard part of the game in the U.S. and it is usually something away from the field. Campusano fit the mould. "The States is okay," he said. "Things are tough. Restaurants. Finding a room, a place to live. The minors, they're hard for Americans. For Dominicans they're extra hard." Not once did he mention anything about the game.

We talked about his family. He was the last of eight kids. He said he wanted "to help the family.... That's the only thing to do with the money." And it is the universal goal, it seems, among the young Dominican players, to be the provider of the best possible life for their family.

There was an innocence about him that players have at eighteen but lose before they make the majors. When I asked him if it was harder to hit Double A pitching than the stuff in A-ball or rookie league, he said no. "The guys in Double A throw harder but it's over the plate," he said. "In A-ball...," he motioned with his hands: balls up in his eyes, down in the dirt, way outside, and even by his face. "A-ball, they don't know what they're doing."

I wanted to talk to Campusano about the scouts' ratings of him. But with someone unaffected as he was by his accomplishments to date, and by his all-but-inevitable success, I chose not to risk spoiling his unassuming attitude.

The next morning I sat at a table with Earl Rapp and Bill Monbouquette in the Hotel Lina's breakfast restaurant. The Lina played home to scouting and coaching honchos from nearly every team in the majors.

Monbouquette, a former twenty-game winner with the Boston Red Sox, had worked that season as the pitching coach with the New York Yankees. The position of guru and mentor to pitchers in the Bronx has long had no more security than that of a tail-gunner during wartime. A few months later, Monbouquette would find himself working in the Yankees' minor-league system. That winter he was in the Dominican working with the Yankees' prospects.

Rapp filled in Monbouquette on the game from the previous night. And though Rapp talked about Campusano, stopping just short of raving, Monbouquette was unimpressed.

"The Jays have had a lot of success with these Dominican kids," Monbouquette said. "You give them credit for that—Gillick and Guerrero. But there's some organizations that just don't think they're worth the bother."

Rapp nodded. He understood even if he didn't share these sympathies. When I asked Monbouquette to explain what bother, he went on at length, complaining about how he had to check up on a few boys who had signed with the Yankees.

"You sign a kid," he said, "and you give him some money. The team invests a little more money in him and brings him to the States. All this time, you don't know what they're doin'. You can't predict what they're gonna do. You work with a kid who you think is gonna be the future of the organization and when he comes back to the Dominican in the off-season he's livin' in some goddamn barrio, in some house with dirt floors and no running water. He could be catchin' some goddamn disease. Dominican kids, I tell ya', some of them can really play. But some of them can be hard on your nerves. They can break your heart."

It wasn't a tirade, not spoken in anger. It was just a lament spoken in exasperation. What Monbouquette was defining was the Old School's view of Latin players in general, and Dominican players in specific.

"What kills you," Monbouquette concluded, "is that there's a part of these kids that you know you can never reach."

The reasoning with some members of the baseball establishment is plain: if you know you can't reach them, it's not worth the bother to try. It sounded blatantly prejudiced. I thought that Monbouquette might change his tune if I talked about some talented young players, so I mentioned Campusano.

"He's looked pretty good so far," he said, sounding like a man who obstinately refused to be impressed, "but it doesn't mean anything till he gets to the majors. Look, Toronto's had some luck with the Dominicans but it isn't all good—the stuff with George Bell. You don't just want a good player. You want a good person. I'm not saying Dominicans are bad people. I'm just saying it's hard to tell if you got a good person, if you got a team guy, good character, when you sign these kids. The American kids it's a helluva lot easier to know what you've got. It's a helluva lot easier to know what they're gonna do."

Monbouquette's exasperation with the unpredictability of prospects, particularly Latins and especially Dominicans, brought to mind a discussion I once had with the Pittsburgh Pirates' Howie Haak, a scouting legend in the tropics. On Haak's recommendation the Pirates acquired Roberto Clemente from the Dodgers' organization and Clemente's stellar play brought a rush of scouts into Puerto Rico and other parts of the Caribbean. Haak also signed two Dominican stars—former All-Star second baseman Julián Javier, who played for the world champion Cardinals team in '67, and Tony Peña, who has given the Pirates and Cardinals many good seasons. Haak first scouted in Cuba in the 50s and then spread his attentions all over Latin America. In the Dominican he is known as El Tiburón, the Shark. He earned notoriety as the most hungry of scouts during the revolution in '65; when bullets were pelting down like raindrops on the streets of Santo Domingo, Haak, as legend has it, was crawling on his belly under snipers' gunfire to track down and sign prospects.

I met Haak one year in spring training and I asked him if Clemente was the best prospect he'd ever scouted. "Clemente was the best player," Haak said, "but Alfredo Elmeada was the best prospect, the kid who had the most potential, the most promise. He was faster than Clemente and could do just about everything else—hit for average and power—that Clemente could. He had a great attitude, great feel for the game. First-rate kid."

In part the conclusion of Haak's story was already clear: if I had to ask Alfredo Who? then this was one prospect that didn't pan out. But the reason Elmeada never made the big leagues was tragic.

"Alfredo tore up A-ball," Haak said. "He was just eighteen and hit .310, had more than sixty stolen bases in a short season, hit seventeen triples and eighteen doubles, a flier with power. What a prospect. But anyway he was playing right field one day and Pablo Cruz [today the Pirates' scout in Santo Domingo] was playing second base. Cruz always had a bad knee and he had on one of those knee braces you don't see any more, the ones with the big steel hinges on both sides. So anyways, they're out in the field and a boy hits a little fly ball that's coming down between them. Cruz runs back and Alfredo is flying in, neither of them are looking at the ball. Alfredo dives for the ball and his head hits Cruz in the knee. The brace goes right through his skull. He died right there at the ballpark. The best kid I ever scouted dies right there.

"Now I end up going to the funeral in the Dominican. I can't believe this kid is dead 'cause, well, 'cause they're not supposed to die. In the back of my mind I couldn't believe it—I kept thinking they're trying to steal this kid from me. Anyways at the funeral it was the hottest day in the Dominican ever. Even the Dominicans were sweating this one out. So when they lowered the casket in the grave I knew this kid was gone. His father went up to the side of the grave and he was supposed to throw some dirt on the casket, but instead he faints and falls dead away into the grave with his son. At that point I felt like jumping in 'cause I figured I'd never see another one like Elmeada. I've seen some good ones, sure, but I never saw one like him again. You don't send anyone to the Hall of Fame off what they do in A-ball, but get me clear on this, this kid would have been a major-league star like Clemente, no doubt. This kid gave you everything he had to play—it ends up he gave everything he had to catch a little Texas Leaguer in A-ball."

Haak's story is not typical, of course. Prospects who die on the field are extremely rare. Still, many prospects die in a figurative sense every season. For every prospect that makes it there is bound to be another ripping at a scout's heart.

By the spring of '86, Campumania had extended beyond the Dominican and scouting circles and reached the U.S. media. During spring training, *Baseball America*, the bible of minor-league baseball, issued its evaluations of the best talents in the minor leagues. The evaluations were based on a survey of scouts, managers, and other insiders. The newspaper contributed to the legend-in-the-making by deeming the nineteen-year-old the second-best prospect among outfielders in all of baseball. The top-rated outfield prospect, José Canseco, went on to win an American League Most Valuable Player Award three seasons later.

Not long after that, once the minor-league season began, *Baseball America* printed a feature story about Campusano. The headline loudly pronounced him "The Best Prospect in the Minors".

The Canadian media picked up on what looked to be a fast-developing story. Campusano received occasional mention in the Toronto press, and television commentator Tony Kubek enthusiastically told everyone, "Wait till you see this!"

While Campusano was being touted by one and all, he was not honing his skills and putting in the hard work that would speed his climb to the major leagues. For much of that early spring he was sidelined and in convalescence with a broken bone in his foot, an injury he suffered late in the Dominican winter-league season. After spring training he was assigned to return to Knoxville; the Jays' front office had every right to assume that Campusano, once recovered, would again tear up the Southern League as he had in the late summer of '85.

In August of '86 I was in Memphis, home of Elvis, and of the Chicks, the Southern League affiliate of the Kansas City Royals. Mike Jones, then the manager of the Chicks, had his own bundle of unpolished talent, a precocious halfback-outfielder named Bo Jackson. Jackson did not make *Baseball America*'s list of the minor leagues' five most talented outfielders behind Canseco and Campusano. When I asked Jones about the good young outfielders in the league, he offered a surprising evaluation of the Knoxville Jays' prospects.

"There's no doubt that, right now, Rob Ducey's already passed Campusano as a prospect," Jones said. "Campusano's game is based on his speed, and since he broke his foot he's lost a step, a step and a half or something. In '85 he was running a lot, stealing bases, hitting .300, lots of doubles and lots of range in the field. But this year, he hasn't shown any speed at all. He doesn't beat out infield hits. He can't steal. Campusano in '86 is half the player he was the year before. Coming out of the '85 season, if you went to the scouts and said that they could have one player out of the league, they would have taken Campusano. Now, if you went to the scouts and told them that they could have two outfielders off the Knoxville roster, they'd take Ducey first and probably Glenallen Hill second."

The manager might have been blowing smoke—it is a manager's prerogative—so I talked with a couple of the Chicks to see if Jones's was a minority opinion. To my surprise they all agreed with him. First baseman Jere Longenecker was in his third year with the Chicks and evidently at the end of his minor-league career. He had seen prospects shine and advance, others fade and vanish. "Last year Campusano looked like Roy Hobbs, the Natural," Longenecker said. "He could do a lot of things when he got here last summer. Why isn't he playing well now? He's supposed to be hurtin' but when I saw him he just looked like another guy. The thing I've learned is that in this league you're either moving up or moving out. You're either improving or falling behind. If you're standing still, the guy behind you is gonna pass you. Campusano's game probably hasn't changed much—he hasn't got worse, he's just stood still. Now everybody knows about him. The pitchers throw to him different. He hasn't figured out how to hit them this season. Maybe he hasn't even figured out that they're throwing him different."

Eight months before, scouts spoke of him in glowing words; but in his second tour of the Southern League, Campusano was a disappointment.

A few days after talking to Jones, Longenecker, and the other Chicks, I arrived in Knoxville and was surprised to find that Campusano wasn't even playing for the K-Jays. He was nursing a sore wrist, a trainer said. But even in the weeks leading up to this small hurt he had been struggling terribly. Ducey was playing well, hitting around .300 with some pop; he had won regular duty in centre field. Glenallen Hill was on his way to a thirty-homer season. Campusano was banished to the bench.

Larry Hardy was then the K-Jays manager. He had an explanation for Campusano's woes and, in a way, Karl Kuehl's assessment of Campusano's hitting—that "he hits everything to left"—foreshadowed difficulties the youngster was having in his second go-round in Knoxville. "Every time a boy moves up a level, he sees players that are not only better, but smarter too," Hardy said. "Everybody has to make adjustments in Double A. From A to Double A might be the toughest jump in the minors.

"Last year the pitchers in this league had never seen Sil. They threw him fastballs to see if he could hit them. Sil made them pay. He's fast enough to get around on a major-league fastball. But Double A pitchers aren't stupid. They're not gonna keep throwing him fastballs so he can watch them go out of the park. They started throwing him breaking stuff and they started pitching him outside and out of the strike zone a bit. And they found out that he tries to pull everything, no matter where it is. All that stuff away, he just hacks at it and hardly gets any wood on it at all. He has to make that adjustment now—he has to learn to hit that outside pitch into right field. When he does that he'll see some fastballs inside again."

Hardy didn't sound worried about Campusano. When I mentioned this to Hardy, he nodded.

"I'm not," he said. "This might be a good thing for him. You want to see how a boy handles a little adversity. You don't want him to go all through the minors real easy. You want to see how they take a challenge. With Sil, after the year he had last year, you know he can handle things when they're goin' right. You want to see how he handles things when he's goin' bad. Besides, it's better if pitchers in Double A find your weak spots. You don't want to be learning to cover your weaknesses when you get to the majors."

I found Campusano in the pre-game and asked him about the stories in *Baseball America*, about being the best player in the minors—at least, the best before the season began.

"They said I was the best?" Campusano said with an expression of wide-eyed disbelief. "No, I never heard about it. Who said it?"

Despite these protestations, Campusano most certainly had heard about it. *Baseball America* may not have impressive circulation numbers in the general public, but it is indispensable in minor-league clubhouses. *BA* is the only authoritative and complete record of major- and minor-league transactions and events. It is the only way players can keep track of who's biting at their heels behind them and who's ripe to be passed at higher levels. *BA* is to the minor-league clubhouse what the *Wall Street Journal* is to corporate boardrooms. Though Sil Campusano's English is limited, his teammates, particularly the American ones, were aware of the stories, as was Larry Hardy. Campusano was probably ribbed about his reviews.

Campusano was not convincing in playing dumb to the expectations and pronouncements of scouts and media. He could not be blind to the advances he had made in the organization or deaf to the attentions given to him by the reporters in Knoxville and in the Dominican.

"I'm just a player," Campusano said. "There's a lot of players. I'm just a player working every day. The best, I don't believe that. I never heard of it before."

When I asked about his poor season and his long stays on the sidelines, Campusano was a little defensive. "I don't think I'm having a bad year," Campusano said. "I hurt my wrist but it's no problem. My foot is good, no problems there."

Mindful of Jones's assessment, "a step, a step and a half or something," I asked Campusano if he was running as well as last year. Again he played dumb. "I'm running the same," he said. "The start of the season it was hurting, now nothing, no problem."

Helping with the rough spots in the conversation was a young man, an outfielder named Bernie Tatis. When Campusano and I were finished, Tatis told me that "Campusano can't miss, he's a major leaguer for sure." Again the can't-miss label. Tatis added that he was going to make the majors too, but that he could only hope to be "a player, not a star like Campy." I told Tatis that his English was excellent and he said that it's all part of getting to the major leagues.

Tatis's assurances aside, Campusano's E.T.A. in the majors seemed, at the end of the Southern League season, well off in the future. In fact, it did not seem a certainty at all. When *Baseball America* offered its season's end assessment of the Top Ten prospects in the Southern League in '86, Campusano did not even receive honourable mention.

In 1987, Campusano rebounded somewhat from the desultory second season in Knoxville. He spent the full '87 campaign in Syracuse. It was not a complete return to his form of the glorious '85 season, but a certain improvement on 1986 and the benching in Knoxville. It was a time of small triumphs for a player who once seemed destined for sensational ones.

In Syracuse Campusano stayed clear of injury, played regularly if not spectacularly, and hit in the .270s, though not with home-run power. He had reason to go into the 1988 season with optimism. Though he had already known the heights and depths of the minors, heard the acclaim, and been passed over, Campusano was still only twenty-one, still learning to be a ballplayer. To borrow the shop-worn sporting cliché, his future was still ahead of him.

In the months before spring training in '88, Campusano was again playing for Licey, and Epy Guerrero was touting him to anyone who would listen. Campusano was doing nothing with Licey that warranted such optimism; nonetheless, Epy was predicting that his young find would be the centre fielder for the big club, the Toronto Blue Jays, in the major-league season.

"This spring he's gonna get his chance," Guerrero said, "and when he gets it he's gonna take off. He's still gonna be a star."

I told Guerrero that some people wondered whether Campusano deserved all this hype. I didn't detail how his stock had plummeted in *Baseball America* or how Southern League players and managers had concluded that he was no longer a prospect. Those same people would probably protest that Epy's awarding Campusano a position, even a back-up's position, with the major-league squad was premature. Or completely out of line.

"A lot of people expected him to hit forty homers, steal forty bases, everywhere he went," Guerrero said, oblivious of the notion that his hype of Campusano may have fuelled such unrealistic expectations. "They can't think he's gonna do that all the time. But no matter what he was doing, you could always see something. If he was swinging and he missed the ball, you could see how fast his wrists are. Nobody's got wrists like that. When he was throwing the ball, maybe he wasn't throwing guys out, the throws off the bag or something, but you could see he's got a strong arm. With guys in the minors, it isn't always what you do that's important—it's what it looks like you can do, what it looks like you will do."

I talked with Campusano in January of '88, just weeks before he would be reporting to a training camp.

"I don't know where I'll go, Syracuse, Toronto," Campusano said in the Licey clubhouse before a game. Though his destination had to weigh heavily in his mind, he put on a fairly phlegmatic front. "A *pelotero* just goes and plays. I don't ask questions. Young players don't say anything—I don't say anything. They pick somebody to play in Toronto this year. If it's me, good. Somebody else, OK. I keep playing."

Even if Campusano was in the dark about his immediate future, Guerrero knew something. Going into spring training the Toronto Blue Jays' front office was considering—and probably committed to—starting either Rob Ducey or Sil Campusano in centre field with the big club. Ostensibly this was to shore up the outfield defence. George Bell's range in left was decreasing; Lloyd Moseby's arm in centre in his best years had been just adequate and was by then a liability. By moving Moseby to left and George Bell to DH and by placing either Ducey or Campusano in centre, the Jays would have shored up their outfield defence, protected the American League MVP's aching knees, and promoted a young player who should have been ready to advance.

The fall-out from the move had a negative effect on the ballclub. Bell, at best a testy soul, was told that he was too poor a fielder to play left every day; to him, the move to designated hitter was an insufferable affront. It was much the same for Moseby, being shifted and slighted to accommodate one of two rookies, players who had yet to prove that they could hit Triple A pitching.

The media build-up had Ducey as the favourite for the spot. The Blue Jays' brass may have been presenting it that way to lighten the pressure on Campusano.

On Opening Day in Kansas City in '88, Sil Campusano was standing in centre field and George Bell was on the bench when he wasn't at the plate hitting three home runs. That may have been the last good day for the system.

The experiment was an utter failure. "Campusano was under a lot of pressure," Epy Guerrero says today. "You don't want to start a kid off like that. Maybe as a fourth outfielder or something. But all the problems [with Bell and Moseby]—it was bad for the club, that's most important. But for Campusano, it was really bad. He tried to show he belonged there right away. When you're like that, you try too hard and you just can't play."

In early summer Campusano was placed on the injured reserve list. Soon after he came out of the sick bay, he was returned to Syracuse, where he finished the season. He was not part of the call-up at season's end. And in early winter, after the winter-league meetings, Campusano was dropped from the forty-man protected list. There were names on the list so obscure that even the most dedicated follower of the Jays would not recognize them: Dennis Jones, Steve Cummings, and others. There was Junior Felix, who was in rookie ball when Campusano was tearing up the Southern League three years before. But in November of '88, Sil Campusano, this conspicious talent, the starting centre fielder on Opening Day, was considered dispensable, and these near-anonymous players and relative neophytes had supplanted him on the honour roll.

Bernie Tatis's luck in baseball has nearly run out. He can be excused for any self-pity. Any bitterness can be understood. He is wearing the green of Los Estrellas Orientales, his second uniform of the week. During the summer he was sold from the Toronto Blue Jays minor-league system to the Pittsburgh Pirates. It's not that he can't play anywhere. Teams are still interested in him. It's just their quality of interest in him that dispirits him so. He has been designated a minor-league journeyman in the States and with this trade to Estrellas, he's on his way to similar status in his homeland.

Tatis has the cheekbones and strong jaw and flawless complexion of a male model. He has the powerful athleticism, lean build, springing step, and rippling forearms that a baseball uniform cannot hide and need not flatter. He looks great—great, that is, until he steps to the plate. Bernie Tatis isn't hitting. "I haven't seen him hit yet," the Contract God tells me. "I don't know how a guy looks so good and swings so bad."

Bernie Tatis is making the transition from a prospect to an organization player. A prospect is a youngster with much promise who is moving up the ladder and learning to play at more advanced leagues every season. An organization player is an older fellow, perhaps once a prospect who has proven that he lacks a certain fundamental skill which prohibits him from playing in the major leagues. Bernie Tatis can't hit well enough to be anything more than an organization player, a warm body to fill the roster. Not every minor-league team in every organization can fill its roster with players they project will be in the majors one day. Where there are no prospects, organization players fill in.

Tatis knows that this transition entails a redefinition of objectives. He cannot think that if he works hard now it will pay off in big-league stardom down the road. Bernie Tatis has advanced precisely as far as he ever will. He can only worry about keeping his spot on a Triple A or Double A roster, making a few hundred dollars a month in the States and the Dominican, and perhaps landing a job in baseball—coaching or managing or scouting—once he's finished playing. To this end, he is still working hard on his English.

Back in 1986, when Tatis was still something of a prospect, he was a teammate of Sil Campusano and Rob Ducey in Knoxville. According to Tatis, Ducey has remained a prospect but Campusano is in danger of becoming an organization player, fodder in a minor-league line-up.

"What happened to Sil doesn't surprise me," Tatis says. "The Jays sign Dominican kids—Epy signed me and I thank Epy—but when the Dominicans get to the minor leagues, the Jays forget about you. They don't talk to you. They don't care about you. They don't look after you."

It is a blanket generalization, and it is not the first time I've heard it. The Jays seem to put the Dominicans in diamonds far-flung around the minors.

"Bobby Mattick just doesn't like Dominicans," Tatis continued. "I know that. He never comes out and says this but he doesn't hide it. What happens is you see guys who get through—Tony Fernández, Liriano, Lee—but there's a lot of guys who get lost in the organization. A lot. That's what happened with Sil. They wanted Ducey to make it. Now they want Derek Bell maybe or some other American player. The Dominican kid can show a lot in Medicine Hat or some place, but it doesn't matter. A lot of American guys get through because these are the guys that Mattick loves."

Perhaps it was not a breaking point for Bernie Tatis, but it was in Knoxville that he soured on the Jays' treatment of Dominican players. Tatis was a second baseman when he was signed and came up through the system at that position. He didn't hit poorly for a middle infielder; they're glove men rather than big swingers. Tatis was hoping to develop either into a major leaguer at second, or into a utility infielder.

In what was his first full year in Knoxville, he was told by coaches that he was going to be the starting second baseman for the K-Jays and that he would have an opportunity to play every day there. It was the type of talk that a minor leaguer likes to hear.

Then came an unanticipated development, the type that changes the course, not only of a player's year, but of his career. The Jays signed a pair of minor-league veterans, free agents with six years in the minors, eligible to sign with any interested club. They were given second base to share with the K-Jays. Tatis couldn't even hope that an injury would throw him back into the fore—it would take two. The vote of confidence given him in spring training could not have been less sincere.

According to Tatis, nobody from the organization told him of the move. He says that he read about it in the Knoxville papers. And, he says, nobody explained to him why they wanted him to move to the outfield. "I was a second baseman always," he says now. "I was ready to quit. I was proud of how I played second and I always thought I did a good job at it. Nobody ever said, hey you better play better or your job was gone. People in the organization told me that they liked me, that I was doin' a good job. I knew I was gonna have trouble hitting enough to make the majors as an outfielder, especially when the Jays had Moseby, Barfield, Bell, and a lot of good minor leaguers. When I got back to the Dominican after the season, people asked me, 'Hey Tatis, how was Knoxville?' I say I was playing outfield. They thought I was joking around. They know I can play second. It didn't make any sense." As it turned out, Bernie Tatis never played second again.

"What was worse was that they released the guys after the season was over. It didn't make any sense."

The only other time that Tatis might have got his hopes up about his future in the Jays organization was before the '88 season. In the weeks before spring training, scuttlebutt in the media had Tatis making the big club that spring as a back-up outfielder, as a utility man.

"I heard people talk about it," Tatis says, "but after Knoxville, I knew not to listen. I knew that if they were talking about me like that either something good or something really bad was gonna happen. They were gonna promote me or they were gonna trade me." The latter, it turned out, was closer to the truth. He was not traded, but in fact sold to the Pittsburgh Pirates. The talk about moving him up to the big club may just have been some type of leverage in commanding a few thousand dollars more.

I suspect that some of Tatis's allegations of poor treatment, heartfelt though they are, smack of sour grapes. His attitude is fairly common among Dominican players who don't advance to the big club. And from what I have seen of Bobby Mattick, he is innocent of Tatis's charges.

In spring training one year I watched Mattick work with a young Dominican kid, a catcher, at the minor-league complex, away from the bustle of the big-league workouts at Grant Field. For an hour, Mattick worked with the kid on the proper way to chase a passed ball or wild pitch: sliding on knees, reaching for it bare-handed, squaring to the plate while still on the ground. It was just one drill among the hundreds that the minor leaguers have to endure. Mattick struggled away with the kid. He was telling him to drop the ball, but the kid just stood there, frozen and intimidated. Mattick knows a few words of Spanish—but not nearly enough. I stepped to the other side of the cage and helped him with my pidgin *español*, and together we were able to convey the message.

When Mattick later spoke to me about Dominican players, he sounded nostalgic. "They remind me of the players I grew up with and players from the Depression years," he said. "There's a real difference between wanting to play, no matter how bad you want to play, and bein' hungry to play, *havin'* to play to live. When you look at the chances these kids have back on their island, you understand that they're playing something more than a game. The stakes are different." He spoke with a respect that was not grudging.

Only once did I hear anything that might suggest something remotely resembling prejudice. I mentioned to him the successes of Epy Guerrero's scouting in the Dominican and he was quick to rebuke me with a harrumph and an abrupt statement of cold fact. "Guerrero's only ever signed one player who made the big-league club," he said. This was early 1987, and he was, in essence, correct. If Mattick was sounding a cautionary note about Epy's achievements, however, they were easily explained: as director of the minor-league system, Mattick might believe that, among the scouts, Guerrero's finds are often heralded in the press, while other productive scouts receive no real acclaim.

But the issue is not the question of any sort of prejudice that Mattick or any other member of the Jays organization may have against the young Dominican players. What is important is that some Dominican players, with good cause or not, believe that they are not given equal and fair treatment by management. For the Dominicans it is easy to believe that the old-time baseball men, the vast majority of them white, and middle-aged or older, are pro-white, anti-black, pro-American, anti-Latin.

In talking to Mattick on a few occasions, I have never heard or seen anything that might suggest that Tatis or any other Dominican player has good cause to believe that he was treated unfairly by him as a result of his nation of origin. But as with the young catcher in spring training, Mattick had trouble trying to get across simple directions and instructions to his non-English-speaking players. He asked the ballplayer to put the ball down and go back to his position. The kid kneeled with the ball and held it in his hand and was frozen in fear. Mattick tried to get the kid to reach for the ball with his right hand, with his bare hand, but the kid did not know right-hand from left-hand, only *derecho y zurdo*.

It is in this failed communication that bad feeling can grow. The worry on this catcher's face showed through his mask. Such a rudimentary, almost insignificant, skill could not be explained to him. Could Campusano accept instruction outside his mother tongue? Could he retool a swing when he was unsure of the directions given him? Ballplayers are often defensive when it comes to coaching. They do not like to tamper with a skill that has been successful for them. They must make a leap of faith to put themselves in the hands of a coach. It is an impossible leap, however, to put themselves in the hands of a coach they do not understand.

When Campusano hears about his removal from the forty-man roster, he is not fazed by it. He shows up at Estadio Quisqueya for another game. He shows up though he will not be starting, only watching players who have passed him by. He does not seem surprised at being dropped from that roster, from the list of the forty best players in the organization. He made this list when he was only eighteen, when he was a young, valued property. He is a little older than when we first met, already older than a few of the players on the list. "I'm not worried about the forty-man. I don't know what happened last year. I'm not worried about it. That stuff isn't important. They think I need to play in Syracuse another year. I don't know. I don't think so but I work for the Blue Jays. I do what they want. That's all."

Once, Campusano's teammates beheld him as a legend. Even that has now passed.

I told Doug Jennings how scouts raved about Campusano's arm, how they compared it to Clemente's arm. He was not impressed. "He's got a good arm," Jennings said, "but saying it's great is an awful lot. Look, there's a couple of kids on this club, not guys playing but young kids down at the end of the bench, kids eighteen or nineteen years old, I don't even know their names, and they throw even better than Campusano does. You see it with all the kids down here. They all can throw. I guess it's just something that they work on more than we do in the States."

Up at El Complejo, where Sil Campusano learned about eating every day a few years before, Epy Guerrero shows me a plaque he received from the Topps Baseball Card Company. It honours him as Topps Minor-League Scout of the Month. He received this award back in '85 when Sil Campusano was tearing up the Southern League. The day he is showing me this award, he has just heard that Campusano has been dropped from the Blue Jays' forty-man roster.

"Maybe I get a few more of these awards," he said. "Maybe I get one for Domingo Cedeño some day. You remember the name 'cause this kid is going to be special. And Junior Felix, I think Junior Felix is going to make the ballclub. You can't keep this kid down too long."

Guerrero then points to two other Topps awards he has garnered: one for signing and scouting César Cedeño; the other for the obscure Eddie Dennis.

César Cedeño, who may one day be known as Domingo's cousin, was an All-Star in the early '70s. Despite his winning honours in The Show, César Cedeño is in many ways Epy Guerrero's Alfredo Elmeada. After several seasons of great play for the Astros, Cedeño earned a reputation as one of the best young talents in the game. His combination of power and speed had scouts comparing him to Mickey Mantle. Then, the unthinkable: a woman was shot and killed in Santo Domingo, and Cedeño was charged and convicted of manslaughter. Cedeño served a brief prison sentence. "After the shooting in '77, he was never the same player," Guerrero says. "He made All-Star again, but he was never the same man." According to Guerrero and those who played with Cedeño, grief and shame consumed him. He might have been able to overcome almost any physical injury but the psychological damage was irreparable.

Eduardo Dennis, on the other hand, just faded. Despite having promise enough for Topps to bestow this second award on Epy, Dennis never played a game in the majors. "Eddie Dennis, he should have been a major leaguer but he never made it. He could run. Fast man, maybe not like Junior Felix, but fast."

What happened to Dennis? I ask Epy.

"I don't know. It was nothing like Cedeño. Not one thing. No injury. Nothing. Just one day he came to the ballpark and it looked like he was running in sand. He lost it. Gone."

I ask Epy about Campusano, a kid he touted just as vigorously a few years before. I mention it must be disappointing that Campusano has been dropped from the forty-man roster.

"He still gets invited to the big-league camp," Guerrero says.

This is, of course, small consolation for going from being the most talked-about minor-league prospect in baseball, the starting centrefielder on Opening Day, supplanting a League MVP for his spot in the line-up, to being a non-roster invitee to the big-league camp, just fodder for the big guys and a quick ticket to the minor-league camp.

"He just has to move his hands from here...," Epy assumes a right-handed batter's stance and holds his hands high and tight to his body, "...to here...." He show his hands a little lower and a little more removed from his trunk. "It's not tough. Just mechanics."

Only then did Guerrero's exasperation show through.

"I don't know why he hasn't done it already. It's something he should have done three seasons ago. I said he was gonna be a great player. I still think he's gonna be a major leaguer, but sometimes a kid surprises you. Not the kid with some talent who works hard and does his best and makes the majors. A kid like Liriano doesn't surprise me when he gets to the majors. What surprises me is the kid with everything, like Campusano. You think he's gonna be great. One day you wake up and you hear he's released. He's run out of time."

Guerrero's experience with Campusano recalls Bill Monbouquette and his stereotyping of Dominican kids. "It kills you when you know that there's a part of these kids you just can't reach." But Epy Guerrero's frustrations with Campusano suggest something more painful: perhaps there's a part of the young Dominicans even one of their countrymen can't reach. Sometimes those who would be great just find themselves running in sand.

*

The game continues to move briskly in the bottom of the third inning. Licey's Juan Guzmán steams along. He sets Wilfredo Tejada down on strikes, induces an outfield fly from Nelson Liriano and then runs the count full on Junior Noboa before whiffing him on a fastball up.

Campusano watches all of this. If he were a young player, one of the nineteen-year-olds out of A-ball, he would be satisfied just to be around major leaguers, just to be a part of the winter league for the first time. The kids are always happy in the dugout, learning about the game, making friends. Campusano is not a kid any more. He was once a star on this field. He must now feel like an intruder in the dugout. He must feel as if time is passing him by. But if it bothers him, he has not shown it so far.

CHAPTER FIVE

The World's Oldest Thirty-Two-Year-Old

LICEY	000	0 0 0
ESCOGIDO	000	0 2 0

Going into the top of the fourth inning, José De León has yet to yield a hit to Los Tigres and has allowed only one ball to the outfield. But the first suggestion of trouble comes when Miguel Santana draws a walk on five pitches and then steals second on the next pitch. Any rally seems thwarted when Rafael Belliard goes down swinging and Luis Reyna pops up to short for two quick outs. But Domingo Michel—"*el primo de* Pedro Guerrero," the radio man announces—sharply smacks a fastball deep in the hole between third and short. Only José Vizcaíno's range and a belly-flopping stab keep the ball in the infield and hold the fleet Santana at third base. But with men on first and third, Doug Jennings, the recent arrival from the Oakland A's, chops a routine two-bouncer to Liriano at second. The half inning is over. De León walks to the dugout.

In the morning papers that day, De León had threatened to abandon the Escogido side, not because of friction with the

management of Los Leones, but because the St. Louis Cardinals
had been slow to negotiate a new contract with his agent, so the
threat of injury may force him from the line-up. If he were to
come up with a sore shoulder or some other ailment, it would
damage his negotiating position. The Cardinals would not race
to the table to ink damaged goods.

While Licey takes the field for the bottom of the fourth, De
León tells manager Regan that he's feeling his shoulder tighten.
Regan could probably see this coming. This isn't De León's
doing; his agent has warned him to be extremely cautious. Regan
tells John Davis to get up in the bullpen and get ready in a hurry.

In Escogido's tiny dressing room the veteran De León is
showering. In Licey's dark and squalid quarters another veteran
is already in his street clothes. Dámaso García is talking to
Silvano Quezada, the pitching coach for Los Tigres. García
arranges a time with Quezada for batting practice before Licey's
scheduled late-afternoon session.

When this is done, García walks out the back exit and makes
his way to a white Mercedes. Like De León, Dámaso García is a
veteran in search of a contract. But De León is hoping to improve
on an existing pact. So far in this winter no ballclub has expressed
any interest in García. A couple of clubs have told him that he
can attend their spring training camps but without a contract or
guarantees. García finds this insulting. His workouts are sporadic
and half-hearted; he hasn't played in the winter league in five
years. He might be able to showcase himself to ballclubs if he
played in the winter league this season; but long ago, when
he signed a multi-million-dollar contract with the Toronto Blue
Jays, García decided that the Dominican league wasn't worth the
risk. He still thinks like a million-dollar ballplayer, but the fact
that no team is making concrete offers this late in the off-season
suggests his value as a player is a fraction of what it was short
years ago. And if he succeeds in fooling himself, he isn't fooling
the fellow who'll be throwing batting practice for him tomorrow.

*

Even though sportswriters are supposed to be above fandom,
to have left idolatry back with bubblegum cards and bedsheets

with hockey players and gridiron heroes dancing across them, and to be paragons of objectivity, many are secretly passionate fans. I, for one, must confess to a personal prejudice: when he was at the top of his game, Dámaso García was my favourite ballplayer. I feel no guilt about this particular enthusiasm of mine, but I will undertake here not to be overly partisan about Dámo. Henceforth, fair-minded objectivity.

But you cannot ignore García's achievements. Back in 1980, his first season in the majors, García hit .278 (with thirty doubles) and combined with shortstop Alfredo Griffin to give Toronto one of the league's best defensive middle infields. He was the best first-year player in the American League but finished fourth in the A.L.'s Rookie of the Year voting. You who would dispute the claim to García's superiority, look at the winner and the first runner-up: Joltin' Joe Charbonneau and Britt Burns. A flawed hitter with home-run power, Charbonneau was only distinguished by his ability to eat light bulbs. He was playing semi-pro ball just five years later. Britt Burns was a fine pitcher whose quality years were ruined by injury. García deserved a better fate. In hindsight, voters realized the error of their ways.

Two years later García was the Jays' first position player to be named to the *Sporting News* American League All-Star team. (In that same year Dave Stieb was the *News*'s A.L. Pitcher of the Year.) García hit .310 that year and stole fifty-four bases. Though eclipsed later by the achievements of George Bell and Tony Fernández, among others, García was the first prime-time talent produced by the Toronto organization. He hit .307 the following year and again won League All-Star honours in '85.

I talked with García for the first time in November of '85, shortly after his heroics and the Blue Jays' Eastern Division title. Well, to be precise, it was the first time that we had a conversation; I had spoken to García once before, at a banquet in Toronto during his rookie season. He looked uncomfortable on that occasion, so when I approached him I told him in Spanish that I admired his play. He smiled and said nothing. When I told him that I thought he would be a great lead-off hitter if he drew a few more walks, he glared at me and stomped away.

Five years after that rebuke I went into my appointment with García expecting nothing better than our first meeting. García's manner shocked me. It was the first of many surprises.

We agreed to meet in the bar at the Hotel Lina in downtown Santo Domingo, and when García first walked in I was amazed by his size. Back in 1980, in his business suit, he seemed to be the size listed on his baseball card: a bit over six feet and 175 or 180 pounds. But five years later he looked an inch or two taller and filled out. He seemed dynamic. When they first meet García, most people are surprised at his stature—he is bigger than they imagined—and they tend to be filled with admiration for his physique—physically, he could only be a professional athlete.

Before he made his way over to me, García made a round of handshakes, greetings, and best wishes with several businessmen (not baseball executives, but financial power-brokers) who were into their rums at the exclusive bar. García had a reputation for being able to turn on the charm when it suited him. I thanked higher powers that he considered the magazine story I was working on suitable for his charm.

"It's different if you come to my country to talk," García explained. This sentiment would be echoed later by George Bell and others. "And I want to speak in English, not Spanish. I've worked hard on my English. I'm proud of it. I want to use it."

I mentioned that Blue Jay banquet years before and García had an explanation for his silence. "It was difficult for me," he said. "I was young, still working on my English. I was in the majors for the first time and I wanted to do everything right. I worried about playing. I worried about talking. The game is more than playing. It's everything you do. That's what teams think. Maybe it shouldn't be that way. Maybe the game should be everything. But [major-league teams] look at everything you do. I wanted to do everything right."

The game of sportswriting demands a little amateur psychology. By the time the waitress came to take our orders, I had already selected the theme for the evening: pride. García is one of the proudest people I have ever met, perhaps even proud to a fault.

García talked about his youth without much prodding and he measured his story well, pausing not for questions but only to organize the story he wanted to tell. It is a difficult thing to do in your mother tongue, all the more difficult to do in an adopted language and certainly something to be proud of if it can be done successfully.

"We were not poor," he said. "My father worked at a church. Like a superintendent. Our family was never hungry. My father had a good job and he was proud of it. He wanted the kids in our family to go to school, to be professionals. That was important to him. We lived in Moca in the north, near Santiago. It's different than the life in Santo Domingo. It is not a poor town. And the people are big. They eat well. The farms are there.

"I was a good student. My father told us to do well and I did. No matter what we wanted to do, he wanted us to do well, do our best. 'Never be lazy,' he told us. 'Other people are lazy but not the Garcías.'

"I played baseball when I was young. When I was in university I played on the junior national soccer team. I had a chance to go to Italy to play soccer. I was the best on the team, probably the best on the team, sure.

"I only played baseball when our Moca team needed me. I played shortstop. That's where they always put the best [athlete]. When our town team played other towns, that's maybe the only time I played. For me it was soccer that I liked. I played baseball just so other towns didn't beat Moca.

"Epy [Guerrero] saw me back then and signed me to a contract with the Yankees. I was studying at Madre y Maestra University in Santiago, in my second year of engineering. Epy gave me eight thousand dollars. My father wanted me to stay in school but eight thousand dollars then was a lot of money. I had to take it. My father understood. He told me to do my best at baseball, to be the best there is.

"When I signed and got my first dollar, I knew that baseball wasn't a game. It was a business. I wanted to be the best and to be paid as the best. There are some guys who love to play the game. For me it is different. I play it because I can play it well. I play 'cause I can play second base better than anybody else. But if I wasn't being paid, if I wasn't in the major leagues, I would never go to the ballpark. I will never be a coach or a manager. Nothing. I only want to play well for money. When I can't play I'll go and I'll never come back to the ballpark."

At this point I asked him about how he played the game. More precisely, I asked him about his attitude. He knew what I was getting at and laughed.

"You mean The Look."

Indeed. If anything coloured the public's perception of García, it was his face. Or rather, it was The Look, a dispassionate gaze that irritated fans. García's defenders—they were few—called The Look "concentration". His detractors—they were legion—considered it an expression of uninterest in the diamond, perhaps even a disgust with the inconvenience of having to play the game.

Too often how a player looks overshadows what he does. For the fans, at least, appearances count for more than performance, style more than substance. If García had displayed enthusiasm but contributed no more to the team's good, he would have fared better.

"I never want to look happy when I do well," he began to explain. "And I never want to look mad when we lose or when I strike out or something. I never want to show the other team what I'm thinking. If I show them I am mad it gives them something to play for. If I [look] happy, they think I'm [showing them up]. No expression. *Nada.*

"People think I don't try in the field all the time because I look that way. But I don't like to talk it up in the field. I give everything but I don't smile. Off the field I smile and I laugh with my family and friends. But with others, they see those things in my face. I can't do anything about it. That's my face. That's the best way to play. Play hard, show nothing."

No writerly turn could better explain García's approach than his own words: "Play hard, show nothing." But why, I asked, do fans see something there? Why do they see something negative?

"The fans don't understand baseball first," he said. "They don't understand how tough it is to play all those games. They don't understand how tough just one game is. And they don't understand that this is how Dámaso García has to play every game.

"And Toronto fans, they don't understand Dominicans. They look at my face and see something, something they don't like. Dominicans look at my face and then they look at what I do at second base and they see something they like. Americans, Canadians, they look at Dominicans and say we're moody. I'm not moody, I'm quiet. I never said a lot in English till I could speak it. I stayed quiet and they called me moody. It shouldn't matter how I am in the clubhouse. Hey, on the field I have one mood. Player."

He stirred his drink. "You don't like my face?" he asked and smiled. I told him that I liked how he played second base and that he'd be the perfect lead-off hitter if he drew a few more walks.

That winter of '85, on one trip with García to Estadio Quisqueya, he introduced me to a former teammate: Silvano Quezada, the pitching coach for Licey. García and Quezada played with Los Tigres for several years and both ducked out at the end of the 1983–84 winter-league season, García because of the risk of injury, Quezada because he had too few pitches left in his right arm.

One afternoon before batting practice at five o'clock, García took me to Licey's bullpen where Quezada was warming up. At 6'4" and 190 pounds he was, I assumed, one of the pitchers for Los Tigres. While firing in fastballs to a kid in borrowed catcher's equipment, Quezada was holding court with a few players, coaches, and members of the press corps.

"Twenty-two and two," he said. "I was twenty-two and two in the Mexican League a few years back and they just said, 'Silvano, don't come back 'cause we can't hit you.' That was maybe the best I played."

"You see this guy," García explained. "Forty-six years old."

When Quezada spied García, he stopped pitching and, hands on hips, pretended to get on his case. "When you come back, I'm going to come back," he yelled with feigned irritation. "I'm ready. Are you?"

García did an about-face and walked off laughing. I stayed behind to talk to his tormentor, his former teammate and keeper of the Quezada legend.

Silvano Quezada did indeed look more fit and trim than many of the hurlers he coached. The years had eroded a couple of feet off his fastball but nothing from his stature. He had played professional baseball for twenty-four years—year-round for twenty-four years—and yet neither he nor his arm seemed tired of the game.

With García's interruption at an end, Quezada picked up where he had left off with the story of his twenty-two-and-two season.

"How old were you?" someone asked.

"I don't know," Quezada said. "Maybe forty. I stopped counting."

I came to suspect it was more than years that Quezada stopped counting, or at least stopped counting accurately. I view the 22–2 record with some suspicion. When I looked to his Dominican winter-league stats, I found evidence that Quezada was an effective pitcher. His best year was with San Pedro's Estrellas Orientales in the winter of 1967–68; that season Quezada led the league in innings pitched with 136 in fifteen starts and seven relief appearances. Though he recorded an earned-run average of 2.05, Quezada won eleven games and lost seven. And across his career, which was the longest in Dominican baseball, with twenty-four seasons, he was only a handful of games above .500, sixty-four wins and fifty-nine losses. This low number of games won and lost in his career is the result of his dispatch to the bullpen as a reliever in 1969; thereafter he was only a spot starter in the Dominican winter league. To ring up a 22–2 season in the Mexican League as a starter ten years after relegation to the bullpen…well, the word dubious springs to mind. To call it a lie would be too absolute; after all, at age forty, Quezada did lead the Dominican winter league in ERA with a minuscule 1.50 mark in fifty-four innings of relief.

Though he was never specific about his age, Quezada seemed to know virtually pitch-for-pitch proceedings in his starts in the Mexican League that season. "The first game I lost was 2–1 with both runs unearned. An outfielder dropped an easy fly ball and the guys scored from first and second. That game was one of the best I pitched that year but the only real loss. The other game was extra innings of the second game of a double header. I pitched a shut-out, complete game, in the first game [of the double-header]. The second game they used me as a reliever and the ump wouldn't give me a strike. He wanted the home team to get at least one game or else he was gonna get shot getting out of the ballpark. So he kept calling balls until I walked in the winning run."

In everything that Quezada said and did that evening, he expressed a love for the game, a love for the ballpark. It was not absolutely requited love: in all his twenty-four years, Quezada did not once set foot in a major-league park. For more than a decade he pitched in the American minors—he says he's been in every bus station in the U.S.

"This is the best place to be," he said. "The ballpark, the best place in the world. When I was a kid, we played because there was nothing else to do. And then we kept playing because we loved the game so much. I played twenty-four years, never made any money really. Enough to live, but I was never rich with money. I'm rich with baseball. If I made the majors, well, maybe. But it didn't happen. I'm not unhappy about that. I played the game. I saw a lot of things and I thank God that when I stopped pitching Licey kept me as a coach. I love to coach, you know, not as much as pitching but to help young players, to talk to them, guide them is a special thing."

Silvano Quezada's philosophy was the antithesis of Dámaso García's. He said that did not unsettle him. "Dámasito is one of the new ballplayers. I came over to Licey just for the last couple of years of my career and Dámaso was already a major leaguer. Players are different today. We never had ballplayers who thought so much about money, who thought it was that important. I pitched against the Alou brothers, Rico Carty, Manny Mota, men who loved the game. They took the money paid them, sure, but on the diamond, in the dugout, in the clubhouse, it meant nothing. And I don't think it's the kids who are different. It's just the money—the millions of dollars—that makes them different than we were. Today, ballplayers have to think about contracts, money. I like the old way better. We were free to play without worries. I know we were happier than they are."

Quezada then bade me goodbye and walked over to the mound where José Rijo was throwing. The coach gave the young fireballer some instruction and demonstrated the proper mechanics. He did not berate the young pitcher. He did not sound stern. No, Quezada spoke softly and sought the young man's trust. When Rijo got it right, Quezada smiled. His contentment in this place was the best evidence that his generation was indeed a happier one.

This was not to say that Dámaso García seemed unhappy by comparison to Silvano Quezada. In fact García, though viewed by many as a truculent malcontent, was more agreeable and talkative than I had ever hoped. But as Quezada might have presumed, the economics of baseball preoccupied García. In the course of small talk Dámaso managed to mention that he would be secure for life when his contract expired—he was in the middle of a five-year deal that awarded him $800,000 U.S. per annum for services around the middle bag—and that he expected to go into business with Mario Soto when their playing days were over, probably in commercial real estate and development in the Dominican. Though García's brother and sister had recently moved to New Jersey, he said he had no ambitions to live in the United States or Canada.

It was not long after our discussion that García's standing with the Jays took a precipitous fall. In García's own definition, a team values a player for what he does both on and off the field. García was in jeopardy for non-performance on the diamond, and for a few excessive performances off it.

Before the 1986 season started, the newly appointed manager, Jimy Williams, stated that García would probably be removed from the lead-off spot in the Jays' powerful batting order. The reasoning was sound: García did not get on base often enough. García went public with his dissatisfaction. Though expressionless on the field, off the field García expressed nothing but hostility towards Williams and contempt for the notion that this All-Star should have to bat ninth in the order.

From Opening Day of '86 on, García's game faltered horribly. Once a free-swinging .300 hitter, he saw his average plummet into the .240s. Beyond that, his base-running ability vanished overnight. Though he remained sure with the glove, his range diminished. In just a few months he had deteriorated from an All-Star to a marginal major leaguer.

The Jays would have been loath to sustain García for the '87 season even if he had the sunniest of attitudes. But he assured his departure from the club when, one night after a tough loss on the West Coast, he set his uniform on fire. Somehow fans and management failed to view García's act of burning his uniform as a joke, or as a release of frustration. They saw it instead as an unpatriotic act. The Jays wanted rid of García not only because his game was going south, but also because he had defiled the uniform. The club wanted rid of him because, on a symbolic level, this was tantamount to torching the flag. If that reaction now seems extreme, well, remember: most baseball executives are registered Republicans.

The next time I talked to García was during batting practice at Toronto's Exhibition Stadium not long after he torched the team colours. I was working on a story not related to Dámaso, but I thought it was only polite to say hello and to thank him for the time he had given me in the Dominican. After his round of batting practice I walked over to him, only to be greeted with The Look. After all the ice breaking in Santo Domingo, after the warm conversation, after I'd even picked up the tab, he gave me the same frozen greeting that he had in 1980. He shook my hand, said nothing and went back to work.

It was disconcerting, to be sure. García had been warm and friendly in the Dominican and then cold as a glacier in Toronto. I wrote it off to the pressures of the moment, and a season-long bad mood.

Dámaso García was dispatched before the 1987 season to the Atlanta Braves. He was moved with Luis Leal, the highly paid Venezuelan farmhand, in trade to Atlanta for Craig McMurtry, a pitcher of no consequence. The Jays were responsible for some of the salaries they were dumping but the team had to be happy not to have those names cluttering the roster.

The Braves organization couldn't have been pleased that García's name was printed indelibly on its injured reserve list. García did not play in a single major-league game that season. In fact he only appeared in one game with Triple A Richmond while on a rehabilitation assignment. Though the skeptics thought he was malingering, García had problems with his knees in Toronto. The best evidence was the drastic fall-off in the totals of his stolen bases—from his career high of 54 in '82, down to 28 in '85, and just 9 in '86.

The next time I talked to García was in January of '88. He was one of the star attractions at "The Dominican Baseball Fantasy Camp", a week-long vacation during which grown men tried to play baseball like the big leaguers. Epy Guerrero was hosting the campers and García was one of the instructors. I was attending, hoping to add colour both to my complexion and to a magazine story.

Before the first practice, I went up to Dámaso, not sure if he would recognize me. I did not know if the iciness of the last meeting would have thawed by now. Happily, he did remember me and was again the gracious García from the hotel bar. He was in good spirits because, as he told me, he was almost healthy. "My knees are good," he said. "And Bobby Cox [the general manager of the Braves, who, as manager of the Jays, had a good relationship with García] says he wants to use me at third base. Not too much to field, so I'm going to have to hit for some power. I'm going to have to put up some numbers."

He would indeed, for, though he didn't allude to it, this was the last year of his huge contract. If he was to be guaranteed lucrative employment, he would have to demonstrate his prowess from bygone years.

It seemed odd that García would come out to this camp. He had earned the reputation of being as thrifty with his time as he was with a peso. Yet he came out to the camp for two full days—players such as Tony Fernández and Nelson Liriano put in only half a day. Besides that, García was the only player from a team other than the Blue Jays to put in time.

García explained his motivation to try to help us *gringos*. "I can never thank Epy for what he did for me," García said as he laced up his shoes before the first practice. "He changed my life when he signed me to the contract with the Yankees and then when he got the Jays to take me in the draft. I can't thank him enough. I left the Jays, but I still have to thank Epy. Anything I can do for him is no problem."

Guerrero later confirmed that García's gratitude wasn't limited to his appearances at the fantasy camp. "One time when I wanted to get some ground made flat and to put up fences, Dámaso paid for it," Epy said. "I never asked. I never had to. Dámaso just did it. He comes out to work out here and help me. He needs a place to work out, sure, but he could do that in Santo Domingo. He drives out here and helps the kids. They see García working hard so they work hard. They see the Mercedes and say that they want that too."

The fantasy camp was a peculiar nexus of contrasting social strata. In this one setting were about twenty pale northerners on expensive vacations; Epy and his coaches; a millionaire major leaguer and his Mercedes Benz; a pack of struggling minor leaguers; and a few peasant kids from Punta.

During the warm-ups, the campers pursued García with balls and gloves to autograph and with questions to answer. They all wanted to know if he was going to play next year, if he'd be back in Atlanta. "No way am I hanging around if I can't play," García said. "I know I can play. I have a few years, maybe five years left. I'm not going to be the guy who plays too long. I don't have to." I had my doubts that he had a good reason to play at the major-league level. If money had been his motivation for playing, then the life-time security granted him by his five-year contract could easily snuff out his competitive fire.

On that first day, we staged an intramural game between the campers. García pitched for our side and I played a rotten first base, no range and a glove that went clang. In the early going, the second baseman made a throw that came in knee high to me. It was an easy put-out, but I muffed it. Just shut my glove too soon. When I looked up, García's eyes looked like twin suns in eclipse and he cast on me a look so dirty that I wanted to shower immediately. It forced me to reconsider, though; if he could take a game at the fantasy camp that seriously, then the fires must still be burning.

By December of '88 I realize that I may have been wrong about those competitive fires. Or that Dámaso García's talent has eroded to the point where no amount of determination will land him a spot on a major-league roster. In the 1988 major-league season Dámaso García played in only twenty-one games with Atlanta before the Braves released him. He did little to justify a spot on the Atlanta roster (.117 batting average, just two extra-base hits in 60 at bats). Opinions vary about his chances of getting a deal. Epy Guerrero says García will be back, but the scout is a lone voice. Whispers say García is spent.

García is running wind sprints at Estadio Quisqueya one afternoon and Ralph Avila is watching. When I ask about García, Avila doesn't seem impressed. I say that it's a sad that an All-Star at twenty-nine becomes flotsam at thirty-two. Avila looks at me quizzically.

"Who?" he asks.

"García," I say. "He was an All-Star in '85 and now he's out of work at thirty-two."

Avila casts a dubious look. "Dámaso García is the world's oldest thirty-two-year-old."

I assume that he is alluding to the wounds that García suffered during those thirty-two years, physical wounds that have prematurely aged him. I am wrong, of course. The Dodger honcho is not speaking figuratively at all.

"I don't know how old García is for sure," Avila says. "But he's thirty-five for sure, maybe more."

A few years back a friend of the Blue Jays organization told me that García was "maybe two years older than the age listed in the media guide, but you can never write that." That García was a couple of years older than his February 7, 1957 birthdate was now a theory that had reached a stage somewhere between locker-room rumour and certified fact.

How pronounced and widespread such white lies are among these vain, age-conscious athletes was not clear to me until I asked a few of the baseball reporters.

Roosevelt Comarazamy, now a writer for *El Nacional*, was a member of the junior national basketball team at the same time as García was kicking the ball for the junior national soccer club. In this the winter of '88–'89, García's age in the guide is thirty-two. Comarazamy, not a vain man and never a tradable commodity, is forty-one. There can be no possibility that García was, say, a nine-year-old phenomenon with the national *futbol* club.

"He has to be thirty-eight or thirty-nine years old," Comarazamy said flatly. The others at the table nodded. "What's he say his baseball age is, thirty-two?"

That phrase, "baseball age", explains a lot of things but requires a little explaining itself first. Documentation of births, like any sort of documentation in this country, is primitive. At age eighteen, many Dominican kids can pass for fourteen- or fifteen-year-olds. Comarazamy explains this as a phenomenon peculiar to the Dominican: "We mature late in the Dominican, especially the kids from the poor families that don't have enough food." Young-looking baseball players try to use their lack of physical maturity to their advantage. Twenty-year-old ballplayers tell scouts they are sixteen or seventeen. They flash their younger brothers' IDs.

In this conspiracy, the scouts are sometimes willing participants. Rarely do they try and sniff out the real ages of the prospects. "Scouts know these kids develop later than American kids," Comarazamy says. "It's not as if the kids fool the scouts. They have a good idea what the ballplayer's real age is. But, again, what the scout is interested in is how far the kid might develop once he does mature, and not what age he is when he gets there."

Soon after talking to Comarazamy I broached the subject with one of the agents for Tony Fernández. "Oh yeah," he remarked, "they all do it, two or three years." When I asked about his own client, the redoubtable shortstop, he said that Tony's age is accurate. When I looked a little skeptical, he corrected himself: "Okay, so he's a year older maybe."

A few days after that talk with Avila and Comarazamy, I saw García being interviewed on a baseball show on one of the Dominican television networks. They were covering the familar ground: García's health, his chances of landing a contract, his workouts in the off-season. Just before signing off, the host of the show asked García: "How old are you anyway?"

He looked the host in the eye then turned away as he said, "Thirty-two."

The host smiled and said, "Baseball years?"

And García laughed and stroked his chin like a story-teller.

Dámaso García stands in the batting cage at Estadio Quisqueya and turns Silvano Quezada's fastballs into line drives to all parts of the park. Six kids, gloveless and shoeless, run down the balls and throw them back into the infield. When García tops a ball or fouls one he shouts out "*coño*". Quezada doesn't say anything. When a ball hits a fence or lands beyond it he stands and admires it.

"Scouts from Montreal are coming down to see me," he says as he swings away in the cage. "I think I can play for them. I'll work hard, maybe even play a few games for Licey. I'm older now, but I'm smarter too. The money doesn't mean anything now. Just want to play."

Before every game Silvano Quezada, in full uniform and with his pre-game work done, sits in the stands behind the Licey dugout. He communes with friends, with loyal fans, with the children and men who work at the stadium.

During one of these breaks, I ask Quezada about García and getting out of the game.

"Dámasito will one day leave the game. I know he can play the game. He knows baseball. I don't know if he will do what he has to—the work, the running—to play in the major leagues. You know when you can't do it anymore. The players know it. Some are afraid to quit then. Some feel they should have to stay. When I was a young player, the older guys, the coaches, told me to get out right then. They said the worst thing in the world is to hear a manager tell you to pack your bags."

When we get around to how Silvano left the game, his recall of his last stand is so vivid that it sounds less as if he played in the game and more as if he watched it from these seats behind the dugout.

"The last game I played was in 1983. I came in and pitched to two batters with bases loaded at the end of a game. The first guy popped up to first but the second guy took the third strike, a fastball right down the middle. That was the end. For a couple of years it had been coming. It was the best way to go."

After that game Quezada did no celebrating, "nothing special, just a shower and a beer and a cigarette". His teammates gave him handshakes, but only for saving the game. They did not know then, and few could remember now, that it was his last game.

"I didn't know that it was my last game for sure. I could still play and I thought about coming back next season. But I was forty-six. I wasn't as good as I used to be. I didn't want to hang on." His face is uncreased, his smile white and gold.

"I never got into trouble doing things my way, never had a sore arm, never missed a start, never missed a game. I didn't see any reason to change what I was doing. I didn't want a ceremony. Ceremonies are for the dead. I was still a coach. I still came to the ballpark every day, the best place in the whole world. I never left baseball. I never left the game. I just stopped playing."

Now it is a dream scenario, this one told by Quezada, and the reader might think the old-timer has probably enhanced the tale just as he improved the 22–2 season. But according to everyone in the clubhouse, that's just the way it happened: Silvano Quezada saved the game, showered, and retired.

I only wish that Dámaso García could make an exit as dignified as Quezada's. I hope that García will be remembered as an All-Star and not as someone who hung around too long. I hope that he will not be shown the door but rather will have sense enough to leave when it's time. These things I hope for a guy who's all through. I tell all this to Silvano Quezada and he shrugs sadly.

"Today the older players can't leave," Quezada says. "The money won't let them."

*

Juan Guzmán is still overpowering in the bottom of the fourth. Leading off, Junior Felix swings weakly and misses a 2–2 breaking ball. Then Luis de los Santos looks at a called-third-strike inside. Finally Geronimo Berroa flies out to right field for the third out. The Licey players jog from their positions to the dugout. Mariano Duncan comes in from second base; though he was once a shortstop he knows as he grows older and his range diminishes he'll be playing second more frequently. Rafael Belliard, another shortstop, comes in from third; he knows that his future is as a utility infielder, and that he'll have to practise at as many positions as possible. The winter league is a place where established major leaguers can learn new skills that will prolong their careers, earning them hundreds of thousands of dollars as they near their mid-life. So it would seem that Dámaso García should be working on his game, working at third base. But this proud man and millionaire is on his way home; he does not deign to wear Licey blue.

CHAPTER SIX

Julio and Juarino

LICEY	000 0	0 1 0
ESCOGIDO	000 0	0 2 0

In the top of the fifth inning, John Davis starts shakily for Escogido. The first batter he faces is Mariano Duncan. Davis has difficulty finding the strike zone and walks Duncan on five pitches. When Davis goes to three-and-one on the next batter, Henry Rodriguez, the Escogido fans boo him unmercifully and the Licey fans laugh and taunt him. Davis grooves the next pitch, a fastball, right down the pipe and Rodriguez lines into right field for a single. With none out and the ball hit sharply right in front of Sammy Sosa, Duncan holds at second. This crosses up Rodriguez who makes a wide turn at first base. When Liriano cuts off the throw from Sosa, he fires over to first base. Rodriguez dives back to the bag in time, but when he gets up and calls for time, he is limping badly. Silvestre Campusano, the dormant prospect, comes on to pinch run for Rodriguez. Joe Ferguson, the Licey manager, will have to juggle his line-up a bit because of this mishap.

For this inning I sit in the section directly behind Escogido's dugout. It's one of the more expensive seats—ten pesos or about a buck and a half—and usually the friends and relations of the players can be found here. A couple of rows in front of me John Davis's wife Misty is agonizing over the threat posed to her husband.

Ramón, a sixteen-year-old serious fan of Los Leones, is an usher, and he does not ask to see the ticket-stubs of those who want to sit in his section. He knows the faces of people who have an affiliation with the club; others can gain entry with a golden handshake, a couple of pesos or so. Of course, one hundred pesos wouldn't buy a seat in Ramón's section if you were wearing Licey blue.

Ramón comes down to talk to me as Gilberto Reyes comes to the plate. He waves his hand dismissively at Davis and says the American is no good. Though he has allowed Misty a choice seat, he will not tone down his criticism just to be diplomatic. To avoid a nasty incident, I try to change the subject.

"Where's Julio?" I ask Ramón. Julio is Ramón's best friend. Julio must sometimes wander through the Licey seats, so he dresses neutrally and lets out the cheers appropriate to the section of the moment. By the middle innings Julio finds a seat among those policed by Ramón. Julio has his honoured place among them, in the back row, on the aisle, next to the orange crate that Ramón sits on while he works the chain. Tonight, however, Julio has not come by Ramón's section. Even on a busy night—and Licey versus Escogido is the busiest of these—Julio manages to stop by to say hello and to ask Ramón to save him a spot.

"Julio's not here," Ramón says, sounding envious. "Julio's not coming back here any more."

Julio's is not a typical ballpark story. He is not an athlete, despite protestations otherwise. He is, in fact, a small-time hustler. He might prefer to be called a entrepreneur and perhaps with justification. Nevertheless, the ballpark and the game of baseball attract a few individuals who scratch out a living on sheer guile. Julio is one; a kid named Juarino out at El Complejo Epy is another. One prospers; the other has his come-uppance.

*

This winter, on the night that I first attended at a game at Estadio Quisqueya, I arrived at the ballyard at four o'clock, four hours before gametime. Julio was already there.

"You remember me?" he asked.

I did. He was hard to forget. Five-five or five-six. About the same weight as a jockey getting into the hot-box. His skin was the colour of *café con leche* and it was pulled tight over a face locked into a broad smile. If I had forgotten his face, I would never have forgotten his smile. His mouth was studded with gold and silver teeth. I imagined that he brushed his teeth with Brasso. His wardrobe consisted of a very polyester pair of pants in a sickly green colour, and a long-sleeved baby-blue shirt with an oversized collar. His sneakers were holey and aromatic, long past wearable but entering their Dominican prime.

Four years before, on my first trip to the island, I found him where he had been for many years and where he still was this winter: in the dugout of Los Leones de Escogido. On my first trip to Estadio Quisqueya I found him doing what had been his routine for more than half his young life: operating in the margins around the ballpark. Wherever I ran into him, whatever he was doing, he was smiling, all gold and silver, a mixture of contentment and mischief, as if he was scamming you but liked you all the same.

Julio's age was, like that of slightly shaky prospective short-stops, a matter of some speculation. When I first met him four years before, he said he was fifteen. Four years later he claimed to be seventeen, ageing like one of the Gabor sisters. I pegged him to be nineteen, maybe more. Ostensibly he worked as a *mani* salesman. If there was reason for the lie it was this, for even at seventeen he was four years older than any of his peers in this the most junior of positions. At worst Julio should have been selling pop or *pica pollo*, a bony equivalent of Kentucky Fried Chicken; if he had real initiative, he would have been selling beer and rum, the only job with tips and a chance to bilk patrons out of a couple of pesos. But in spite of his lowly designation, Julio made ends meet. He spent most of his time at the ballpark as a valet and guide for visiting *gringos*. Vendors who wished to sell their wares to the Yanquis under his care were obligated to give Julio some sort of kickback, a half-peso here, a peso there. He would find baseball hats and T-shirts for his clients, fetch them pizzas and chicken and beer and rum. He would take on a commission and work a tip into the cost. The prices remained cheap, and for all his hustling he would in the end make a couple of bucks and usually little more.

At the Estadio Quisqueya before the games he looked more the peanut salesman and less the enterprising young businessman. He walked around the infield giving out rolls of peanuts to the players and coaches. He sat beside the stars in the dugout and got them to autograph balls. I never knew if the players realized that these autographed balls were being sold in the stands but I imagine that many of the Dominican *peloteros* understood that the vendors were more interested in commerce than sentimentality. Still, I think Julio attached some value to talking to players. He wasn't just making money; it was Tony Peña making him money, or José De León, or Nelson Liriano or Junior Felix. I'm sure that the money he made through his association with celebrity meant more to him than the pittances he won from fans munching his *mani* and from *gringos* gargling beers he fetched them.

Julio had little time for visiting American scouts and others in the baseball community. "Too cheap," he once told me. "They don't like to pay. The players don't have to but they give me a couple of pesos anyway. The scouts don't give me anything." The hard labour of the *mani* salesman is not in the hawking of his wares, he explained. Demand is constant, collection easy. All payments, a half-peso per, are made in coin, thrown rather than passed down the rows to the aisles. And, like vendors of like items in ballparks in North America, the *maniceros* throw the little rolls behind the back and under the leg like Globetrotters in miniature. But the hard work and expertise are in the rolling of the peanuts into the grey paper wrappers. The result looks something like a joint. As I had expected, Julio had this angle covered too. He had his own retinue of ruffians. They gathered in the Escogido dugout before games and rolled the mani for Julio at a furious pace and, it seemed, for no reward. Before every game Julio transformed the dugout into a sweatshop.

On my return to the yard this winter he was happy to see me. In other years I had always tried to be generous with him, and pay rather than service was foremost for Julio. He loved the game, but the smell of the grass wasn't enough to bring him to the ballpark. His attachment to the game was more pocket-felt than heartfelt. He commuted crosstown to the games from his parents' shanty home down near the docks just east of downtown. He lived in a barrio that was considered depressed by Dominican standards. "It floods a lot, the water comes, but I like it," he said. "It is better to live here than in the country, better to be where they play baseball than out on the farms."

On this our return meeting he felt obligated to reintroduce himself. "Anything you want I can get," he said. By rote, he rhymed off an impressive catalogue of goods and services that he could provide. This was virtually the same list he first gave me when he was thirteen. Ballpark food. Good seats. Taxis. Cars. Beer. Liquor. Good restaurants. Nightclubs. Women. The last of these suggested a precocious level of sophistication for a self-proclaimed seventeen-year-old. At women he stopped his solicitations. Not that his services ended at the moral line of prostitution—rather that anything more illicit was by customer's request only. He was able to do this in fractured English, though he was much relieved whenever I could say something to him in Spanish. Most of all he offered for free something that he did not bother to list, entertainment.

He walked among the ballpark urchins but he stood apart from them. It was not merely that he was so much older than them; he was established. He had gone from ballpark employee to ballpark personality.

There is a substratum in the society of the Dominican ballpark: a group of fans who are entertainers and oddities. Sometimes a team will carry a mascot for a season or two. Los Leones had one strange creature a few seasons back, a skinny fellow in a chicken suit with red feathers and big yellow feet. What made this mundane fowl exceptional, however, was the head. Instead of beak and plume, he wore a lion's head. This hybrid mascot was without name and did nothing but stand on the sidelines, perhaps hiding out of tremendous embarrassment. When he was terminated, no cry went up. Other mascots have proved as unsuccessful. Because of that, teams consider it wiser to give *gratis* admission to fans who can provide a laugh and diversion in a blow-out or rain delay. They are ballpark grotesques, not quite exhibits from freak shows, but definitely different.

On my first trip to the Dominican one boy named Oscar Manuel was frequenting the park. His head was disproportionately large; to the layman's eye it was twice the size it should have been. Oscar had not a voice so much as a growl, a low rumble. His mouth was like a torn pocket. He entertained crowds by putting his whole fist in his mouth. This was more impressive than it first sounds—his hands were huge and he was able to palm five or six baseballs quite easily. Yet his fist fit so loosely in his mouth that he could move it around without obstruction. He would take a baseball in his mouth with ease and even manage to smile or talk with it resting on his tongue. Fans would bring other household objects to try. He was not always successful but he would try even the most preposterous objects and for this fans would give him a few pesos and guards would allow him free entry to the stadium. He could enliven a dull game. They called him El Tiburón, the Shark, because his open mouth recalled the mechanical shark in *Jaws*.

Perhaps the only guy that outdistanced Oscar Manuel was a chap at Estadio Tetelo Vargas out in San Pedro. One Yanqui ballplayer described him as the Ear, Nose, and Throat Man. He was not a doctor of any sort, but more of a tailor, adept with needle and pin. He could take a needle and thread in his mouth, thread the needle with his tongue and then, after a sequence of coughs and wheezes and disgusting noises, make the threaded needle pass out one of his nostrils. He called himself the King and wore a tin crown painted yellow. Among the jesters at the yard he surely reigned. Evidently he made a decent living "entertaining" the fans a little indecently. I thought, however, that most fans, sickened by his act, paid him to go away, like the Rat Man of Paris.

Oscar Manuel and the Ear, Nose, and Throat Man were certainly the most unusual of the entertainers. Others were more pathetic, more tragic. A few regular beggars, their bodies swollen and misshapen by elephantiasis and other maladies, manned spots near the exits or outside the bathrooms and waited for donations from passers-by, often regular benefactors.

Julio was by no means an act or an unfortunate. But he was so painfully skinny and his way of moving so clown-like that his spot among the ballpark entertainers was deserved. He was less a side-show freak and more a cheerleader. When Los Leones began to rally, loading the bases or whatever, the sale of Julio's wares halted outright and any requests from *gringo* clients went unheeded. The cheers for Escogido often took the form of a rhythmic whistling and clapping. Julio conducted the whistling as if he were Zubin Mehta, standing on a box seat behind Los Leones' dugout and waving his hands in 4/4 time.

At the end of each night that he ran errands for me—even running down players for interviews—I thought that maybe, maybe, Julio was doing some of this work out of friendship. But every night came the plaint: "Me hongry," even when he had just eaten half my pizza; "I have to pay thirty pesos or no school tomorrow," even though he was most certainly not attending; "I have to buy my brother shoes tomorrow or he no can go to school," although there was no chance that his brothers would see coin or shoes with Julio's take. He would point to young vendors to whom he bore not the slightest resemblance and say that he had to look after his brothers.

Once I had slipped him twenty pesos, about three bucks or a night's wages for someone working the concessions, he would hail a cab for me. And when I got in the cab, I would usually see the driver shaking Julio's hand and slipping him two or three pesos more.

The Contract God once said to me that in ten or fifteen years, when he comes down to the Dominican, he'll be talking to Julio in the owner's office in the Escogido clubhouse. Or perhaps even the president's residence. I didn't dispute it. At an early age, Julio understood that the cheering sounded nice but that you couldn't take it to a bank.

At one game Julio was tied up and couldn't attend to me. Two female flight attendants, well proportioned, blonde, and British, had somehow arrived at the ballpark. This was of course a ballpark urchin's dream assignment and Julio left me behind for them. I sat a few seats away from them and heard Julio's pitch: eleven children in the family; father dead; "go hongry," he said, rubbing his belly. If it didn't have them sobbing, it at least kept them distracted. The hot-blooded Escogido fans nearby let out a number of wolf whistles, growing louder and more frequent in the later innings as their mickeys of rum fast emptied.

While Julio was preoccupied with the stewardesses, another ballpark urchin took me over. His name was Rinso, like some Latin detergent, I suppose. Rinso had not a tooth in his head and was a light-skinned kid of sixteen or seventeen. He spoke not a word of English and even his Spanish was incomprehensible because of his toothlessness. His breath just whooshed through his mouth turning all his words into slushes and whistles. He wore what had once been beautiful white linen pants, rendered gross by daily wearings, infrequent cleanings, and indescribable stainings.

Rinso ran the errands; the cigarette run, the pizza run, the beer run, and the rest, that Julio usually looked after. In fact Rinso had a bit more bounce in his step than Julio did when doing these tasks. After a few weeks of twenty pesos a night, Julio had grown complacent. At the end of the night I gave Rinso twenty pesos, the same gratuity I'd given Julio all those times. He gave it back to me and told me to give him only ten. Twenty, he said, was too much.

The next night the British women were gone and Julio was again at liberty. When he saw Rinso standing beside me and talking, he approached us but made no secret of his displeasure. Julio did not have words with Rinso, did not seek a confrontation or anything unseemly. But as soon as Rinso's head was turned, Julio whispered to me, "He's bad."

We three moved into the stands at the start of the game. Rinso again carried on a running commentary of the game, with a few editorial comments about politics, a brief summation of his own skills as a ballplayer, and other themes lost in his toothlessness. Julio stared forward in stone silence. Perhaps there was a code among the urchins, that the rights to a mark, once acquired, were not transferrable or subject to competition.

At the end of the game Rinso went to the washroom and only then did Julio lash out. "He's a thief," Julio said. "He act nice but he wants to rob you, that's all. Don't listen to him."

At the end of the night, once I climbed into a cab, I gave Julio twenty pesos and Rinso ten. It probably would be too expensive to retain both of them as my agents.

The next day when both came to me, I told Rinso that I wouldn't need him. Mild and incomprehensible invective followed as Rinso traipsed off. I felt no remorse. Anybody who declined twenty pesos for ten probably wasn't sharp enough to help me.

Wherever a *gringo* travels in the Dominican, he will be surrounded by young boys who, in chorus, beseech him for a *pelota* (ball) or *guante* (glove). A *pelota* is for those who think small; most think big and appeal for a *guante*. I have never been able to understand this: how can they expect someone travelling quite empty-handed to produce a dozen or so gloves on demand? I sought the foundation of this behaviour—perhaps there was a mythic *gringo* who went about the countryside planting gloves on the hands of needy kids; perhaps there was some sort of Johnny Appleseed with a bag of Rawlings instead of apple pips. An old-timer once told me that American servicemen always left baseball gloves behind when they shipped out, but the story did not have the ring of truth.

Julio always regaled me with tales from his league. He claimed to be a third baseman and always pointed to third basemen in the winter league and said that one day he would have their jobs. It was a bit of a stretch. He couldn't have been more than 5'5" standing on the bag at third base and 120 pounds carrying a full load of *mani*. "I'm going to be strong, be big, keep growing," he said. All doubtful.

Always during these tales he told me that he was a good fielder, but that he was undermined by a well-worn glove that his father gave him. "No pocket," he said. "Torn."

It was an inventive if obvious play for a glove.

A lot of our conversations boiled down to Julio's hidden agenda and my playing dumb to it. It was a sparring session, though I'm sure he's more unrelenting and I'm more patient. When he first brought up the glove issue, I mentioned that if he gave it to me, I could take it back to Canada to be repaired. That ended the conversation that night. He couldn't quite hide his disappointment that I couldn't understand, let alone sympathize, with his plight.

The next night he again approached me. He said that there was a championship game on Sunday morning and that he needed a glove, that he couldn't play in this important game with an unreliable mitt. I ignored the stuff about the glove but acted enthusiastic about the prospect of seeing him play. I asked where the game would be played and what time they'd start. He was peeved. He said six o'clock in the morning in San Cristóbal, about forty-five minutes to the west of Santo Domingo. He was so peeved that he wanted to dispatch me out of town—and at so un-Dominican an hour. I told him that I would see him there. When next I saw him, I apologized and told him I had spent the morning in church.

Every night for two weeks this went on. He found a new reason to have a glove and I either considered the options or ignored him completely.

One night the Contract God and I went to the casino at the Hotel Lina. He was supposed to introduce me to the fellow who shot the Polaroids of the naked Dominican women that the Contract God always had in his possession.

A novice at blackjack and a skeptic of card-counting systems, the Contract God went into the hole a bit. I covered about twenty-five dollars' worth of his debts. He promised repayment. At the end of the night he found himself, like so many patrons, a few dollars short of his good intentions. The Contract God asked if I would take a baseball glove in lieu of pesos. I asked if I could see the mitt first. He then took me to his car and showed me a brand new Rawlings, a major-league glove with the guarantor's tag still on it. It was easily worth twice the debt, so I agreed.

This would be Julio's Christmas gift, the glove he had appealed for. He didn't have to know that I would never have acquired it for him if the Contract God hadn't hit on seventeen.

I carried a gym bag to Estadio Quisqueya on the last night before the Christmas layoff. In that bag I carried Julio's glove.

When I presented the glove to Julio, his enthusiasm was contained, to say the least. He began with a suspicious and disbelieving inspection of the glove. He finally granted me a smile and a *gracias*, but nothing more; perhaps he was still disbelieving.

Within a few minutes, however, he was on the field, showing the glove to his friends. But rather than guarding it cautiously, he was offering it around to others to try out. It seemed unusual behaviour—to at last secure the sacred object, only to pass it casually around. I heard him bragging about how much it was worth, inflating it some. I realized that I couldn't imagine how much that must seem to a ten-year-old working at the ballpark—a month's wages, maybe more.

I didn't see Julio at the games after Christmas and I let myself imagine why. I asked Ramón the usher if some sort of bad fate had befallen the King of the Urchins. "He's the lucky one," Ramón said. "He got some player's glove, sold it, and then got on a ship for Puerto Rico."

It occurred to me then that baseball can be almost anyone's ticket off the island, that it doesn't have to be one of the star *peloteros*. And I thought that calling it "some player's glove" was a nice touch by Julio.

I got used to kids disappearing in the Dominican. Juarino was another one. "Where's Juarino?" I asked Epy Guerrero. Guerrero would know. At El Complejo, if Epy sneezed, Juarino would be there to hand him a hanky. Juarino was not second in command, like Ignacio Javier. He was a step up from Linke, the cook, and the groundskeeper. In the baseball division Juarino was just a corporal, the last in the chain of command, just a step up from the troops who take the field each day.

"Juarino," Epy said. "I had to let him go. He can't come back here any more."

Outsiders could easily have mistaken Juarino for one of the prospects at El Complejo, at least at first. There were, however, subtle differences between Juarino and the young players. Though he looked no more than seventeen, he was in fact twenty-two, at least a couple of years older than most of the players. At 5'9" and 175 pounds, he was stockier than the others. His disposition was different from that of the players: more relaxed, more playful, more talkative.

Juarino wasn't a prospect at El Complejo. He was an employee. Epy kept him around as a handyman on the diamond. He pitched batting practice. He hit grounders for infield practice. He caught in the bullpen for pitchers warming up. He tossed the ball for batters who wanted to hit into the nets. The players did not regard him as a coach. They did not accord him the formal and dutiful respect that they gave to Ignacio Javier or Melvin Perez, nor would he be the first they sought out for instruction or advice. Yet if they were trying to overcome a flaw, such as hands dropping too low in the batting stance, they would ask Juarino, because he would play it straight. The players did not trust each other because of the competition. Juarino was not competing for a job, so he could remain friends with everyone. He ate with the players, and was occasionally offered a beer with Epy, the coaches, and vistors.

Juarino's job brought him to El Complejo seven days a week, fifty-one weeks of the year. Among Juarino's responsibilities was Epy's Little League, his youth program. Though the Little Leaguers wore Epy's name on the backs of their T-shirts, the league was, but for the title, Juarino's. He called himself *el jefe*, the boss. When the players and coaches went home on weekends, Juarino organized games at El Complejo for the children of Punta and the nearby countryside. And as peaceful as the camp was during the week, an ordered and controlled environment that barely changed from day to day, and from year to year, the weekends were raucous and unruly. Games were played on the main diamond, on the little-league diamond opposite the mess-hall, and, for the youngest, on the practice infield. These locales were always filled, and the spillover—there were always dozens who could not be worked into a game—tried to play on any open area around the camp. Foul lines might be a barbed-wire fence, second base a cow. The grounds were overrun with young boys and girls, though the latter did not play—they were usually keeping an eye on a male sibling. There were no quiet moments for Juarino: any group of a hundred excited kids knows no level of noise below screaming. But in spite of the cacophony, the games were as organized as any in the Republic—that is, the rules were strictly adhered to; cries of balk went up against a ten-year-old trying to hold base runners on. The officials and players were knowledgeable if not well equipped. Catchers did not have the usual protection, and many players did not have shoes, let alone spikes.

As keyholder for the equipment, selector of teams, arbiter of close decisions, and leader of baseball-skills clinics, Juarino was a man of considerable power and celebrity in the town of Punta. The kids all cried for Juarino. They shouted his name at every dispute. He was a Pied Piper. He walked the grounds carrying his bat and glove and ball and behind him trailed skinny young boys, skipping, smiling, shouting his name.

I once rode on the back of Juarino's motorcycle from El Complejo to his home in Punta. The bike was a rather lofty status symbol for a young man whose job in baseball paid him six hundred pesos, or about one hundred dollars, a month. Juarino explained this to me. He and his brothers have a small auto-body business in their backyard. "All day I spend at El Complejo," he said to me. "All night I work on the cars. The cars will be my family's business. My brothers can't work at El Complejo. There aren't enough jobs there. So we work here. One day we'll get a garage, a shop in the city."

Helmetless we rode to his house in Punta. We passed tractors, were passed by overloaded buses, dipped into potholes, barely slowed for parts of the road washed out. Smiling and waving to those he recognized, Juarino sang *merengue*. The pistons and my chattering teeth provided percussion.

Every kid we passed yelled his name. A couple of young women, almost voting age, gave him seductive looks.

"I am a big man in Punta," Juarino explained. "Big man, the baseball coach."

Juarino's home was like many others in Punta. The highway cuts through the village, but other than that there are no roads. The houses are assembled along its sides two, three, and four deep with paths trodden down between them. The houses are surrounded by lush tropical growth in which bugs nest. Often insects hover outside the houses in clouds as thick as smoke. Trash piles along the side of the highway and between the houses burn around the clock, untended, sometimes out of control. Juarino's family lived in a small frame house, a pastel shade of blue. Worked into the façade of the house was a simple cross made of two of the same rough-cut planks that make up the siding. The cross was coloured the same pastel blue, so it was not at all conspicuous. Unlike Tony Fernández's old home, or Alfredo Arias's in San Pedro, unlike Julio's home near the river in Santo Domingo, there was a serenity about Juarino's home in Punta. If it were better tended, it would have been almost pastoral.

"This is the biggest moment of my life," he said, showing me a photograph from a baseball tournament. It depicted him accepting a trophy that was as tall as him. "This is Venezuela. The time I went on a plane. I pitched for a national junior team and we won a Caribbean tournament in Caracas. I was the Most Valuable Player. That is it—the best of my life. We put the picture in the living room and every day I look at it. Then I thought I would be a ballplayer. Other players from the team were signed by the big-league clubs, but they did not want me. A little too short, don't throw hard enough. Epy told me."

I remembered what Epy told me about Juarino too. "He was as good at sixteen as anybody," Epy said, "but at sixteen he was as good as he would get. He wouldn't throw harder or better. He was a very good pitcher, smart, knows the game, but an average or below-average prospect. I told him this but he told me that he still wanted to work in the game—coach, batboy, anything. So I kept him around. I think at first he wanted to be around so he could show me how he could play, but he's not stupid. He saw what I meant, that others would improve and he wouldn't."

Though he had a couple of trophies and a diploma from school, it was the photograph that made him proudest. The large trophy did not come home with him—the national team kept it—but the house would have been scarcely large enough to contain it.

When his mother came in, Juarino introduced me and she waxed enthusiastic about her son. "He makes us so happy," she said. "I don't understand the game but I know he likes baseball and he is paid well to do what he does. He helps our family so much. I know that he will always do well in this game."

In the backyard the auto-body business was flourishing. His brothers were welding a Volkswagen bug that was probably past the half-million-mile mark. "You see, the way I got my motorcycle was because of the auto-body business," he said. "Most people in Punta can't afford a motorcycle, but we buy our cars from somebody who sells wrecks. I was able to get the motorcycle very cheap because it needs work. Somebody probably was killed on it so the family doesn't want it any more."

That night we went to the disco in Punta. The mix of music was dated and eclectic, the stereo system loud but distorting, the atmosphere one of smiles disguising despair. Unfamilar faces received unfriendly inspection. Any show of money or material wealth drew covetous stares.

"Can you get me into the States, into Canada, Toronto?" he asked. "I can coach baseball. I can make them as good as Dominicans."

He was disappointed, even disbelieving, when I told him that baseball coaching in Canada is for the most part a non-paying pastime, a hobby, not an occupation.

"No money?" he asked.

For the Jays, yes. For a neighbourhood team, no.

"I'll stay here in Punta then," he said.

It seemed that he had it good in Punta. The deejay played Bob Marley's "Buffalo Soldier", and though a few patrons danced by the bar, nobody took to the floor. "The women love me here," Juarino said. "I come here every night. Have some rum, a beer. I have a motorcycle. I work in baseball. The women think that I am a player, but I never tell them different. What they don't know...."

I told him that the major leaguers don't have it much better and within the confines of El Leicy Disco this is probably true. Dark-skinned women, smelling of hairspray, approached him and asked him to dance. Until the small hours of the morning, Juarino was having a good time, the King of Punta.

"Where's Juarino?" I asked Epy.

"I had to let him go," Epy said. He was mad. This was another upset to him, like a prospect who diappointed him, who did not fulfil his potential. "It turned out that Juarino was taking ten pesos a month from all the kids who came out here, maybe a hundred and fifty or two hundred kids were giving him ten pesos a month. That doesn't sound like much to you, but it's a lot down here and a lot for the kids in Punta. The kids could not say anything. Juarino scared them into not saying anything and the parents didn't want to take a chance that their kids might not be able to play."

I told Epy that it was hard to imagine that the kids and especially their parents would remain silent about this.

"I don't know why they didn't say anything," he said. "But in the Dominican you don't talk about a lot of things. A soldier does something wrong, you don't report him. Too much trouble later on."

It was not fear that influenced the people of Punta, I imagined. Though Juarino might make a reprisal, some type of retribution, a socket wrench or bat in the side of the head, there were other prospects scarier in the daily course of their lives. It was probably more a sense of inevitability. I recalled what Ralph Avila had told me about Dominican coaches, about how they do what they do here for money more than for love, and about how they weren't willing to sacrifice a few things in order to learn how to coach at the Dodgers' expense. I realized that the citizens of Punta were so accustomed to officials raking in kickbacks and commissions that they were not fazed by a kid at the diamond demanding the same.

Still, Epy was moved to some sort of righteous indignation. "I paid Juarino good money," he said, "but he was making three times as much by collecting off the kids."

No doubt Juarino's contemptible actions deserved such sanctions. Juarino sought to profit from Epy's contribution to the community and betrayed his employer's confidence. But the hazy ethics of this nation extend from the government down to baseball. I thought of Mario Guerrero, Epy's brother, the agent. Though Juarino's profiteering represented small change, the Guerreros seemed in a distinct conflict of interest: one a scout, the other an agent. The monies at stake in the Guerreros' realm made Juarino's small monthly take seem like chump change.

Juarino is out of baseball for now. Epy made it sound as if he will not let Juarino set foot on the property again, but like all things apparently written in stone in the Dominican, this is subject to change. Whether he comes back to the camp or not, Juarino, like Julio, King of the Baseball Urchins, has already shown instincts that will stand him in good stead in the business of baseball.

*

To Misty Davis's relief, her husband John somehow gets off the hook in the fifth inning and shuts down the Licey side. First he fans Gilberto Reyes and then strikes out Juan Bell. He gives up a walk to Miguel Santana to load the bases but Rafael Belliard strands three runners when he hits a slow grounder to Nelson Liriano, an inning-ending 4–3 putout.

In the bottom of the inning, Campusano goes to centre field, the fleet Santana to right field, and Doug Jennings from right field to first base. Licey's outfield defence is tightened considerably, though Domingo Michel does not cover much grass in left.

Juan Guzmán continues his impressive pitching. He retires the Escogido side in order. José Vizcaíno lines a shot right back at Guzmán for an unassisted putout; Sammy Sosa flies out to

Campusano; and to end the inning, Hector de la Cruz strikes out looking. The game remains scoreless.

CHAPTER SEVEN

La Prensa

LICEY   000 00 0 2 0

ESCOGIDO   000 00 0 2 0

The game breaks open in the top of the sixth. Luis Reyna leads
off the inning for Licey with a grounder to first. Hector de la
Cruz fields the ball going to his right and pitcher John Davis, tall,
ungainly, has to hustle over to beat Reyna to the bag. One out.

Domingo Michel is next up. Michel, leading the league in
average and homers, is also near the leaders in runs batted in, and
has the potential to become the first-ever Triple Crown winner
in the history of the Dominican league. A list of those who
have played here and not accomplished the trifecta is impressive.
Among the Americans are Hall-of-Famer Willie Stargell; future
Hall-of-Famer Dave Parker; Negro League star Ray Dandridge;
and Cincinnati star George Foster, who hit fifty-four homers in
a major-league season. Among the Dominicans are the Alous;
Manny Mota; and Rico Carty. All this makes Michel's situation
more puzzling. Can a player who leads the Dominican league in
these power stats *not* be on the Dodgers' forty-man roster? And

further, did all the other major-league teams pass on acquiring Michel for a few spare bucks at the minor-league draft a few days ago? The answer to both questions is yes, and though he is slow of foot, Michel, it would seem, should be able to play left field for somebody in the majors.

On the first pitch from Davis, Michel hits a titanic shot to dead centre field, a homer in any major-league park. Junior Felix races after it, even catches up to it, but the ball hits high off the fence and rebounds behind him. Meanwhile Michel is chugging around the basepaths as if a gale-force wind were blowing in his face. But the ball is hit to such a deep part of the field that Michel comes into third base standing up. His batting average is up to .315.

Doug Jennings is the next batter and he is aware that it will take a fairly deep fly ball to cash in Michel. Davis mows Jennings down on strikes.

Next up is Mariano Duncan. Davis appears to be home and clear when Duncan gets under a fastball and lofts a fly to centre field. Junior Felix, however, slips when he breaks for the ball and though he is there in time to make the catch, he is rattled and the ball caroms off his glove. Michel trots in with the game's first run and Duncan is safe at first. The Licey fans exult while the Escogido fans are livid. Money changes hands up in the all-standing gambling section—all those who bet that Licey would score first cash in.

Sil Campusano steps up to the plate and no one can be expecting too much of him. All season long he has batted a few points over .200 and has shown no power. But he turns on a first-pitch fastball and slams it into—where else—left field. The ball is within a few feet of the line and Geronimo Berroa has to chase it down into the corner. Duncan is coming all the way around to score. Campusano appears to have a double, but Berroa misses the cutoff in to second base and throws wildly. Campusano gets to third on Berroa's throwing error, the second error of the half inning for Escogido.

Phil Regan is livid. Felix's error was bad luck. Berroa's was bad judgement. Berroa is spared any further indignity. Gilberto

Reyes grounds to Liriano, 4–3, to strand Campusano at third and end the inning.

Juan Baez, the radio announcer who does Escogido's games, relates the bad news to the team's faithful listeners: two runs on two hits and two errors. Both runs are unearned.

Baez probably is taking this worse than Regan. Many of the experts are saying that Regan is in danger of being fired—this despite Escogido's win at the Caribbean World Series last season. But if dismissed, Regan can concentrate on coaching at the Dodgers' complex or just return to his home in Michigan for the rest of the winter. Baez's fate is tied directly to the team; if Escogido doesn't make the playoffs, he won't be working; if they win the winter league, he'll get a working vacation in Mazatlán where the C.W.S. is being staged this year. His is not the voice of objectivity when he recounts the game during his broadcasts. With his own fortune tied to the team's, who'd expect him to be neutral?

The members of the baseball press, both the print guys and the broadcasters, are the envy of the *fanaticos*—they stand shoulder to shoulder with the national stars and bask in reflected glory. A few are content with a hectic but comfortable living scratched out in the stadium; these men are able to separate the diamond from the island. But a few, including Baez and his friend Roosevelt Comarazamy of the newspaper *El Nacional*, confess that *beisbol* today troubles them. The Dominicans' excellence in the big leagues cannot obscure the troubles on the island; and though major-league baseball awards million-dollar salaries to a few of the very best ballplayers, this big business does little to help the citizens of the Dominican. For Baez, Comarazamy, and others, there is a crisis of conscience, though speaking of it too freely might endanger their professional security. They do not wish to bite the glove that feeds them.

*

Beginning at 11:30 this morning, braving a rainstorm that floods the streets of Santo Domingo, a steady stream of customers, all regulars, all men, pour into the Lucky Seven, a modest tavern and restaurant on Avenida Pasteur near *la playa* and around the corner from the most posh of Santo Domingo's hotels. Though the waiters there will recommend the red snapper, the luncheon special this day, as it is seven days a week throughout the year, is baseball. From the moment these customers arrive the air is thick with baseball talk, equal parts hyperbole and opinion. The smoke glass windows can scarcely contain the booming voices. Out on the avenue, a residential street darkened by shade from trees and exhaust from mufflerless cars, traffic noises are occasionally drowned out by the din of disputes over the merits of George Bell versus those of Pedro Guerrero. As a rule, a decision is rendered—there is always a winner and, through submission, diminished support, or lower volume, a loser—but rarely is it unanimous. Indeed if one of the boys put forward that the infield comprises four bases, for the sake of sustaining debate and to infuriate a rival somebody would come forward and interject that there is a fifth base in the game, as yet unused. Or, better yet, maintain that there are three bases and a plate.

The substance and nature of conversation at this bar are typical of those in other establishments in the Dominican. What makes the Lucky Seven different from the others is the clientele: they are from *la prensa*, the sportswriters and the broadcasters who work the winter baseball league. If there is one subject beyond dispute, it is that those who shape the public opinion of the Dominicans' national pastime call this place home.

Caricatures decorate the walls. Each figure carries in his right hand the tools of his trade, tape recorder and mike, and in his left hand the inevitable tumbler of rum. (The one exception is a fellow carrying a bottle of mineral water. A waiter explains that this *periodista* is diabetic.) Also on the wood panelling are photographs of famous players who have dined and, perhaps, had a glass here, among them the aforementioned Pedro Guerrero, the power-hitting outfielder late of the Dodgers but traded to St. Louis, and Mario Soto.

Besides its patrons, both expert and famous, the Lucky Seven can lay an even greater claim to being the most respected baseball forum in this nation preoccupied with the sport: throughout the day, from noon until the wee hours of the morning, *los periodistas* broadcast their barroom banter on radio and the resulting programs are the nation's most popular listening. So this discussion on the merits of Bell versus Guerrero is being heard all over the island.

For more than twenty years, radio shows have originated from a back room in the Lucky Seven. Legend has it that one of the broadcasters suggested to his superiors that he move his show to the bar for "better acoustics". Through the years broadcast facilities have improved, and what was once a closet now houses a sound board that is state of the art in the D.R. Occasionally guest luminaries appear at the Lucky Seven for interviews, but for the most part the show is strictly news and commentary.

In any nation and any language the task of radio announcers is not enviable. The difference between their work and that of the daily press is like the difference between tightrope walking with a net or without one. Unlike their English-language peers in the U.S. and Canada, these Dominican sportscasters work not only without a net, but also without support, either technical or human. There are few if any commercial interruptions to provide them with a chance to catch their breath. Because of the makeshift facility, they make do without pre-taped interviews or segments from the radio wire. They go wall to wall with words, a torrent of verbiage, seemingly at the speed of sound in the moments of greatest excitement. A six-team league, and at best three games a night, would seem to provide only the barest of fodder for so many hours of news and commentary. It is a tribute to the sophistication and dedication of the journalists and their audience that the press can round up so much detail and that the fans will listen to the most minute developments. In instances when American and Canadian fans would, by and large, be content with the scores or, for the most obsessed, with a glance at the boxscores, the Dominicans are prepared to pore over the papers, listen to radio shows all day long, and watch the games, either at the park, or on one of the five-times-a-week television broadcasts. In a country where many go hungry, the population remains hungry for baseball. If they could be sustained by baseball, they would be well fed.

On this day, a Monday in November, a couple of weeks into the Dominican winter-league season, the talk-radio guys have to stretch a bit. By any standard, this is a slow news day. Monday is a dark day in the winter league: no games are scheduled. Later in the season Mondays will be the make-up days for rain-outs, but tonight there's no action. There's no news from the U.S.—the MVP awards will come later in the week, as will the Associated Press All-Star team, always hot topics of conversation. Compounding the tension is the fact that this is the Dominican equivalent of sweeps week, the period of the year when audience numbers are highest, because of allegiances to teams in the winter league. If, on this day, the announcers find the prospect of filling time daunting, it's easy to understand their need for an extra shot of Barcelo in the front room before they take the mike.

Juan Baez, a short, stocky man with a voice as sweet as molasses, takes his seat behind the mike, flips the switch and, before cupping his right hand over his right ear, checks his watch. Thus commences this edition of "Perspectivas Deportivas", a show Baez has hosted for twenty-three years. He works with no script, only file cards, newspaper clippings, and a few sheets of stats provided by the winter league. He introduces himself with a flourish and the natural reverberation of a *basso profundo* that would make James Earl Jones blush, a voice too precious to risk on house rum. He walks through a thumbnail sketch of the Sunday game—there was only one, Licey versus Estrellas Orientales of San Pedro de Macorís at Estadio Quisqueya. The other games were rained out, a frequent occurrence in mid-November. He reels off the standings and records, as well as the statistical leaders. Baez is not unaware of the entrances made by friends and waiters—indeed, he acknowledges their every entry, smiles or gesticulates outrageously—but never once does he break stride, never once does he break rhythm.

Three or four minutes into his show, it appears that Juan has exhausted any subject worth pursuing. It is this point that he flags over to the table and introduces to the listeners Maximo Lovaton, the owner of Caimanes del Sur, the team ostensibly based in San Cristóbal. Lovaton is a pudgy, balding man in his fifties. He has the look of a man who has walked into one too many open man-holes. In a chain-smoker's rasp, he tells Baez and the listeners that his team will be playing home games in far-flung cities and towns in the provinces.

"We'll be playing in San Francisco de Macorís [a town deep in the interior] because that's the hometown of our manager Julián Javier," Lovaton says. "We're playing another game in Moca. We want to show all of the Dominican people some good winter-league games."

Baez and Lovaton continue their discussion of Caimanes del Sur and its player movements. Lovaton says that his team has a player-development deal with the Chicago Cubs, a deal that will help defray the costs of the American players' salaries.

"We've got a few Cubs' players down here this year and so the Cubs should help us the way we help them," Lovaton says. "And I'm trying to work out a player-development contract with Epy Guerrero and the Blue Jays."

Everyone in the room, including Lovaton, knows this is a dubious claim. Mario Guerrero, Epy's brother, once told me that Epy's the only guy in the Dominican with an exclusive contract with all six ballclubs.

The discussion between the two proceeds cordially until a waiter walks into the back room and points fretfully to the front room. Baez is talking into the mike, but Lovaton, looking worried, interrupts and says that he's being called away. The owner then runs out the back door and into the downpour. Baez is left in the lurch and has to cover himself quickly. He waves to Roosevelt Comarazamy and Tomás Montes, a fairly mountainous young reporter who covers Santiago games; Baez's two friends step in and the announcer hardly misses a beat.

Seconds later, Jerome Walton, a young outfielder from the Cubs' minor-league system, storms into the back room and looks around. Without saying a word he walks into the bathroom and then into the restaurant section. Walton is looking for Lovaton and Lovaton knew he would be.

Maximo Lovaton has bounced the cheques on the payroll of Caimanes del Sur. If there's one sure method of forging team togetherness, it's writing rubber on payday. It disenchants the entire team together. The first payroll went through, but this and every subsequent payday will be uncertain.

Caimanes del Sur and Maximo Lovaton are teetering on the edge of insolvency. In fact, it appears Lovaton may have to disband his ballclub. If it happens during the season this will have a calamitous effect on the winter league—players out of work, the season's schedule effectively ruined.

When Baez, Comarazamy, and Montes go off the air, they explain to me how the crisis of Caimanes is, in fact, just a symptom of a malaise in pro ball on the island.

"We'll probably see more players looking for paycheques," Baez says. "A few rain-outs left Maximo without enough cash— the players don't get paid by the game, they get paid by the week, and if you have four rain-outs, there'll be trouble making the payroll. It's simple."

But even in good weather Caimanes would have cash problems. Lovaton is staging games in San Francisco de Macorís and Moca because the gates at games in San Cristóbal have been abysmal. "Caimanes just doesn't draw," Baez says. "There probably isn't enough money in San Cristóbal to keep a team there and Max might be looking at these other cities—San Francisco de Macorís for sure—as a place to move his team. There are a couple of other cities with enough money to have a team—like Puerto Plata—but they're so far away that the travel makes it too expensive or too difficult."

According to this roundtable and all Dominican baseball executives, the winter league on the island has never been in such financial straits; Escogido and Licey may be the only teams breaking even. Compounding this is a significant drop-off in the quality of the competition.

"If you look at a roster from the early '70s," Comarazamy says, "you'll see a lot of great American players. A Dominican had to be Triple A or major-league just to make the roster."

Back in the '70s winter-league teams could carry twelve American ballplayers. In the 1972–73 season, Licey featured big leaguers such as Gary Matthews, Garry Maddox, and John Mayberry; San Pedro's line-up included George Foster, J.R. Richard, Ralph Garr, Joaquín Andújar, and Rico Carty. These two teams didn't run away with the league title; it took a star-studded roster just to compete. None of the Dominican players thought about sitting out the winter league.

These days teams can have seven Americans on their roster. The ceiling on the monthly salaries for import players is $3,500 a month. For Dominican players, even major leaguers, salaries are limited to $1,200 a month. Not only will major-league players laugh off such salaries, but a good number of minor leaguers are opting for Venezuela, Puerto Rico, or even Mexico. And at $1,200 a month, few Dominican big leaguers think the winter league is worth the inconvenience in the off-season. In the estimation of Ralph Avila, the level of play has dropped from "between major league and Triple A in the '70s to decent Double A in '88, no better."

Truth is, the Dominican winter league is in danger of collapse because the nation's peso is very weak. Latin America is about $400 billion in debt. While the Dominican Republic's portion of that debt is only $4 billion, consider that the nation's population is only about six million. Per capita the D.R.'s debt is proportionately as burdensome as that of many of the biggest debtors. What makes this frustrating to the Dominican people is that many of the projects for which the nation went into hock—dams, power dams, highways, and public works—were ill-conceived and are either falling apart or were never finished. Most were part of pre-election posturing by former presidents Antonio Guzmán (who committed suicide shortly before his term ended) and Salvador Blanco (who was recently sentenced to a long stretch in prison for serial frauds and misappropriation of funds). With an election a couple of years off, Joaquín Balaguer has embarked on an equally ruinous initiative. To give the country a superficial appearance of smooth operation, Balaguer has ordered the construction of new hotels, highways, and attractions that are to be ready for 1992, the 500th anniversary of Columbus's arrival on the island. Work is behind schedule on many sites and the financing may develop into an economic apocalypse. The birthday party may turn into a wake, the time when hard times finally lead to collapse. If Columbus could have known that his discovery of Hispañola would later result in such misery, corruption, and confusion, he might have bypassed the island completely.

According to Montes, the weakened economy has staggered baseball fans and the winter league. "They say inflation is 60 per cent a year but in the last four months the price of milk has doubled. The average income is about $100 U.S. a month. People can't afford five or ten pesos [seventy-five cents or a buck and a half] to go to the stadium. With a weak peso against the U.S. dollar, owners would like to raise ticket prices but nobody would go to the games. The costs for all the American players are in American dollars and teams are losing money offering salaries that don't attract good ballplayers. The Dominican just can't compete with countries such as Puerto Rico or Venezuela— the more financially secure places. And Mexico is just so much bigger, they have the numbers. The Dominican winter league is just about dead."

Though major-league baseball can't do much to help the national debt, Comarazamy says it will take the intervention of major-league baseball to save the Dominican winter league. "Teams will have to sponsor and pick up the cost of teams down here," he says. "Because the peso is so weak, it really wouldn't take a lot of money to do that. And the way they can make it profitable is if they can sell television [rights] in the States and Canada. If they can get major-league fans interested in winter-league baseball—not just in the Dominican, but in all the Caribbean—they can make money here."

Baez's solution to pro ball's woes in the Dominican is a hard-line contrast to Comarazamy's. "If a major-league organization signs a Dominican player, it should be committed to pay a certain amount of money into player development here. All the young men in the sand-lots and sugar fields learn to play the game on diamonds owned by the government. Think of the players as a national resource. If a big company wants to mine in the Dominican, it has to pay the government. So if the big leagues want to take precious goods out of the country, they should have to pay the government too."

In the room this idea does not go over well. Even a waiter who has strolled in rolls his eyes when he hears the suggestion of handing over large sums to the government. During the long tenure of Trujillo, the direction of government funds was none of the public's business; in the three decades since his assassination, government misappropriation of funds seems to have been honed to a fine art. At least, many Dominicans believe that money funnelled into official hands for development of ballplayers is likely to land in a numbered bank account in the Turks and Caicos.

Montes has a cynical opinion of the positions that the United States and baseball have taken on the island. "Since the beginning, the Americans have come to the island and taken things away and the Dominicans have let them. The Americans set up sugar mills and had a store to sell them things to keep them amused—the Dominicans just smiled and worked. That's what our nation is—the Dominicans can't build things up on their own. So other countries come in and take things away. They make money on the Dominican people."

And for Montes, baseball is what religion was to Marx: an opiate of the people. "The Dominican people look to the baseball fields in the States and see the stars playing. They think this is great. And then they see the stars shaking hands with politicians so they think the politician is okay too. Maybe the ballplayer doesn't know better, but the scouts should. They are more experienced, older. They can tell you what they do is good and for a small number it is. But the way their business is, the scouts know that it is bad."

Montes is perhaps too dogmatic for Baez's and Comarazamy's liking, but what he says is true. Epy Guerrero and Ralph Avila can be viewed as makers of dreams or as agents of imperialist exploitation. But they are less buyers than sellers, for they must sell to young men the promise of baseball improving their lives. For stars it does; for others it is only a temporary alternative to the sugar mill or the factory. One job in professional sport parallels that of Avila, Guerrero, and the others: the job of recruiting players for U.S. college basketball. The Latin American scouts acquire talent at a price far below U.S. market value, but hungry, underprivileged kids at the sugar mills know no better; college basketball recruiters sweet-talk kids, many of them nearly as hungry and underprivileged as the Dominicans, and tell them that college will prepare them for the exclusive pro ranks. Both the scout and the recruiter sell the young athletes false goods; the deals they strike are tantamount to fraud.

I ask the group if they think that their lionizing of ballplayers is counterproductive. "Wouldn't it be better to make heroes of doctors or lawyers?" I put to them, offering role models that might be more appropriate.

"We can't do that," Montes says. "The people won't stand for that. For the kids it's easier to look up to a ballplayer whose game they understand. They can't understand what a doctor does or what a lawyer does. A lot of them have never seen a doctor. Besides, a lawyer or doctor may have a good life, but he's still on the island. A ballplayer goes to the States and makes millions. Medicine or law doesn't get you off the island. Baseball does. We all know we make gods out of the ballplayers but it's only what the people want."

Comarazamy interrupts. "The Wade Boggs story [his philandering liaisons with Margo Adams] wouldn't be written about here. We couldn't write about a ballplayer and a woman other than his wife. We have to be friends of the game and the ballplayers."

Baseball's troubles in the Dominican and the foibles of its star players are not fit subjects for publication because of this "friendship". In the United States and Canada, the major leaguers consider a reporter as an inconvenience, possibly as someone who would want to do them harm. But even George Bell, who considers himself an expert on media harassment, claims that it's different at home, that his friends in the press corps aren't intrusive: "The reporters here treat you like a regular guy, they give you respect so I give it back them." This amounts to elevating the players and owners and scouts above reproach.

Comarazamy maintains that the friendship is genuine. "The pressure is on these guys here. Everybody wants something— usually money—from these guys. I've heard about kids who sign minor-league contracts and when their families hear about it everybody—parents, brothers, cousins—quits his job and expects the young guys to support him. The reporters, hey, all we want is to talk. We don't want money, and we don't write anything that hurts."

"And we have good jobs so we don't make problems," Montes says.

"I used to be a lawyer," Comarazamy says and smiles, "but now I've got the second-best job in the country."

Baez, Comarazamy, and Montes adjourn to the bar where a pack of the pressmen are watching the U.S. cable sports network on the satellite dish. They will have a drink and talk about their obsession, and the nation's, till the small hours. And tomorrow they will spend another day and night at the bar, revelling in the joys of the moment rather than dwelling on the tough issues, which are too numerous to consider.

*

Juan Baez's enthusiasm for the game is waning by the sixth inning. It looks as if this will just be one of those years. Though Escogido covered itself in glory at the Caribbean World Series last year, this just seems a season destined to be wasted. Down 2–0, Los Leones go out like lambs in the bottom of the sixth. Wil Tejada bounces a one-hopper back to Guzmán for the first out. And then Nelson Liriano and Junior Noboa both strike out swinging.

CHAPTER EIGHT

BELL Y FAMILIA

LICEY	000 002	2 4 0
ESCOGIDO	000 000	0 2 2

Before the seventh inning, the field crew runs out onto the basepaths to smooth down any rough spots. With Licey fans howling, Torito, the tiny assistant batboy, comes sprinting out of the dugout with a stuffed toy tiger on his back, its tiny paws taped together around his neck. Torito is so low to the ground that the tiger's tail is dragging. After rounding the basepaths to laughter and applause, Torito dives head first into home plate. The umpire camps it up as he signals safe and Torito walks back to the dugout surely wondering what might have been if he were a foot taller.

The first batter in the top half of the inning is shortstop Tito Bell, the younger brother of the Blue Jays' George. In the press box before the game, the *periodistas* were discussing the trade of young Bell to Baltimore. For most of the winter-league season, Tito has been a more frequent topic of conversation than his famous brother. During the summer of '88 he made a breakthrough with the Los Angeles Dodgers' Triple A farm club in Albuquerque and was rated as the top prospect in the American Association. Scouts said he had an excellent chance to make the defending world champions' line-up in the spring of '89. And yet there were whispers that the Dodgers were unhappy with Bell's attitude, that he did not take instruction well, that he had feuded with management. Of course many people expected nothing less of George's brother.

After weeks of rumours, the Dodgers did to Tito Bell what the Blue Jays have often threatened to do to George—that is, they traded away the problem child. Los Angeles sent young Bell and a couple of prospects to the Baltimore Orioles for first baseman Eddie Murray. While Bell remains in the starting line-up for Los Tigres, he harbours bad feelings towards Licey's manager Joe Ferguson, who is also a coach with the Dodgers.

On a one-and-one pitch Tito lines a shot into centre field. He has hit in the .250s all season, nothing spectacular, but solid enough for a twenty-year-old. His fielding, however, has been erratic and a few suspect he has arm troubles (a possible explanation for his dispatch to the Orioles). Tonight, so far, so good.

Miguel Santana hits a sharp one-hopper to short, and Tito Bell is erased on the front end of a bang-bang 6–3 double play. Bell returns to the dugout with a look of disgust. He looks up to the guest boxes where George is having a beer. Tito Bell has expectations of more, expectations higher than anything he can achieve in the winter league. He will only be satisfied when he is as successful and famous and wealthy as his brother.

*

An old man five feet tall holds a shotgun four feet long and stands outside cinder-block walls eight feet high. Out in the noonday sun, without the relief of shade, he has both hands in his pockets, and the gun rests over his forearm, its stock tucked into his armpit. The gun is loaded and, with a few more shots from his flask, so too may be the gun's bearer. He comes to his post shortly after dawn and leaves late at night, spelled by another like him. He does this seven days a week.

The residents on this street just east of downtown San Pedro de Macorís represent the city's élite. Their houses are protected by security measures—high walls, barbed wire, electrified fences, video cameras, dogs. And it is no surprise that a good number of the well-guarded, well-moneyed class are ballplayers. Joaquín Andújar, one-time twenty-game winner now fast fading, was the first to come here. Andújar erected his sprawling manse about ten years ago. Alfredo Griffin, millionaire shortstop of the Los Angeles Dodgers, soon followed with a split-level ranch house. Andújar's is enclosed by a high wall and Griffin's sits behind wrought-iron fencing. These measures are typical in a neighbourhood wary of intruders, thieves, and encyclopedia salesmen.

The house under armed guard is the neighbourhood's latest addition and still under construction. Though the house is as yet unoccupied and without contents, the building supplies alone warrant special protection. Atop the walls shards of glass have been dropped into mortar to provide a more intimidating line of defence than barbed wire. Inside these walls, a weary, underfed German shepherd is chained to an iron post. Anything remotely precious is shackled and locked away. Indeed the design of the house is fortress-like: an illuminated moat protects the front door; corners of the house rise up like turrets; the coach house has the look of an arsenal.

Parked out front, a Mercedes blocks the driveway. The old man warily eyes any pedestrian who strays too close to the big-ticket auto. He stands beneath a sign that announces RES-IDENCIA DE BELL Y FAMILIA. The sign is not necessary. When locals pass the site, they know this could only be the home of George Bell. There is no need for personalized licence plates on the Benz. All of San Pedro knows its owner.

Behind the walls, and behind Ray-Bans, and behind a spotty off-season beard that isn't quite menacing, George Bell inspects the site as he does every day. He is at once owner, developer, and chief trouble-shooter. Today the source of concern is the Jacuzzi on the second floor. Bell oversees a session bringing together chief engineer, chief plumber, and attendant workmen. Though there is something a bit sinister in Bell's appearance, his manner at this meeting is not intimidating. Rather he is gregarious with friends. He goes about the work site with handshakes for all and looks up at the cathedral ceiling in the main foyer with something of a child's fascination.

"When I was a kid, back in school, I wanted to be an engineer or an architect maybe," he says, staring up two and a half storeys to the cathedral's peak. "That was before baseball. But design, that was something I was interested in. Now with this house, I'm here every day, making sure things go the way that I want them to." In talking about this house he builds, George Bell, born Jorge Antonio Bell de Gomez, lets me know that he is the master, if not the mastermind, behind Residencia de Bell y Familia. Indeed, the house looks like a child's imagination was loosed upon it, and his vision of splendour realized. But on this point Bell is adamant: "I didn't draw anything like this," he says. "It's not like I'm building the house I always wanted. It's just the house I want now. It's a house for the rest of my life."

Over an off-season girth stretched by Christmas and New Year's excesses, he wears a white golf shirt. Above the paunch, dangling from his neck, are pounds of gold: BELL spelled out in script a half-inch wide in the strokes; a round saucer-sized medallion with 1987 AMERICAN LEAGUE MVP inscribed; various religious artifacts and chains as thick as your middle finger. His fingers, similarly bejewelled and diamond-studded, are as yet pristine of the ballplayers' most-desired fashion accessory, a League Championship or World Series ring.

Dominican machismo comprises many character traits—honour, courage, and bravado, among others—but in the most powerful men in the republic there are a couple of peculiar patterns of behaviour.

Rafael Trujillo was, like Bell, the self-styled champion of the Dominican people. In the halls of power he had the same sort of clout that Bell has on the field. Trujillo held the nation spellbound with his macho style. He was a man's man, they said; many were able to ignore his murdering of countrymen because they so admired his adultery with countrywomen. Like Bell, Trujillo had a penchant for outlandish accessories. Trujillo's predilection for a chestful of trinkets contributed to the caricature of the "banana republic" leader—listing to the left, weighted down by the hardware over his heart. In addition to the dozens of honours from foreign states, from the Vatican to the Soviet Union, Trujillo bestowed awards upon himself: Order of Military Merit; Great Cross of Benefactor of the Country; Collar of the Order of Merit; Order of Merit of Juan Pablo Duarte; Great Cross of Valour; Heraldic Order of Cristóbal Colón; Order of Trujillo (something of a meta-honour); Order of Merit of the Air Force; Order of Merit of the National Police; Great Collar of Peace. He took on official titles of somewhat dubious distinction: Meritorious Son of San Cristóbal; Benefactor of the Fatherland; First and Greatest of Dominican Chiefs of State; Restorer of Financial Independence (that's rich); Commander and Chief of the Armed Forces; Father of the New Fatherland; Loyal and Noble Champion of World Peace; Chief Protector of Dominican Culture; Maximum Protector of the Dominican Working Class. For Bell the honours are not so numerous: MVP; Silver Slugger; major-league All-Star; Latin All-Star; Blue Jay player of the year; and others more mundane. Yet he wears them proudly, as if each were the Red Badge of Courage.

Like George Bell, Trujillo had a lust to build. Though he knew nothing of drafting and blueprints, Trujillo was the architect of the Dominican Republic. Under his rule he did more to shape the Dominican nation than all subsequent presidents and administrations combined. To Trujillo nothing was as beautiful as a construction site. In his first twenty-five years in power he built 103 Roman Catholic churches, and 380 bridges that linked more than 1,800 miles of new highways. He built baseball stadiums throughout the country, not just in the major cities of Santiago, San Pedro, and Santo Domingo, but also in the outreaches, in cities that couldn't possibly support a winter-league team: Moca, Puerto Plata, San Francisco de Macorís, and others. In towns not large enough for a stadium, Trujillo built fine amateur baseball diamonds. His influence upon the Dominican agenda is still obvious three decades after his death. Before every election these days, the leaders in power embark on overly ambitious construction projects, weakly imitating Trujillo. Unlike Trujillo, today's

leaders, including Balaguer, do not have the wherewithal to finish projects. Their efforts further bankrupt the economy and
cause inflation rates to spiral.

Bell is Trujillian in his self-decoration for triumphs on the field
and in his interest in erecting monuments to a career that he and
others will tell you is monumental, worthy of lasting memory.

When he first secured tenure in the majors he built a modest
home for his parents on Avenida Mauricio Baez, the street in
San Pedro where the Bell clan had lived for ten years. It is not
a grand neighbourhood. Still, the Bells' two-storey cinder-block
home is as conspicuous as the Trump Tower would be. The Bells'
neighbours live in a frame house with a sheet-metal roof and a
dirt floor.

When the money came in more by the bucket than by the
handful, he built a place in La Romana that has, as his friends
assure me, a whirlpool bath shaped like home plate. This house
was in addition to a luxurious home in San Pedro, about twenty-
five minutes away.

Now that acclaim, fame and, most of all, money are in place,
Bell is constructing this garish dream home. The San Pedrans
walk up to it, gander, utter oaths, laugh about their own cruel
fate, and move on. Traffic on the road slows as rubber-neckers
lean out their rolled-down windows.

This is not just the latest of Bell's large gestures. This is his
Crystal Palace (done with glass brick) or even his Graceland
(granted, bats and baseballs will likely replace guitars and gold
records as a design motif). Whenever a tourist-loaded bus drives
through San Pedro de Macorís it passes by the Residencia de
Bell y Familia. Indeed, given the scale Bell works on, perhaps
the pilots of jets coming in to the Santo Domingo airport will
point out the Bell mansion from the air.

"One more year, one more good year," he says to no one in
particular as he walks through the premises. The way he utters
the line suggests that he does not mean that the 1989 season
will be another great tour of duty, another high-numbered line
to be entered in his career statistics. He is resigning himself to
"one more year", another commitment of 162 games, so that he

can complete this latest home and earn security enough for his family.

Bell is abrupt in tone, distracted in manner. He goes to lengths to remind me that I am an intruder and an imposition on his valuable time. When talk about the house turns to the hard numbers, pesos and centavos, Bell dismisses me, pointing me downstairs and telling me to wait there. A half-hour later, Bell returns, giving me a perfunctory explanation for his absence: "Business."

It has always been Bell's way, in Toronto and everywhere else, to point the fourth estate away, to dismiss them without reason or explanation for months or seasons. Trujillo also had his way with the press, dictating to them what they could and could not write. I ask Bell about the reporters he faces in Toronto and the United States, those people from whom he retreats.

"They're okay but I don't like to talk. That's all. Some guys like to talk even more than they like to play. That's their problem. I don't mind talking about the game I just played or what I do on the field. But they always want to know personal things. One guy in Toronto asked me what type of food I like. It's a stupid question but I told him seafood. So he asked what type of seafood. And I said, 'Seafood'." At this point he gestures downward with an open hand in a chopping motion, exasperated. Evidently there is nothing more to seafood than, well, seafood in Bell's world, or at least on his dining table. "So then the guy asks me what's my favourite restaurant. 'I can't go back there if I tell you,' I told him. Stupid questions. That's how publicity messes your life up. You say what your favourite restaurant is and then you can't go back there because all the people are bugging you. I don't like publicity.

"It costs me money not to talk," he says, as if this is the ultimate sacrifice he makes in the name of his privacy. "It costs me money not to be the nice guy. My agent tells me that if I do interviews and talk nice and do the other stuff I can make another hundred thousand, maybe more. But I don't care. I'm a ballplayer. I play ball. I don't talk. I don't like publicity."

It must be a problem, I say. After all, if a guy on the end of the bench doesn't like publicity, he won't get it. But an MVP, a guy who drives in a hundred runs a year for a contender and makes $2 million a year, can't avoid it. Doesn't building a new castle, driving a Benz around town, draw attention that he doesn't want?

"Yeah, it's a problem," he says impatiently as a few Canadian tourists drive up to the gate. By the time the *gringos* step out of their rented car and bang off a few Polaroids of the palace, Bell is safely inside, out of sight.

On a night in late October, George Bell digs his heels into the batters' box at the stadium in La Romana. The pitcher who has just walked to the mound is introduced over the scratchy P.A. and there follow jeers, boos, and name-calling. The pitcher ignores the noise and fires a ball in, a floater out of the strike zone. Bell takes a mighty cut. A swing and a miss. His body contorted. Bell smiles.

The pitcher is the most hated man in the Dominican Republic, Jimy Williams, the poor bloke who manages the Toronto Blue Jays. Depending on which report you read, Williams either said or did not say to Bell in the middle of a horrendous fielding slump, "If it weren't for baseball you'd be back cutting sugar-cane." Or words, perhaps more profane, to that effect. Dominicans, and most probably the sugar-cane cutters among them, took offence at this. In myriad contretemps with Williams during the latter's tenure with the Jays, Bell has mentioned that he will "outlast" Williams. Bell did not specify whether outlasting referred to employment or living.

Yet on this night Bell is playing the fool, archly swinging at a ball that you would think he'd be trying to line back at his tormentor. It would be sweet vindication for the power hitter. Williams, you would think, would likewise be throwing the ball at the unhelmeted head of the millionaire. But this is a social call that Williams is paying Bell and before these fans, press, and the rest they claim to have buried the hatchet—and not in each other's backs. Williams, along with general manager Pat Gillick and assistant GM Gord Ash and broadcaster Fergie Olver, will be attending and hacking away in the George Bell–Alfredo Griffin charity golf tourney in La Romana. This opening-pitch ceremony is to publicize that event, with proceeds to go to a not-as-yet-constructed-but-much-talked-about orphanage *cum* youth centre in San Pedro de Macorís. Bell and Williams even put their arms around each other's shoulders and mug shamelessly for photographers in aid of underprivileged youth. Bell says something about being "realistic" about playing left field for the Jays. Williams tells the Dominican reporters that George Bell is his everyday left fielder for 1989.

This is just the latest paradoxical situation for this monstrously contradictory character: hated by opponents, perhaps even by management, yet loved by teammates; perceived as a malcontent by Toronto fans for whom he performs his heroics; yet lionized by his countrymen before whom he has not deigned to play for several years. A superior batsman who takes great offence, personal hurt, when management casts aspersions on his glovework.

The improbable outrages of George Bell, even those that are printable, are legion.

Bell first came to prominence in the U.S. and Canada when the Blue Jays won the Eastern Division of the American League and met the Kansas City Royals in the Championship Series. When certain calls seemed to favour the Royals, Bell levelled charges against the umpires and the baseball establishment, saying they were at once anti-Dominican and anti-Canadian. The charges were termed ludicrous, yet, speaking about the alleged anti-Dominican sentiment, Bell was only giving voice to an opinion widely held though infrequently expressed by many of his countrymen.

One of the Dominican television stations introduces its broadcasts of winter-league games with a montage of major-league highlights. On one occasion, George Bell's contribution to this was not a homer, a bold swing, or a stellar play in the field, but rather a brawl with Boston Red Sox pitcher Bruce Kison. A brushback pitch incited Bell to riot. He charged the mound and let loose something described in the press as "a karate kick", though as one knowledgeable source told me, "He must have learned his karate from watching Bruce Lee movies." The blood feud between Bell and the Bosox has lasted for a few years and shows no signs of abating. "The Red Sox hate George Bell's guts," wrote baseball diarist Margo Adams.

After one uncharitable story written by John Robertson, then of the *Toronto Sun*, Bell took bat in hand to threaten the born-again, middle-aged recovering cardiac patient with bodily harm. Robertson refused to blame his subsequent circulatory problems on this challenge.

Other stories are more fleeting, though no less incendiary, but on this night they are, for the moment, forgotten. As we go from dusk to darkness, La Romana wins the game easily over Caimanes del Sur, the team from Trujillo's hometown of San Cristóbal. The game on the field is barely noticed by Bell and his guests. Bell hosts a party—no music, only drinks—in the stadium's presidential box, in the same place where Trujillo danced and frolicked with a bevy of mistresses, where he traded stories with cronies whom he would later bury or float off to sea.

On this night Bell poses for photos with Williams, his chief tormentor, and hosts the visiting dignitaries, drinking elbow-to-elbow with them, smiling, and talking with Roger Clemons, the Boston pitcher who'll play in the tournament. It's hard to believe that this same Bell says, "You can't trust anybody in baseball. I don't have any real friends on the Jays. I don't have any friends in baseball." It is hard to believe, so it is completely in character.

When pressed on the issue George Bell will admit that, at one time, he had a friend in baseball, but "they traded him away.... After that, no more friends in baseball." Alfredo Griffin, formerly a shortstop with the Jays, later the Oakland Athletics and, in 1988, shortstop for the World Champion Los Angeles Dodgers, was the man who befriended Bell when the young outfielder first came to Toronto. It is no coincidence that Bell is building his latest home just a few doors down the street from Griffin's house. "We were teammates," Bell says. "In a few years I want to be business partners. We'll build malls, apartment buildings, condominiums." He says this as if sharing the construction of commercial and residential buildings is the ultimate expression of friendship.

The man in George Bell's good graces is stretched out on
the couch in his recreation room. At home Alfredo Griffin is
a quiet man, a gentle man, who, in sleepy repose, looks older
than his listed age, in "baseball years". In this room, a shrine to
baseball, he has hats from every major-league team. Photographs
of himself and other great players. Half-dozing, he watches a
videotape of a game from the summer of '83. Toronto baseball
fans will remember that night, a Monday night, the Jays against
the Kansas City Royals. It was Toronto's first appearance on
nation-wide television in the U.S. On that night Alfredo Griffin
did something that George Bell will likely never do: he won the
player-of-the-game award on a night when he went hitless. And
here in his recreation room, more than five years and two teams
later, 3,000 miles away, he watches his glorious times when he
wore Toronto blue.

"This was my best game," he says. He runs and reruns a play
where he goes deep in the hole and throws across his body to
nab a base runner at first. Howard Cosell enthuses, the crowd
goes wild, each of the five times he runs it. "The best moment
was winning the Series, 'cause I'm older, I might not be there
again. But that game in Toronto, that was the best I ever played.
I remember the cheers. I remember Dámaso and George shaking
my hand."

Despite all the dissension that has racked the Toronto ballclub
in the last four years since he was dispatched to Oakland, Griffin
remembers nothing but good times in the city. "They've had a
lot of talent for four or five years now," he says, "I don't know
why they've never won." When I say to him that maybe all the
club needed was a leader, someone like, say, Alfredo Griffin, he
is not flattered. "I know what I can do for a ballclub," he says.
"To play every day, every inning. Hurt, healthy, doesn't matter.
To be a good man in the clubhouse, to talk to the young players,
to make a team. That's what I do. I've got a year more, maybe
two, but that's it. I'll keep doing what I've always done."

The qualities of a good leader, the *rara avis* always found on
a championship team, are usually tough to define. Not so with
Griffin, however. In baseball circles he is renowned for being
able to create a peaceful and joyous atmosphere in the clubhouse,

to head off any dissent. "Any new player, young kids, I always go to them and try to help," Griffin says. "That's nothing to do with being a leader. That's just being a good person. It's tough to be a ballplayer. A good life but tough when you're starting. Other people helped me when I was starting. Rico [Carty] always helped me out and there were lots of others. I just helped others the way they helped me."

Among those he helped was a young George Bell. "George was the same as a lot of kids when he started out," Griffin says. "Not talent—not too many kids have his talent—but just being a little nervous, being in a new city not knowing his way around. It didn't matter if it was a Dominican kid or an American. If there was anything I could do to help I did. That has nothing to do with being a good ballplayer or a good leader. It's just being a good person.

"What you are as a ballplayer, you are as a person. What George does on the field is the way George is in life. What I do on the field is the way I am in life. We are different ballplayers, different people. It's that simple."

When I mention to Griffin that it must be difficult for him to be a partner in friendship, business, and philanthropy with Bell, a man of a such a different temperament, Griffin quickly disagrees.

"We understand what we are," he says. "Ballplayers. In the United States you are an athlete. In the Dominican you are something more. You're the hero. You're the hope. You're responsible to the people. I've known about being poor. My family came from a sugar-cane plantation outside of San Pedro. Now that my career is almost over I know I want to help the Dominican people, maybe someone who was like me when I was a boy. If someone is going to help the Dominican people, it has to be the ballplayers. They bring the money into the country. They are the leaders."

Through it all a love of the game pervades the words of Griffin, a love of the game that is never even hinted at by Bell. "I know George doesn't want to manage," Griffin says. "He plays the game and when it's over he will move on. But I love the game. I do. It hurts me that I can't play here in the winter. I would love to play in the winter league, but because of the money— you know, two million dollars—I can't risk it playing here for a thousand dollars. I want to play in front of the Macorístas, at Tetelo Vargas, but I can't do it. I want to show them Alfredo Griffin the ballplayer. I want to show them that I'm a ballplayer and not just a rich man. But I can't risk my security, my family's security. Sometimes you can't do everything you want to."

Later that week, there are two small items in the newspapers. In the first, George Bell has stated that he will wait to report to spring training until March 2. Though this is within the letter of the law and complies with the terms of the players' collective bargaining agreement, virtually all players, from lowly rookies to the most high-priced superstars, voluntarily show up a week or more earlier. This will be the second consecutive year that Bell does not appear until the eleventh hour. That's why fans frequently boo this man whose bat can change the course of any game he plays in.

In the other item, Alfredo Griffin has announced that he will play in the last dozen games of the season for Estrellas Orientales. In his first game back, he will go two-for-four. That's why the fans have always fallen in love with this guy who can scarcely hit his weight. Two different ballplayers, two different people. Once best friends, now neighbours and partners yet the furthest thing from soul mates.

"I always have played hard for my team and my organization, but first of all, the most important thing, I've played for myself. This is what a ballplayer does, the way he has to think." So says the son of Jorge Vinicio Bell, the most famous father in San Pedro de Macorís. Under the glare of television lights, he talks to a Dominican broadcaster before a game at Estadio Quisqueya.

I want to talk to this son of Jorge Bell senior, to talk to this man whose reputation for surliness is an ever-growing legend. After the television interview ends and handshakes are exchanged, I ask if I can have a minute or two. Here follows an abridged version of a statement he issues while wielding a Louisville Slugger in a menacing fashion: "*Coño*. How long you been? How fuckin' long? You never say hi, you never fuckin' talk to me before. I'm not going to talk to you now. Fuck you. Fuck off." With that Jorge's son walks away without a look back.

Though this is a tantrum worthy of George, it is Juan (Tito) Bell who lets loose this purple stream. And though George has on occasion gone on the record with his disregard for management and fans, it is Tito who here espouses this doctrine of looking out for Number One, not coincidentally the number he sports for Los Tigres de Licey. Like George, Tito is, to put it mildly, press-shy.

After this introduction, the beginning of what I assume will be a forever frosty relationship, Juan Bell retreats to the clubhouse. Mario Guerrero, Epy's brother the agent, overhears the barrage and consoles me.

"He's really a good kid," Mario says, despite the ear-singeing evidence to the contrary. "This is just a bad time and he really doesn't know what you want. The trade hasn't been confirmed yet. He doesn't know where he's going to be playing this year. He's confused. It's rough, you know, when you're twenty and two teams are moving you around like you're nothing."

Tito Bell's upset is understandable. Two fellow Macorístas, citizens of San Pedro, enabled the Dodgers to trade Juan Bell. A few experts in the States believe that Juan's Dodgers days were numbered when Alfredo Griffin, San Pedro's elder statesman, signed a $2.2 million contract after the World Series this autumn. However, even more important was the emergence of shortstop José Oferman, the kid so highly touted by Ralph Avila.

The consensus among the baseball press is that Oferman is the outstanding young prospect this season in the winter league. "No insult to Tony Fernández, but Oferman has a good shot at being the best shortstop ever to come out of San Pedro," says Juan Baez, the commentator. "Juan Bell is a fine talent, a future major leaguer, but there wouldn't be room on one team for both Tito and Oferman. And to choose between them is easy: Oferman."

And Baez adds that Bell probably expedited his own transfer to the Orioles. "His attitude is bad," Baez says. "Whether it's true or not, he has a reputation for being hard to coach, for not listening to managers and for not taking instruction. Oferman is a coach's son. Bell is a ballplayer's brother. One's a good kid. The other spoiled."

Says Joe Ferguson, Licey's manager and Tito Bell's tormen-tor: "It's just amazing that Oferman, with just one year of rookie ball, can come in and play well in this winter league. He has incredible tools, raw ability, and he makes spectacular plays sometimes. Other times he looks green. When he can make the routine plays consistently he'll be in the majors real quick."

Mario Guerrero takes me into the Licey dressing room. Bell is laughing and talking with his friends but stops when he sees me. Guerrero approaches him first and, talking calmly but firmly, tells the prospect that interviews have to be done, that the best thing is just to give reporters a little time, not too much, and be done with it. Shirtless, Bell looks down to his bare chest all the while. Though far leaner, it is during this lecture, in this moment of despondency, that Tito Bell's features most resemble those of his brother.

"I'll talk," he says.

Guerrero says that young Bell can speak English, but I have yet to see proof that he can speak in words longer than four letters. I ask Guerrero to stay on to translate Tito's words from Spanish to English to avoid confusion.

No matter which language he speaks, Tito echoes the philosophy of his older brother. They share a vision of the game, one utterly stripped of sentiment. "I don't care if I go to Baltimore or if I stay in Los Angeles," he says. "I'm a ballplayer. This is what a ballplayer has to do. I know this."

He says that no game in his life has ever been more memorable and meaningful than another. He has no career highlights. "I hit two home runs in a game in Triple A, a grand slam someplace else, but there was no game, no season that means that much to me. It's like asking a worker did you ever have one good day at work. For me baseball is a job. Just a job. My job, but just a job. When I make the major leagues and get a hit, I'll keep the ball, sure—but I'll give it to a coach and try and steal second. If it's a homer, I'll grab my glove and get ready to go back in the field.

"I knew I was going to be a ballplayer after George signed. That was it. I was going to do what he did. I knew I could because I was his brother, same flesh. Maybe I can't be the same ballplayer. Maybe I can't hit forty homers. But he can't play shortstop so it doesn't matter. What matters is that I can be a ballplayer in the majors, that's all. I will, it's that simple.

"There was never something else. School wasn't important after George signed. I started working from when I was about ten and I worked on becoming a major-league ballplayer. Nothing else. No back-up plan. Not interested.

"I talk to my brother every day," Tito says. "He's giving me advice all the time."

What sage counsel does his tempestuous older sibling provide? "Play hard, work hard, get along with your teammates and manager." About the last, it seems the younger Bell has yet to develop any sense of irony.

Tito says he's looking forward to playing against his brother when Toronto faces Baltimore. "The first time that I play against George," Tito says, "he won't be my brother any more. Just another player. And when I'm out there at shortstop, I'll stop taking his advice—at least when we're playing Toronto." At this point, Juan Bell almost lets the mask slip, almost lets himself smile.

"Where a ballplayer plays isn't important. It could be Toronto, Baltimore, Los Angeles, Houston, Milwaukee, Detroit, anywhere. In the end he must be paid and that is what is important," says the father of George, of Tito, and of Dodgers farmhand Rolando.

To thine own self be true—yourself and your accountant first. Señor Bell has imparted this philosophy to his children and, though reasonable in print and in casual conversation, it has caused problems for the oldest, promises the same for Tito, but likely won't affect Rolando, the least talented in the group. The word in baseball circles is that the Dodgers only kept Rolando around to keep Tito company. With Tito shipped to Baltimore, Rolando's days in pro ball are numbered.

Señor Bell can easily rationalize his play-for-pay beliefs. "The player can only play so long and he lives in pain. Look at George. His knee hurts. His back hurts. He had a broken jaw from a pitch. He has to take from the game what he can while he can. To play you have to be aggressive and not think about injuries. But when it comes to contracts, you have to think that maybe this is the last one you will ever have; that it is all over the next time you step on the diamond."

The fifty-six-year-old Jorge Bell took from the game what he could. The son of a truck driver, Bell senior played amateur ball in San Pedro on Saturdays and Sundays and holidays. Pro ball was not even a dream. He was an engineer on the sugar train to Santa Fe, and sugar was the lifeblood of the community; baseball was a mere diversion. "It's almost the other way now; as much money comes in from baseball when sugar prices aren't high," Bell senior says.

One storey above roaring traffic, on the balcony of the house that George built his father, Señor Bell holds forth on a player's motivations and the game's rewards. He even sports an ornate, solid-gold "G" about his neck. Jorge is his son, but George is his benefactor. It's no surprise that in this family the hand-me-downs include jewellery.

A safe distance from George, Señor Bell confesses that he was, in the beginning at least, doubtful about his son's ambition to be a pro ballplayer. "He would always say, 'Come watch me, I'm going to be a major leaguer.' I told him to go to school and he could practise after school. I always wanted my sons to do well in school. We moved to the city so they could go to school and have a better life than I did. I thought that school was the way to do it. But after I watched him once, I guess he was fifteen or sixteen, I knew he had power. Right then I told him he could practise more. He had my approval. If he wanted to practise he could practise all he wanted because I knew he was going to be a ballplayer.

"I gave him some help. He used to hit all left hand (motioning that the right hand was releasing from the bat early). I tell him that the right hand is the power, that until his right hand is there he will never have the power. I was never a coach. I didn't work hour after hour with George or Tito or Rolando. But I always watched them and I know their games. I still ask questions or give advice."

Señor Bell isn't worried by Tito's trade to Baltimore, though he doesn't know the city well. Or even which coast it is on. "I don't know what Baltimore will do this year. I think he may be ready to play in the big leagues but if they want him to stay in the minors another season or half a season that is okay. He will play in the majors, that is for sure. I saw him play in Florida in rookie ball and I see him with Licey at the stadium or on television. I am not surprised that he is a ballplayer. I'd be surprised if he wasn't. I'm happy that he will go to Baltimore and get a chance to play. Even though he's ready, he would have to wait a year at least, maybe more, with the Dodgers."

Reiterating what George has said, Bell blames many of the Dominicans' problems on a lack of understanding in both the media and the public. "I understand the problems George has had in Toronto. They don't know how the Dominican people talk. If the press asks him about money and he says that he can make more money playing in Japan they write, 'Bell going to Japan.' They misunderstand him. With Jimy Williams he didn't know how to handle George and other players. Jimy Williams was never a player. It takes a player to manage players. The Blue Jays with Bobby Cox would never have had the problems. Cox was a player. I think that for three seasons Toronto would have been another team, a better team, a champion."

Despite the lack of championship success, George has a fierce defender in his father. "With all the troubles he is still the best player on Toronto," Señor Bell concludes. He motions to me for approval or opinion. Politely, I say that nobody else has hit forty-seven homers in a season for the club, nobody else has won an MVP award or been voted to the starting line-up of the All-Star Game. Were he George's agent rather than his father, perhaps I would have pursued it, perhaps I could add that Epy Guerrero contends that Tony Fernández, not George, is not only the best Blue Jay but the greatest Dominican player ever.

On this topic I ask Señor Bell who is the best ballplayer he has ever seen: "I am his father," he says. Even in fatherhood a Bell can swagger.

I assume that Jorge Vinicio Bell's claim to having sired the superlative player is a reference to George, but Ralph Avila is not so sure.

"As prospects, as kids, the best of the Bell brothers was Vinicio," Avila says. "Vinicio Bell, a little younger than George and older than Juan and Rolando."

Talk to a scout and he will never mention the one who got away, a prospect he just failed to sign. But he will always ruefully talk about the kid who betrayed great promise, the kid who coulda and shoulda been great—César Cedeño, Alfredo Elmeada, and now Vinicio Bell. Avila has signed scores of players. Only a couple were as good as Vinicio Bell.

In Avila's office at the Dodger complex Campo Las Palmas is decorated with photographs of the many players he has scouted and signed, yet nothing here even hints at Vinicio Bell, except a thin folder in Avila's precious filing cabinet.

"Vinicio Bell was a switch-hitting shortstop," Avila says. "As a fielder—glove, arm, and range—he had it all over Tito Bell. And with the bat, he hit for a better average than George would. Not as much power as George but lots of power for a shortstop. Any power at shortstop is just a bonus. He had power that a lot of All-Star shortstops don't have. Great mechanics, real aggressive, and he had *cojones*, just fearless at the plate. Vinicio Bell...." Avila raises his eyebrows and his voice trails off. Here again just the memory of the prospect's potential tortures the veteran scout.

"It's a shame really," Avila says. "I remember in Instructional League, we played the Mets and the Mets had a kid named Craig Swan who won about fifteen games in the big leagues that year. Vinicio hit Swan all over the yard, lit 'em up, a home run, a triple. Vinicio had just one year in pro ball and he's lighting up a very good major-league pitcher. Vinicio was a real talent." But for all this promise, for the show of power against a major-league pitcher, Vinicio Bell never gained a place on the walls of Señor Avila's office. Avila does not hide his disappointment.

"At the start of what was supposed to be his second year in the organization, Vinicio Bell reported to training camp in Dodgertown [Vero Beach]. He was playing great again, but there was an argument between him and a coach. I can't say what happened but the situation was unacceptable, unacceptable."

Here Avila lets the imagination of the listener race. He does not respond to any questions about the "unacceptable" situation.

Could it have been fisticuffs with a coach? A woman in the dorm? Avila will not even hint at what happened. But consider the many sins forgiven ballplayers—drug use, weapons possession, criminal charges, insubordination—and you get an idea that Vinicio Bell wasn't dismissed for spitting in the showers. "Let's just say that it was bad enough that it didn't matter how good a prospect Vinicio Bell was," Avila says. "We had to release him even though he was one of the best prospects in the organization. And it was bad enough that when word got out, no other team would sign him. By the time we released him, Vinicio's problems were no secret. The Mets sure knew about him.

"Vinicio had the worst temper of the Bells, maybe the worst temper I ever seen on any Dodgers' player. His father had a real temper too. If any of his kids ever got out of line and one of the neighbours told Jorge Vinicio, well, he gave them a whipping for sure. He taught the kids discipline. He taught the kids toughness and he didn't take anything from them. The kids became ballplayers—George a great ballplayer, Juan a pretty good young prospect, Vinicio a great prospect for a year, and Rolando a pretty useful organization player—the kids became ballplayers because of the discipline for the game and the toughness that their father gave them. Unfortunately he gave them his temper too. Vinicio's temper got him out of baseball. I don't know about Juan yet, but George, well, George's temper is nothing compared to Vinicio's."

It is an opinion that is sure to make a few baseball executives swallow their cigars.

"I know what I did was wrong. But the Americans don't understand about the Dominican ballplayers, about the Dominican people. To fail means something else to a Dominican ballplayer. If you don't make it in the States, you can find a job and make money. If you don't make it and you're a Dominican, your whole family loses. If a Dominican makes it, he's really rich. If he doesn't, he's really poor. If someone does something that threatens his career, his chance to make a living and be rich, he's gotta do something about it. I did. People misunderstood why I did it. And the second after I did it I was sorry. I don't want to hurt anybody. But if you think that somebody wants to hurt you, you reach to hurt somebody, anybody."

The confessor here isn't George Bell. Or even Vinicio Bell. It is Juan Marichal, the first Dominican player of prominence in the major leagues and the first elected to the Hall of Fame. He won more than 280 games in fifteen seasons and many experts regard him as the best pitcher in the '60s.

His considerable accomplishments in the field lost some of their lustre when in 1965, in a crucial series between Marichal's team, the San Francisco Giants, and the Dodgers, Marichal attacked Los Angeles catcher John Roseboro. And though George Bell has been vilified for his assault on Bruce Kison, at least George dropped his bat. Marichal used his Louisville Slugger to express his discontent, rapping Roseboro's unhelmeted head with it.

"John [Roseboro] and I became good friends after that," Marichal says. "Still are. It happened in the game. When the game was over I apologized. He said sure. That was it.

"I understand George Bell when he charges the mound when a pitcher hits him. I understand why he reacts bad after Jimy Williams sits him down during the season. This is his living. This is his power, to be a ballplayer.

"I know what George Bell is thinking when he says that everyone—the umpires, the front office, the fans—is against him. For most of his life he was competing to be the best. Nobody helps him, he helps nobody. The guy beside him always wanted the same job that George did. That's the way it is for the young players in the Dominican and in the minors. And George and the Dominican players always are thinking that to be as good as the American players isn't good enough. If two players have the same ability, one an American, the other Dominican, the club will always take the American. So the Dominican player thinks that being [as good] isn't good enough."

I tell Marichal the story of the Blue Jays Player-of-the-Year voting in 1985. The media, those who cast the ballots in the voting, passed over Bell and elected Jesse Barfield. The statistics were quite close—yet Bell saw this as a slight against him.

"That's it," Marichal says. "What else is he going to think? The fans are going to say that he's got a bad temper, another Dominican, stupid, whatever. They don't understand how he feels. Foreign country. Another language. Coloured. He's going to think that it's those things that the sportswriters are thinking about. It might not be true and the fans know it, but how's George going to know that?

"The Dominican ballplayers—and the other Latin ballplayers —the game is all they know. You might see the American guys in the clubhouse sitting around talking about fishing, hunting, bars, anything. The Dominican players are sitting around talking about baseball or they're practising. There isn't anything else. You know they always talk about how American ballplayers and Dominicans don't mix that much. Sometimes I think it isn't because of anything racial. I just think that the American guys don't want to talk about baseball all the time."

Marichal has known all the glories the game holds for the greats: he played in the World Series and was elected to Cooperstown. I ask him how all the wealth and celebrity changed him. I ask him about the pressures he had to face.

"You don't know. You can't know. I know but I can't tell you so you know."

Santa Fe has barely changed through the years. Old-timers complain about the noise from the tractors that nowadays pull trailers loaded with sugar-cane. In days not so long ago horses and donkeys pulled wooden carts weighed down with smaller loads of the same crop. But, as the many piles of dung on the roadside would suggest, horses still work the same routes as their grandsires and granddams did. Technology is finding its way into the refinery. Mechanical efficiency is eliminating jobs and increasing production. Still the refinery is the only employer in town. The low groan from the factory echoes all over town. The townspeople have grown deaf to this ambient noise.

Santa Fe is a *batey*, the sugar belt's equivalent of a company town. When sugar companies set up their mills close to the fields, they constructed barracks and a few amusements and conveniences to attract and appease workers. The rules today on the *batey* are much the same as they were decades ago. A worker has to put in twenty-five years of hard labour, usually six days a week, to draw a pension. Automation has eliminated many jobs and families which have lived for generations on the *batey* are being forced to move into the city. Still the one way to guarantee employment is, surprisingly, to be able to play ball. Those who are good enough to play in the majors leave the *batey* for ever, but those not quite at that rank can secure a position with the sugar company by playing on the *batey*'s team. Managers at the *bateys* want their teams to do well in the company leagues; a winning team promotes good spirits in the work force. Many kids who are signed from the *batey* never imagine that baseball will take them to the States; they only hope it will win them a twelve-hour-a-day job inside the mill.

Over the past twenty or thirty years life on the *batey* has changed little. A few more houses have electricity, but not all of them yet. Running water is still a luxury item; many citizens carry drinking water by the pailful to their homes. The women balance the buckets on their heads. In various states of undress, or absolutely bone naked, the children hoist water in plastic containers back to their homes. Goats and pigs and dogs and horses walk around unattended or lie in the muddy, unpaved streets. And at the end of their shifts the men from the refinery will go to the Barra de las Estrellas Brilliantes, the Shining Stars Bar, for glasses of rum. The proprietress of Las Estrellas Brilliantes says there has never been trouble at her bar—no fights, no angry words—and that her patrons come in during the day and don't leave until the stars shine.

"It's a happy town," she says, optimism unbridled. "Watch the children going to school or coming home in their uniforms. They smile, they laugh. It is a beautiful place, isn't it?"

And there is the train, the train from Santa Fe to San Pedro de Macorís. The train covers a distance that takes a couple of minutes by car. The kids of Santa Fe often walk to San Pedro, passing the dense, high fields of sugar-cane. For the townspeople of Santa Fe, a trip to San Pedro is a special occasion. But the train makes the trip every day, a slow, almost funereal procession of thirty or forty boxcars.

The train is loaded with its sweet cargo beside the baseball and softball diamonds at the edge of town to the east. On this day, the children play on the softball diamond. Theirs is a scaled-down game of baseball, the outfielders stationed barely on the outfield grass or pulled in onto the basepaths.

The baseball diamond is in a state of disrepair. The seats in the stands behind the plate are rotted through and would collapse under the pressure of the skinniest rump. The roof covering the seats has been blown away. There is no shade, no relief from the noonday sun. The shucks from sugar-cane litter the ground beneath the stands.

"This is where my father worked, this train," George Bell says, pointing over to the refinery. "A lot of my family worked there. I rode the train sometimes." As Bell tells it, his grandparents, on both his father's and mother's sides, came to the Dominican Republic and Santa Fe from the British Virgin Islands, Nevis, Montserrat, and St. Kitt's. "The people from the British Virgins are really hard-working people. That's the way we see ourselves. That's the way the Dominicans see us. Our families want more than anything else to work hard. They left their home islands, they left everything they had, to come here to work. That tells you how much they care about work." His paternal grandfather came here to drive the horse-drawn carts and the rarer trucks that pulled the sugar-cane into San Pedro in the days pre-dating the train. George Bell's father drove the train. Given that things change very slowly in Santa Fe, many townspeople may have thought that one day George Bell would assume his father's job. It has long been considered a good job in these parts.

"I was born here and we lived here until 1974," Bell says. "I always loved Santa Fe. All I can remember are good times, happy times, here. When we were kids we just ran around and played. We didn't care about anything. When we moved to San Pedro, I knew why my father wanted to do this but I still loved the country. Country boy. I still wanted that life in Santa Fe. Life in San Pedro was different. Fast. Rush, rush. People rushing everywhere. Lots of cars, noise. Everybody busy. But my father was right. He wanted a better life for us and the only life in Santa Fe was the sugar factory."

George Bell is driving his car, this time a Saab 9000, to the diamond in Santa Fe. His son Kevin, a year and a half old, sits in the front seat beside him. Bell the father asks Bell the son about, well, about having to go pee-pee, and the son is adamant in the negative. Bell then hands his son a bottle of milk and negotiates the streets of Santa Fe.

Bell is returning to his old hometown this morning to work out with the Houston Astros' young Dominican signees, a collection of thirty or so fledglings. In tow with Bell, driving a Jeep, is Joaquín Andújar, former All-Star, one-time twenty-game winner, soon-to-be-neighbour of Bell. It is the first week of the New Year and time for these two veterans, one near the top of his game, the other well past the summit, to round themselves into shape.

"I don't always come here," Bell says. "There's a lot of places I can go. The teams, they like it when you come out. It gets their players excited. They can learn."

After he entrusts his son to the Astros' trainer, Bell takes the field in Blue Jays pants, a white headband, and two blue plastic shirts to work up a sweat. Though it's only ten o'clock, the temperature has already reached 35 Celsius, and the sun is unrelenting in the cloudless sky. First Bell shags balls with the third basemen and then with the shortstops. When one youngster looks a little ragged, Bell, who managed seventeen errors from the least demanding defensive position, left field, in part-time play, corrects the youngster's form and gives him a seminar.

When Bell comes off the field I say to him that I couldn't run around in sweatsuits in this heat. "It's in your head," he tells me. "It's in your head. If you want something bad enough you can do anything. This is nothing. A doctor could tell me that I shouldn't do this, that I can't do it. I do it. That's it. I do it, 'cause I want it." Fault George Bell for his attitude, perhaps, but do not fault him for his work habits; when he does set down to work, he goes about his demanding routine intensely—doing things because he wants to.

With sweat pouring off him, Bell runs back on the field. Bell and Andújar go through the same paces as the youngsters. For the veterans there's still a sense of play. In fact they seem more at play, more joyful and relaxed in their practice, than the young Astros' farmhands. The vets are, of course, working without supervision, working without the weight of having to satisfy coaches. Still, they are going through drills and routines that they are repeating for the thousandth, maybe ten-thousandth time.

I don't know what to expect when Andújar comes off the field for water. Andújar is both Bell's neighbour and his emotional equal, a certified hothead. Though Bell's tantrums are part of growing legend, Andújar may have the shortest fuse and the most explosive payload in all of baseball. He earned infamy by being the only player ever ejected from a World Series game in modern history. Back when he was pitching for the St. Louis Cardinals in the 1985 Series, he was thrown out of Game Seven for charging, bumping, and threatening an umpire. It was simply an act of frustration—Andújar was going badly, throwing badly, and was a prisoner of the bullpen after two consecutive twenty-win seasons.

While I watch him and with some trepidation wait for an opportune moment to approach him, he walks up to me and extends his hand for shaking. "Joaquín Andújar," he says. "Spanish or English?"

I fear that he is offering a tirade in a choice of languages. English, I tell him. I also tell him that I'm a *periodista.*

"You here for George?" he asks. I tell him that's the case. "You know they used to come down here for me. But when you're thirty-seven years old they stop coming down here for you."

Andújar tells me his story without being pressed. This runs against my expectations. To find a ballplayer who will cooperate with an interview is rare enough. One who volunteers himself and is conversational, well, this is like finding an auditor who'll give you the benefit of the doubt.

Has Joaquín Andújar mellowed with age, growing wiser and calmer? A few years ago these questions would have incited Andújar to riot, but today they solicit thoughtful explanations. "You have some ballplayers who are quiet, never angry—peaceful guys that don't make trouble. They are able to do their jobs because nothing bothers them. Other ballplayers do their jobs because they walk around mad all the time. Angry. They do their jobs 'cause everything bothers them. That was me. Always angry. I could throw because I was mad, everything against me. When you get a little older you go back toward the middle. I'm older now. Now I know that maybe a lot of things were against me—but not everything.

"I'd like a chance to play some place," he says. "I know I could help someone." And though Joaquín Andújar, vintage '84, the raging pitcher, could pitch for any major-league ballclub, deep into January of '89 not a single major-league ballclub has extended to him so much as an invitation to spring training. That is all he seeks. He knows to ask for a contract, even a minor-league contract, would be folly. And deep down he knows an invitation will not come.

"It's not sad," he says. "It's baseball. They came here to see me when Rico Carty still wanted to play. I had a house bigger than Rico. Now you come to see George and he's got a bigger house than me. Some day George is going to be coming out to this park with some young kid, maybe Tito. The reporters will be here for the young guy—he's got a bigger house than everybody—and George will be like me, looking for a place to play, trying to stay in shape. I've got no complaints. That's just how it is."

Things run in cycles, no less in the Dominican than anywhere else. For all his past outbursts, a maturing Joaquín Andújar had it precisely right. I ask him if he ever thought it would be like this when he was twenty-nine or thirty, like George Bell today.

"No way," he says, "*Nunca*. I was gonna be Superman for ever and quit the game when I got bored and got too much money. And I never thought I was gonna be a nice guy."

Andújar returns to the fray and shags balls in the outfield while Bell takes about twenty minutes of batting practice. Later they throw long and run wind sprints. Their practice lasts two and a half hours and it seems as though they've worked every blade of grass on the diamond. When they return to the dugout, Bell's son is wearing a glove and yelling for his father. Before they leave for home, Bell goes to his car and pulls out an oversized equipment bag. He opens it in the dugout and dumps out more than twenty pairs of baseball spikes, given him by shoe companies for endorsement or by his Blue Jay teammates.

When the shoes are distributed, he gets into his Saab. "People ask me why I come back here," he says. "People ask me why I don't live in the States. I live here because I want to help the people. I don't owe anything, but I want to help. I make a lot of money. I think I should bring it back here. Simple. That helps the country. I don't want to live anywhere else. This is it."

For George Bell there is no Manifest Destiny. Like Trujillo before him, Bell has not set sights on other shores. He has his fiefdom and is content to consolidate it rather than to diversify. Besides, he has travelled through so many worlds just in the short distance from Santa Fe to San Pedro (albeit via Toronto); if he finds San Pedro too "rush-rush", well, the rest of the world will probably disappoint him.

Bell drives through Santa Fe on his way back to San Pedro. Kevin, who still claims to be dry, sits strapped to the seat beside his father, unable to peer over the dash, unable to see his father's old hometown. "The Dominican's a beautiful country, the best place in the world, a great place to be...." He pauses as he slows down and looks at some sad and desparate faces of Santa Fe, faces probably a lot like that of a young George Bell. "... If you got money," concludes this dark cloud ready to thunder, this unintentional ironist.

*

In the bottom half of the seventh inning, Guzmán again faces the minimum number of batters. Junior Felix flies to left. Luis de los Santos hits a flair to centre that drops in for a single. Then Geronimo Berroa hits a hard shot to short, to Juan Bell's right. Bell runs to it and, without time to properly set, fires across his body to Duncan covering at second, who throws on to first for a very sharp 6–4–3 double play. The Licey fans cheer madly. They have not been quick to embrace young Bell—they seem to think a power hitter's brother should be a wallbanger as well. But on this occasion he is just a shortstop making a major-league scoop. There is some reason to think that a new mansion, a new Residencia de Bell y Familia, will be built in San Pedro and that it will be another Bell overseeing and paying for its construction.

CHAPTER NINE

Rico

LICEY	000 002 0	2 5 0
ESCOGIDO	000 000 0	0 3 2

To begin the top of the eighth inning Dave Beard, a journeyman pitcher on the fringe of the majors, replaces John Davis on the mound for Escogido. Los Tigres wanted to get De León out of the game and reach Escogido's bullpen, which has been vulnerable all season long. Beard is one reliever that Licey's ballplayers believe they can rough up. And with a two-run lead and Guzmán smoking in the late going, Los Tigres can swing from their heels.

While Beard throws the last of his warm-up tosses, Juan Baez, the voice of Escogido, flags down a celebrity in the stands to kill a little air time. Baez waves over one of the regulars at this and other ballparks: Rico Carty, former Brave, Indian and Blue Jay, one-time major-league batting champ and ever a gold mine for reporters in search of a quote and announcers seeking to save wear and tear on their vocal chords.

The umpire is dusting off the plate when Baez asks Carty if he remembers the first time he played in the winter league. A reporter from one of the morning tabloids has moved into the seat behind Baez in order to lift quotes for a filler item in tomorrow's sports pages.

"The first time I played here," Carty begins. "The first time was almost the last time. I was maybe seventeen and the first pitcher I got up against was Juan Marichal. That's not the best way to start, you know, to hit a Hall-of-Famer, that's never easy. But to be seventeen, forget it. The first ball he threw me was a fastball, a strike inside. I never saw the ball hit the catcher's glove because I was out of the box about ten feet from the plate. I never saw a ball thrown that hard so I just got out of there. He threw two more like that and I swung at them but I wasn't close. So I said to myself, Rico Carty you're going to do something else in this life because there's no way you can hit this guy. I was thinking that all the pitchers were like this guy with the big leg kick and the ball coming in a hundred miles an hour. I figured I'd go back and cut sugar-cane or something. When I got back to the dugout I started walking up the tunnel to the clubhouse. I was just going to shower right then. But this was Escogido, Trujillo's team, and the manager told me that if I quit on him he was going to give my name to Trujillo, so I stayed in the game. Now Rico Carty was a real hitter and hit a few guys good when I was seventeen, but Rico Carty only went up to the plate against Juan Marichal 'cause it was life or death. I figured getting killed by a fastball was probably better than getting killed by a bullet."

It's a wonderful story, some of it probably true. The reporter scribbles furiously through its telling. At its end, Juan Baez brings the listening audience up to date on what has happened on the field during Carty's tall tale. Beard has retired Licey in order: Luis Reyna on a fly out to Berroa in left; Domingo Michel on a strike-out looking; and Doug Jennings on a routine two-hopper right at Nelson Liriano, 4–3.

Baez thanks Carty for joining him and spelling him for a half-inning, even if it meant that listeners were briefly in the dark about the course of action on the diamond. Baez rushes Carty off because the announcer knows that Carty could easily take over the mike and, without prompting, talk until the players were pulling out of the parking lot.

*

In the mid-'70s, one of Garrett Morris's regular characters on "Saturday Night Live" was the lamentable Chico Escuela, a Latin baseball player. Chico Escuela had a perpetually sunny disposition, even if he was slightly clued out. He was at the end of his career but completely unconscious of the erosion of his middling talents. In gratitude for the game and its gift to him, he frequently uttered a mangled motto: "*Beisbol* been berry berry good to me." With this caricature the comedian—no doubt unwittingly—helped shape a stereotype of Latin ballplayers as simple-minded, at a time when the subtropics were producing ever-increasing numbers of major leaguers. These young men, unfamilar with the language and culture in the northern climes, were easy enough for satirists to skewer. And more than a decade after his last appearance on "Saturday Night Live", Chico Escuela is still an influence. Talk to fans long enough about Latin ballplayers and almost inevitably, "*beisbol* been berry berry good to me" will enter the conversation. The lower the brow, the more frequent the reference.

Garrett Morris did not base Chico on any one player, but many baseball fans, especially in Milwaukee, Atlanta, Cleveland, and Toronto, likely thought some of Chico's mannerisms were borrowed from a player who put in some curious time in these towns: Rico Carty, the "Beeg Mon".

Unlike Chico Escuela, Rico Carty was a player of great talent, an All-Star and a batting champion (.363, Atlanta, 1969). He earned a reputation as the best two-strike hitter in baseball history. Nonetheless, his career was one of peaks and valleys, excellence and agony, rather than consistency. Injuries set him back frequently and often impaired his performance even when he managed to play. For a period he was racked with tuburculosis and his life was threatened. That he was able to return to the majors after these physical set-backs was a tribute to both his ability and his perseverance.

Unfortunately and unfairly, throughout his career and in his years of retirement, Carty's accomplishments have not been as well remembered as his reputation for buffoonery. He was the Dominican equivalent of Alibi Ike. Like the Ring Lardner character, Rico could explain away any shortcomings—if he didn't play up to expectations, it was, according to him anyway, no fault of his own. In his last years, with Toronto, he had a contract that ran sixty-three pages in length, celebrated as the most clause-riddled pact in major-league history. If this established him as a clubhouse lawyer, he went to higher courts to ensure this status. After his release by the Blue Jays in 1980, Carty attempted to file a lawsuit against major-league baseball and the ballclubs that had employed him, claiming that misdiagnosis and maltreatment of his myriad wounds had cut short his career. It was a futile case to argue because Carty had played fifteen years in the big leagues and was released by the Jays at age forty (in "baseball years"). Carty could not prove that some time at a spa would have extended his employment.

The joke about Chico Escuela was always quite simple: try as you might to mine the depths for an important or significant thought, he could not speak anything more revealing than "*beisbol* been berry berry good to me". Somehow any conversation with Rico Carty will return to a line close to Chico's credo.

Rico Carty lives in a one-storey Dominican ranch house opposite a military installation in the east end of San Pedro de Macorís. It is the oldest house in the neighbourhood, a recently developed surburb called Independencia. The house stands on a site selected by his mother back in 1965. It was at her insistence that Rico put his money into a house rather than a fancy car. Back then power lines did not run out to this neighbourhood and Carty had to pay $2,000, an astronomical sum then, to have them installed. Since then, Carty has watched new houses, grander and more grandiose than his, go up in this suburb. This includes the homes of millionaire ballplayers like Joaquín Andújar and Alfredo Griffin. They all draw power from lines run in for Rico Carty. "I'm always the first," Carty says. "I paid $2,000 back in '65 so Andújar can use his satellite dish."

From the outside the house looks just like all the other residences in a well-to-do neighbourhood. Yet with one step in the front door the visitor can tell that this is home to a singular individual. It has the ambience of a live-in shrine, oddly filled with artifacts and fixtures that seem to contradict one another.

The walls are fairly covered with religious knick-knacks and icons. On the wall beside the dining-room table hangs a reproduction of *The Last Supper*. Elsewhere on the wall is a smaller oil painting that depicts Christ wearing the crown of thorns. Crosses abound. Bibles, Spanish-language versions, sit on a table top and a book shelf. Ceramic pieces depicting divinity scenes act as bookends. To all appearances, this is the home of a fiercely religious family.

And yet prominent in a living-room otherwise cluttered with Christian bric-a-brac is a framed-and-mounted *Playboy* magazine. That is, a mock-up of the magazine, for the cover subject is not a barely clad bunny but rather Rico Carty himself, self-proclaimed playboy.

In the living-room, a large bookcase made of dark stained wood is filled with the collected works of the great writers and thinkers, Spanish-language editions. Shakespeare. Emerson. Thoreau. Dostoyevsky. Goethe. Carlyle. The books have a uniform binding, obviously part of a classic book series. Is the visitor to assume that this is the home of a man of letters, an intellectual?

On closer inspection the visitor finds that the spines of these books are uncracked, pristine. They have weathered nothing beyond removal from their boxes and placement on these shelves. The owner may be disappointed if he discovers that his edition of the collected works of Homer has nothing to do with *beisbol*.

And it is obvious from all the photographs of the householder hanging about that this is a celebrity's lair. Exactly what type of celebrity is less clear, for though the master of the house is sometimes pictured in baseball togs, he is more often posing in street clothes with non-diamond dignitaries.

"Here I am with Juan...," Rico says, beginning the tour, pointing at one photograph framed on a wall in the living room. Without success, he tries to remember this gentleman's last name.

"Carlos," I prompt, "Juan Carlos."

"The king, yeah," he says. "King of Spain, you know. When the king comes to the Dominican he's like everybody else. He's gonna see Rico."

He points to a photograph of a benign, smiling man. "Carter," he says. "He was governor when I was playing for Atlanta. When he went to president he never had another good year, y'know." And where world leaders run out he has filled the wall space with photos of sundry leaders from around the Caribbean, every Dominican president in the post-Trujillo era, and other famous figures without portfolio.

Off to the side, displayed without particular prominence, is a photograph, black and white, fading a little. "That's the 1969 All-Star Game, me, Willie Mays, and Hank Aaron, three great outfielders," he estimates, not so modestly. "Two Hall-of-Famers and one that could have been."

Though he has shaken hands and posed with kings of countries and of baseball too, Rico Carty, once a shining light, is now nearly ten years past the game and in certain eclipse. "You send me the story you write. When I was a player, I kept a lot of things, trophies, pictures, y'know, but I didn't know that it would mean that much. I thought I was gonna play for ever."

It sounds a little too maudlin, Carty must be thinking, for then he picks up one of his old Louisville Sluggers and takes his stance. "Y'know I could still swing a bat. I hit a few balls the other day. Maybe I make a comeback. You give me your knees, okay."

He has the physical bearing of a man who would have had a good shot at playing for ever: huge hands and forearms; powerful shoulders and chest; trim waist. He looks closer to thirty than fifty. And yet on closer inspection Rico, in his tank top and shorts, looks all too destructible. Surgical scars criss-cross his knees and line his right shoulder.

Still, retirement allows Rico Carty time to pursue the one hobby that gives him almost as much pleasure as baseball: the creation, the promotion, and the propagation of the Carty mythology. While most present-day players only favour reporters with the occasional quote, former players are more likely to tell stories at length. Carty is a prime example. Not content merely to answer questions, he attempts to educate the questioner and entertain him with something like Rico's Wit and Wisdom. His parables probably emphasize entertainment over accuracy but where they depart from the truth, they seem to improve on it. And each of his stories puts him at the very centre of baseball, as if no great player emerged without Carty placing his stamp on him.

In a taxi, Rico Carty and I head out to his childhood home, Consuelo, a sugar plantation seven miles outside of San Pedro. The Carty family was, like many in San Pedro, new to the Dominican. Carty's grandparents were from St. Maarten, Nevis, Curaçao, and Aruba. They came to the island to work at the plantation. It seemed like an opportunity. But when he was growing up, one of sixteen children, twelve brothers and four sisters, Rico Carty knew of only one life. "It was sugar," he said. "Oh, you had a choice of what you wanted to do with your life. You either work in the fields or work in the refinery. With all the children my mother didn't work there but she worked as a midwife when she could. Back then kids didn't grow up dreaming of playing baseball in the major leagues. It never happened. Baseball was a game we played together for fun, until we were old enough to work."

Baseball was not yet the fantasy of the underclass that worked the plantation, but Jacobo Carty had a sporting ambition for Rico, one more typical for a poor and desperate people. "My father was a boxing fan," Rico says. "He wanted me to be a boxer. He got me books on it. He showed me how to do it, but I tell you, Rico Carty likes too many people to be a boxer. I got love not hate, so I couldn't be a boxer. It disappointed my father because back then baseball didn't take you anywhere. I know it disappointed him 'cause even when I made the majors, he never went to see me at the ballpark. He thought I could have been a great boxer."

Both Carty's mother and father have been dead for a few years now—his father lived to be in his nineties—but both were at home in Consuelo. Though his brothers and sisters have moved on from Consuelo, it is a place peopled by familar faces. Carty is not sure if his success and celebrity haven't changed things for the worse.

"What I did changed Consuelo, changed the *batey*," he says as the car pulls over in the gathering of frame houses. "Before me, you were born here, you stayed here, and you were happy. After me, baseball was a way to get out and some kids did, like Alfredo Griffin and Nelson Norman and a few others. Baseball was the only way. People on the plantation saw the money that I made and they got the envy. They're not happy any more with what they make. Maybe even without Rico Carty the plantation would have changed—more machines, not so many jobs. A lot of people just don't do anything, just sittin' round doin' nothin'. A lot of people are really poor and really sad."

The taxi pulls over on the dirt road that serves as Consuelo's main drag. Rico Carty emerges and the townspeople come running, adults and children, smiling and shouting his name. They look poor but, for now, not sad.

At four in the afternoon, long before an eight o'clock game, Rico Carty is standing in the home dugout at Estadio Tetelo Vargas. The players from Estrellas Orientales are just starting to make their way onto the field to practise and take b.p. Carty, in his street clothes, is not here in an official capacity. He is just an interested visitor, one who drops by the ballpark three or four times a week and watches games on television the other nights. One by one, the Estrellas, some just out of their teens, some who weren't even born when Rico Carty won his batting title, file by to shake his hand. In turn Carty offers words of advice to a few. They assume their stances, and then Carty inspects their posture and re-positions their hands and feet.

"You know I was never a coach or manager," Rico says "but I could have been a good one. I probably helped more players on the island than anybody else. Rico Carty always has time for young players. That's the way it is on the island. You get a chance to help, you help. I did more than anybody else probably."

It is a struggle to look sympathetic, but I give it my best. When I ask him which players he helped, he says that he can't name them all.

"But I tell you who I really helped was Fernández, Tony Fernández," he says.

"You helped him with his hitting?" This, I fear, is something of a silly question. First, Carty can speak with authority about one facet of the game in particular: hitting. Anyone who has hit a .363 for a full turn in a major-league season is entitled to expound on the subject. Secondly, with such a superb fielder as Fernández, it's hard to imagine that he ever needed much coaching from a less-than-average outfielder.

The question, it turns out, is not as dumb as I thought.

"No, not his hitting," he says, to my astonishment. "It was his fielding that I helped him with. Back when I played for Licey in '83 and '84, I watched Fernández. He was our shortstop. I told Fernández, 'You're a good player, good fielder, but you can only go to your right. When you can go to your left and take a hit away from Rico Carty then you're ready for the major leagues,'" he says.

At this point, Carty not only strains credibility, he ruptures it. For those who have marvelled at Tony Fernández's play in the field, his thievery of base hits from deep in the hole to his right, and directly over the bag at second to his left, it's hard to believe that he ever lacked a tool in the field.

Carty continues with his improbable tale: "So I tell Fernández, 'You come out early before games and I hit you balls. Rico Carty works with you.' I made him promise not to tell anybody that I was working with him. You see, Rico Carty doesn't want the coaches to think that he's trying to steal their jobs. Don't want coaches to think I'm trying to mess with their players. No way. If I helped a player—and I helped a lot of them, a hundred, maybe more—I told him that they can never say that I helped him. I don't want no credit."

If this story started out by sounding dubious, it now seems to have taken off into sheer fantasy. Not only did Rico Carty make Tony Fernández the great fielder, but the veteran made the rookie promise never to say a word about it. It sounds too generous, too self-effacing. Further, it's hard to imagine this tutelage remaining as strictly classified information—Carty is displaying no reluctance at all in telling it to me for publication.

"So we kept going out every day," he continues. "We had to get there early, before the coaches get to the park. If they see us,

Fernández is in trouble. They can't do anything to me. I was a big-league *estrella*. But they would be yelling at Fernández.

"I'm hitting him hundreds of balls every day and he's working real hard. Then one day I hit a shot, line drive sinking over second base. That's through, I think. He's not going to get it. And then...." At this point he reaches out with his left arm extended and snaps his hand shut. "...he's got it. I say, 'Fernández, you're ready for the major leagues,' and a few months later he was playing for the Blue Jays."

It sounds incredible. And yet, when I ask Fernández, he does admit to Rico having helped him, though perhaps not to the extent that the veteran claims. "He hit balls to me," Fernández says. "He's a good man. You only get to the majors with the help of a lot of people." Alfredo Griffin, Fernández's predecessor at shortstop with the Blue Jays, makes a much stronger endorsement. "The man who helped me most of all," says Griffin, another product of the sugar plantation in Consuelo, "was Rico. He always told me that I could be a big leaguer if I kept working. He never let me give up. He helped me with the bat. He helped me in the field."

Griffin admits that it's hard to believe that Rico Carty, a pure batsman with a glove of tin in the outfield, could have been seminal in the development of two defensive nonpareils at shortstop, but his explanation is pithy: "Oh, Rico knew what to do in the field and he told you. He just couldn't do it himself. But, listen, if Rico said something, I listened. He told me not to talk, just listen to the older players, and that's what I tell the young guys today. I listened to Rico Carty. He was the town hero. He's still big here."

The young players at Estadio Tetelo Vargas are, like Griffin and Fernández before them, a little starstruck around the big names, the national heroes. Those from San Pedro de Macorís would have heard their fathers talk about Rico Carty, the first great player the town sent to the majors.

If the behaviour of a Dominican ballplayer, particularly a native of San Pedro de Macorís, should ever baffle major-league fans, said fans should be mindful that Rico Carty, as eccentric as a spinster aunt, was an idol, role model, and mentor for an entire generation of players from the island. George Bell, the source of much puzzlement to the followers of the Toronto Blue Jays, has called Rico Carty one of his boyhood heroes. To be an admirer of such a paragon of strangeness is bound to have long-term side-effects: superstition, enlargement of ego, delusions of grandeur, and other traits that North American fans cannot seem to fathom.

Rico Carty is having lunch in a restaurant on the town square in downtown San Pedro. As in many smaller towns in the Dominican, the town square is a small, shady parcel of parkland where bands play for donations, where street merchants sell their wares, where beggars mutely solicit. The town square in San Pedro recalls its past. No longer is it the centre of activity. As the city grew, businesses and markets moved to other places with wider roads. Rico Carty comes to this old part of town once a day to meet with friends, to talk, to kill time.

"People don't know how important luck is in baseball. I'm not talking about if a ball drops in for a hit or if you get a ball called instead of a strike. I'm talking about real luck, like all your career you have good luck. There are some guys that are lucky every year, every game. Some guys don't have luck. None."

This is not mere superstition. Rather, it is the great catch-all, the ultimate rationalization of failure, the alibi for poor performance. Alibi Ike, the Lardner character, would hit a line drive right at an outfielder, and when he caught the ball without moving a step, Ike would return to the dugout saying something like, "That would have been a hit if the guy ain't playin' out of position." So it is with ballplayers who talk not about a single hit or pitch but whole careers being lucky or unlucky. They are to be viewed—as Ike is—with skepticism.

"I got five girls and a son," Carty says. "For a ballplayer that's unlucky, to have just one son. Now my son, he doesn't have luck."

His son is, in fact, a strapping, tall, and muscular kid in his late teens, an impressive figure like his father.

"My son goes to tryouts but nobody wants to sign him. He goes to tryouts and hits the ball hard—I mean *hard*. The thing is, he always hits the ball right at somebody. Other little guys hit the ball not so hard and it falls in for a hit. The scouts sign the little guys and don't sign my son. It doesn't make sense. The scouts should sign a son of Rico Carty, y'know, 'cause maybe the son of Rico Carty can play like his father some day. But nobody signs him. He wasn't born with the luck to be a ballplayer.''

Even those who managed to play in the big leagues and make All-Star teams don't always have the luck with them. Carty cites César Cedeño as the best and worst example. "What happened to Cedeño should never have happened," Carty says. "He had it all, probably the best talent from the Dominican ever. They tried to push him so high, another Willie Mays or Mickey Mantle. But the accident, that was his bad luck. It should never have happened. If he called me, he would have never gone to jail. If I know somebody who gets into trouble I go to the police and say, 'I'm Rico Carty. You give him to me and he won't get into any more trouble.' That's my word. That's me. That's what I can do in this country. I am an important man. If César Cedeño had asked me I would have gone to the police and got him out of jail. But he didn't ask, so...." Carty's voice trails off with the same sadness that Epy Guerrero's has when he talks about his best-ever prospect.

"It's sad what happened to Cedeño," he says. "I knew the girl. It had to be an accident, that's all. But if he had come to me then maybe we could keep the thing under control and he doesn't go to jail. But the girl dies, bad luck. He doesn't call me, bad luck."

I ask Carty the ultimate question about his belief in fated greatness: Does he consider himself a lucky man? He wavers.

"I had the luck sometimes," Carty says. "The season I hit .363, hey, I see the ball real good, the balls drop in. I was lucky for a season sure. But I was unlucky too. Rico Carty could be in the Hall of Fame, y'know, but I have too many injuries. I couldn't play long enough. And a lot of time I was playing hurt. If I stayed healthy, if I had a bit more luck, I'm in the Hall of Fame. I had luck to make the majors, sure, but nobody knows how good I could be if I stay lucky and healthy."

Carty is quite honest about life after the majors. He considers himself unlucky not to have a job in baseball. Other Dominican stars have found regular employment in the game: Juan Marichal as a scouting director with the Athletics; Manny Mota as an instructor with the Dodgers; Felipe Alou as both scout and coach with the Expos; among others. Carty resents the slight but tries to understand it. "Maybe I am unlucky because I did not play my whole career with one team," he says. "If I did then maybe I'd have a job now. But I played with a lot of teams. Each one thinks that another is going to give you a job.

"The Dominicans have a shot at coaching sure. But look at what Al Campanis said about blacks and Latins," Carty says. He refers to the infamous speech on the anniversary of Jackie Robinson breaking the colour barrier. Among other thoroughly racist notions, Campanis claimed that blacks might lack "the necessities" for baseball's front offices. "Al Campanis isn't a bad man. He just got fired for saying what a lot of people think but are afraid to say."

It sounds as if Carty is leading up to a filibuster on affirmative action. But then Carty takes off on a most unusual tangent. "See, baseball doesn't have to hire Latins, Dominicans, anything. American blacks, sure, they should get jobs if they're good. But Dominicans, they don't owe us nothin'. Baseball's an American business. They don't have to hire foreigners. They should hire Americans first and Dominicans only if they have to. So I don't complain I don't have a job. They don't owe me anything. Dominicans, we're all unlucky—if we were born in the States, everybody's workin', right?"

Right. Unlucky to be Dominican, unlucky not to have a job, unlucky not to have more than one son, unlucky not to have a son in the majors, unlucky not to have a son get signed, unlucky not to get in the Hall of Fame, unlucky to come along before he gets $2 million, unlucky to get hurt.

He worries about how he sounds. "I still think I've got it pretty good, y'know," he says.

He returns to his meal, but before he can set in, he is talking again about racism. "Don't get me wrong about the Al Campanis thing," he says. "I'm not angry about that. I've never had problems with whites. It's funny, but the Latin players, black Latin players like me, we never had problems with the white players. If there was prejudice, if some players didn't like us, it was usually the black American players. Now I got some good friends who are black Americans—guys like John Mayberry and Mack Jones are beautiful men, get along with everybody. But a lot of black players in the '60s and '70s didn't try to get along with the white players. Back then they were trying to be proud, like they don't have to get along with anybody who wasn't black.

"When I was in Atlanta, I remember I talked to everybody. I was sitting round talking to some white players. A black guy comes up—I don't want to say who because I don't want to make problems for him—and he says to me, 'What you doin talkin' to whitey? You should be with the brothers.' I said to him, 'Hey man, we all God's children. Underneath the skin we all brothers.' In the Dominican, the colour you are doesn't mean anything. Until I got to the States, I didn't know I was black, do you know what I'm saying? I know I got dark skin, but I don't know what it means to be a black man, especially in the South, in Atlanta.

"One time I was walking down the street in Atlanta with a black guy," he says. "This girl walks by us. A blonde, really beautiful girl. A skirt, y'know, that's what Mayberry called them. Anyway she smiles at us and walks by. I turn around and look, a good look. The black guy says, 'Hey what you doin'? She's white. You don't do that with white girls.' I tell him, 'Hey, in the Dominican, if you see it and you like it, you look and let them know.' Colour, it's nothing."

We come back to Carty's place after the trip downtown. Rico Carty fetches a couple of pops from the fridge and takes me into the walk-in closet that he has converted into his trophy room.

A trophy for Milwaukee Braves' Rookie of the Year 1964 is inscribed to "Ricco Carty" [sic]. The presenters were a group appropriately named "The 99% Wrong Club". The bats that yielded landmark hits, numbers 1,000 and 2,000, are mounted on the walls. Rico says he comes in the room and looks around "all the time—it's like yesterday [that all this happened]". But it's hardly yesterday at all. He has not added a memento or trophy to the room in eight years. And just as he waited for accolades and honours and trophies to roll in, the only recognition of his meritorious service he receives these days is a major-league pension cheque.

"You know they're starting a league for players over forty or over forty-five in Florida. They have some real money. I'm gonna get a piece of that."

Carty doesn't have a job today. In his last few years he was able to put a few dollars away. He says he doesn't need much to live on. "I'm not a young man spending money on jewellery and cars," he says. "I make a thousand dollars to play in an old-timers game in the States. They pay for the plane, the hotel and everything. I play in three or four and take my wife for a vacation.

"When I hit .363, I made $45,000 that season. If I hit .363 today, I'd make more than that for three games. But at least I got to play in the majors. That's the important thing. And I got my house. Baseball gave me my house, my memories. I am happy with that. I have to be happy with that 'cause that's what Rico Carty's got, *comprende?*"

"*Beisbol* been berry berry good to me" was a funny moment on a funny show. In the end, perhaps something close to "*beisbol* been berry berry good to me" is the animating thought and the recurring theme in what Rico Carty says.

*

A few of the less devoted Escogido fans leave after the bottom of the eighth inning; the more devoted are draining the last ounces from their bottles of rum. The home half of the inning begins promisingly with José Vizcaíno drawing a base on balls, but the young Dodger prospect is stranded there when Sosa and a pinch-hitting Mackey Sasser, a good ol' boy and back-up catcher for the Mets, fly out to right and centre respectively. The conspiracy theory—the notion that games are fixed for close finishes—does not seem to be in play tonight. Though only two-nothing, a comeback looks nearly impossible.

As the Escogido nine take their positions on the field for the top half of the final inning, Rico Carty is still talking to the newspaper reporter, who wants to get away. By now he has enough material for dozens of columns, perhaps even a book.

For the latter the only question would be its genre: nonfiction or fiction? Comedy or tragedy? Too close to call.

CHAPTER TEN

Peloteros Romanticos

LICEY	000 002 00	2 5 0
ESCOGIDO	000 000 00	0 3 2

Pepe Lucas, the first-base coach for Escogido, knows the poses of managers. He played for a legion of dugout leaders and coached for that many more. He has carried line-ups to the umpire before a thousand games for, it seems, nearly as many managers. Once a manager himself, he no longer has an interest in this occupation of weighty responsibilities and high turnover. He may be scared off by the thought of tape recorders and television cameras shoved in his face twice nightly. He can go about coaching with muted rage, well practised from years past, and without testimony to the nosy needlers of the media.

Here in the top of the ninth, in the death throes of the tense struggle, Licey's lead-off batter, Mariano Duncan, swings at a three-and-one pitch from Dave Beard and lifts a pop-up to foul territory on the first-base side. Falling earthward, the ball seems destined for the glove of Escogido's second baseman, Nelson Liriano. Liriano steps to the foul ground, calling off the first baseman, Mackey Sasser, the ball directly overhead. For Sasser, a portly catcher playing an unfamiliar position, it would be a long shot if he hauled the ball in. On this play the second baseman has a better angle. But the best angle of all is that of a photographer. At the games in the Dominican winter league, the photographers are not restricted to a fenced-in pen as they would be in the majors. Rather the lensmen roam foul ground, sometimes within a few feet of the lines. Punished by low light, they must venture into play on occasion to get some black-and-whites for *las secciónes deportes* in the morning papers.

This time, however, calamity. Liriano brushes the photographer, loses the ball and watches it fall, within his reach, but not in his grasp. Liriano looks at the umpire, first in silence, then in disbelief that there is no call. The second baseman beseeches the ump for a call of interference and an out to Duncan. The umpire shrugs and offers him something approximating, "Them's the breaks." Phil Regan storms out of the dugout, pointing at the photographer, gesticulating madly, courting an early shower. Sensing the enormity of the game and a situation about to boil over, the head of the umpiring crew comes from behind the plate to restore control. He can do nothing to appease Liriano and Regan, but he also knows the ejection of either would be unwise, for the argument is taking place on the Escogido side of the stands. The umps hear Regan out and early in the debate Regan knows the battle is lost. But the fans expect the manager to protest, and Regan is complying.

At the same time as Regan wails away at the umps, Pepe Lucas steps out of the dugout and begins to dismiss the photographers. He shoos them away from the field of play with backhanded waves that look as if, upon any resistance, they will turn into a backhanded shot in the chops. The crowd eats up Lucas's display as much as Regan's.

But even when Regan returns to the dugout, when Liriano has resumed his position, when Duncan steps back into the box, and when Beard prepares to pitch once again, Pepe Lucas continues to rant at the photographers. They interfered with one ball, but by measuring the abuse Lucas heaps on them you would think he is holding them responsible for all of Escogido's miseries this season. He stands fully out of the dugout, knowing the umpires won't say a word to him. The scorn heaped on them for such an action would be followed by a shower of rum bottles.

In the stands, dressed in Escogido red, a half-dozen well-oiled Leones fans call for Lucas, trying to attract his attention. He hears them. They are loud enough that they can be heard on the other side of the stadium. Doug Jennings, the opposing first baseman, even waves his glove keeping time to the chorus of "Pepe, Pepe" between pitches.

"Pepe loves this," one of the members of the chorus says. He claims to be a friend of Lucas. "Pepe knows the players should play hard. That's their part. That's what they give the *fanaticos*. And he knows the *fanaticos* should cheer and boo. That's what they give the players."

Lucas understands this cathartic exchange. He takes the stage but takes no bows. He can no longer take the lead roles—those of player and manager are long behind him. Now in his dotage he is reduced, or reduces himself, to the supporting roles, the scene-stealers. Now like Buster Keaton, Lucas does not allow a smile to crease his face. He looks sourly and disbelievingly at the unfairness of it all. No words when silence will do.

*

Since the end of his playing days, Pepe Lucas has maintained the same pre-game routine. Sitting in the dugout, chain-smoking Marlboros, wearing the red-and-white uniform of Escogido, the same uniform he has worn for the last thirty-nine years, Lucas holds a bat in his thin long fingers and watches his pitchers run in the outfield. He was loath to do these wind sprints fifty years ago when he was a young man but fully expects it of his charges. With eyes bloodshot from a lifetime of standing in sun-drenched outfields, Lucas watches a couple of his hurlers goofing off in the bullpen, chatting up *chiquitas*. He straightens up and pulls his gaunt frame, a little bent by decades of hard use, to the top of the dugout steps. He doesn't yell or motion to them, but he waits. "They'll run or they won't come back into the clubhouse."

As Escogido's first-base coach and adviser-at-large, Lucas has had bestowed on him a position like an honourary fellowship, for career service rather than for what he can impart to the generation of his grandchildren. Like many former star ballplayers, he is not patient with young players who are not as diligent or talented as he was. He is not willing to work with kids who need instruction. At least, he won't work with those who need help; with the rest, he knows enough to leave them alone. Lucas also brings a unique sensibility to the coaches' box. For other clubs this is something of a cheerleading, rump-slapping, fist-shaking position, but Pepe brings to it all the old-fashioned goodwill and spirit of a customs officer working overtime. His temperament is utterly unsuited to any sort of coaching. His attitude would have to improve significantly just to be cantankerous.

Waiting for the delinquent pitchers, Lucas walks to the top of the dugout steps and looks into the stands for familiar faces and sees none. A few years ago the last of his contemporaries stopped coming to the ballpark as a result of, well, natural causes. All he spies in the stands are American major-league scouts, sitting behind the screen, probably boasting about their golf scores and their last plunders from the Dominican treasure chest of baseball talent.

When Lucas started out in pro ball, the closest these scouts ever came to the Dominican Republic was a golf course in south Florida during spring training. Pepe Lucas was born José Sainte Claire, the son of a noted ballplayer named Lucas Sainte Claire. Managers and players bestowed upon him the moniker Pepe Lucas, something like L'il Lucas, in honour of his father's accomplishments. In the end, however, whatever Lucas Sainte Claire might have achieved on the field paled compared to his progeny.

A talented but untimely outfielder, Pepe Lucas played for more than twenty years, starring in élite leagues in Cuba, Mexico, Puerto Rico, and Venezuela. He also played ball in less likely outposts throughout the Latin circuit, such as Panama and Colombia; in the latter he met his wife, Filta. Yet in all his travels, in this vagabond life of a Latin ballplayer, Pepe Lucas has never even visited the United States. Lucas was ready for the majors long before the majors were ready for him. He goes back to a time before Juan Marichal, to a time before Jackie Robinson, to a time when the major leagues had no use for Dominicans, especially black Dominicans. Lucas dismisses the slight. His attitude was the product of two generations of either hindsight or bitterness; Lucas has told friends that he had no use for the majors, that he could have gone to the U.S. to play in the Negro Leagues but just never wanted to. He lights another Marlboro from his previous, still-smouldering butt.

Jorge Bournigal, an avuncular radio man and chief historian among the baseball press in the Dominican, calls Lucas "a legend, one of the greats of the early days". The era seems like recent history to fans in North America. The big-league superstars of that era, Joe DiMaggio, Ted Williams, and others, live on in the memories of older fans and seem familiar to the younger set for the brightest moments have been well documented by film, in print, in lines in the *Baseball Encyclopedia*, in nostalgia shows. But the early days in the Dominican, as Bournigal describes them, are "those days before a Dominican could play in the big leagues, before Marichal". There are only a few names who live on: Tetelo Vargas, an outfielder in the Negro Leagues; José Llamades, a Dominican pitcher who played in the Negro Leagues even though he was a white man. Bournigal says that Pepe Lucas belongs in the ranks of the greats. "Pepe would have been a big leaguer, an All-Star if not a Hall-of-Famer," Bournigal says. "There were a lot of Dominican players who could have been stars. They had no chance. Lucas was one of the best. He made $100 a week in the Venezuelan League when the whole infield combined didn't make half that. He was a hitter like Pedro Guerrero or Jorge Bell, lots of power to all fields. But he was a better fielder than Guerrero and Bell. If Pepe Lucas played today, he would be a $2-million player."

Unfortunately for Lucas, he came along too early, not only for the majors, but for El Torneo Dominicano; his blooming as a ballplayer long preceded the flowering of the Dominican winter league, thus denying him a proper show-case of his talents in front of audiences of his countrymen. The current alignment of the Dominican winter league was set in 1951, a few years too late for Lucas's glory. "By that time Pepe could still swing the bat but couldn't hit the fastball," Jorge Bournigal says. "He'd lost speed in the outfield. Still it was good for him to be with Escogido, a good way to go out. For so many years he played in other countries—it was good to finish playing in front of Dominicans." Even at that, he posted some numbers that teased the imagination of the fans:

Year*	Team	Games	At Bats	Runs	RBI**	Hits	Ave.	HR**	SB**
1951	Esc	51	195	30	38	54	.277	6	8
1952	Esc	53	195	22	28	50	.256	5	7
1953	Esc	55	209	22	23	58	.278	1	4
1954	Esc	38	145	23	26	43	.297	5	3
1955-56	Esc	48	159	11	6	35	.220	0	3
1956-57	Esc	1	0	0	0	0	.000	0	0

*All games in the first four seasons in El Torneo Dominicano were scheduled in the months before Christmas so as not to conflict with the Caribbean World Series and other more lucrative Caribbean leagues.
**Simply multiply these significant numbers—RBIs, homers, and stolen bases—by three to get a rough measurement against a major-league or minor-league season.

If Pepe Lucas was in his decline and fall by the '50s, he still maintained a high level of play, hitting for power and average in parks that tended to diminish both.

In any media guide provided by league officials, the career numbers of coaches and managers are accompanied only occasionally by birthdates. This should not come as a surprise in this country of fictitiously extended youth. The only way to gauge the relative antiquity of a former ballplayer is by the emphasis coaches, players, and sportswriters place on the word "*viejo*". In referring to Pepe Lucas, their emphasis on *viejo* suggests that his age could be determined by carbon dating. Even if he was thirty-eight in his last full season in 1955–56—and extraordinary as it sounds, that is the athletic mid-life in these subtropics—that would make Pepe Lucas seventy years old. It is just as likely, however, that Pepe Lucas was, like Rufino Linares of Escogido today, playing deep into his forties; that would pin him in his middle seventies.

The sky is clear but for a few flumes of smoke from a fire beyond the outfield fence and from the dart between Lucas's lips. A *merengue* band is setting up in the back reaches of Estadio Quisqueya. A player, a youngster whose father was not yet born when Lucas was already a journeyman *jardinero*, walks by and says that it's a nice day for a game. Lucas doesn't say a word— when you've seen 10,000 nice days and nights for *beisbol*, it's difficult to get excited about another. Whenever he watches his young lions, major leaguers and would-bes, he must envy their timing. A great player at the wrong era, he is now a low-paid coach of lesser men in a bountiful time. Having put in so many years, he's entitled to any bitterness he may feel.

I approach *el viejo* with trepidation. The *periodistas* from the Lucky Seven have warned me that Lucas does not consort with the fourth estate, even its Spanish-language division. They say that Lucas bears reluctant or possibly hostile witness, that as custodian of his personal history he'd prefer to keep it under lock and key, to be a keeper rather than a sharer of secrets. While Rico Carty and others are makers and inflaters of their own mythology, Lucas, they say, is more a security guard protecting his personal history.

Trepidation well founded. His lack of interest in the fourth estate transcends his contempt for the major leagues, major leaguers, and young players. After a brief introduction, I tell him that I want to write about his past greatness. "Reading about it means nothing," he says. "A few watched. A few played. Good players. Good games. Words mean nothing." He walks away, into the clubhouse, not saying anything more, never looking back.

For days and weeks, I try to talk to Lucas. A radio announcer acts as an intermediary and tells Lucas that I am willing to pay him to talk to me, a week's salary for an hour's worth of talk. The radio announcer says that he will act as interpreter to avoid any communication problems. Dates are made. A couple of times I show up four hours before games hoping for a spare moment. When he spots me he hides in the tunnel or takes the other end of the dugout bench. When I ask for his time Lucas always cites an infirmity—a headache, a backache, tired blood—or a prior commitment—a team meeting, work with the bullpen, an appointment with the trainer. I linger after games into the midnight hours, but he always says he is on his way home, that he has to leave right away.

I am able to corner him for a brief question-and-answer only once, during a rain delay before a game between Los Leones and Los Azucareros of La Romana. The dugout is crowded because the rain has a tropical-storm intensity, because the tunnel has been flooded and because a blackout has darkened the clubhouse. Lucas is without escape this time.

When I ask him if he would want to be a ballplayer today, his answer is terse. "I can't be," he says. "It's stupid to ask."

I ask him to name the best ballplayer he has ever seen and he is only slightly more expansive. "There were a lot," he says. "Josh Gibson, [Cool Papa] Bell, Tetelo Vargas. Nobody's the best. Every day comes and one of the ballplayers is the best on the field. The next day somebody else. I saw Josh Gibson hit three homers in a game. That day he is the best. The next day he goes zero for four. The best means nothing."

I adopt the tack that perhaps he will be more forthcoming if he is tooting his own horn. I ask him which was his greatest season. "Puerto Rico, 1951," he says. When I ask him to explain why, he just shrugs. "It's my best." He sounds like George Bell talking about seafood. Bournigal will later tell me that Lucas led the Puerto Rican league in homers that year. Through this circuit a number of major-league Hall-of-Famers passed, including Henry Aaron, Willie Mays, and Roberto Clemente.

Only when I ask him the fully loaded question, "Are the players today as good as or better than the players back then?" does Pepe Lucas perk up.

"We played exhibition games sometimes and there would be a fist fight every three innings. The players are no different from the toes to the neck. But we played when the game—the game that day—was everything. We thought of nothing else. The players today swing like we did, throw, hit all the same. But we thought different about what we did."

At this point his tolerance of the interview is exhausted. He dismisses me. "The game is nothing new," he says. "Go talk to other players." He walks away, up the tunnel and into the pitch-black sanctuary of the coaches' offices, taking with him a lifetime of memories, an age of Dominican baseball that is virtually lost. That's just the way he wants it.

Santiago, the Dominican's second largest city, is a pleasant relief from the overcrowded poverty of Santo Domingo. Situated in a valley in the mountains, the so-called Dominican Alps, in the centre of the island, the city is at a crossroads for all the towns of the region. Santiago is as prosperous and comfortable as Santo Domingo is impoverished and overcrowded. Nearby towns are homes to mines and mills and factories; the hinterlands, those that haven't been open-stripped, are green with cash crops.

But the poor people of the cities in the south do not have an exclusive licence for baseball fanaticism. Águilas, Santiago's team, is the object of fans' affections in Santiago and other towns in the centre of the country. Fans drive every night to see Águilas at Estadio Cibao.

At a café around the corner from Estadio Cibao, Tetelito Vargas, a brown and balding little man dressed in ratty jeans, a baseball T-shirt, and sneakers without socks, is having a Dominican coffee. Served in a plastic container no bigger than a thimble, his brew has the consistency of hot tar, the sweetness of fresh-cut cane, and a jolt best measured in volts. Tetelito Vargas is nearly a famous name. That is, Tetelo Vargas, the Babe Ruth of Dominican baseball, the man after whom the ballyard in San Pedro de Macorís is named, was the cousin of this stooped man who drinks this black dynamite a short walk away from his place of work. Tetelo Vargas was raised by Tetelito's mother. Since both shared the same name, the youngest became little Tetelo, Tetelito. The diminutive came to have almost a mocking ring to it. Tetelito was also a ballplayer of note, playing from 1939 until 1954. Though he had the same name as the legendary Vargas, Tetelito had only a fraction of his power. By his own estimation, Tetelito figures he hit "five or six home runs—my career, not one season". Tetelo went to the States and played for four years in the Negro Leagues, making the Negro All-Star team twice. Tetelito stayed behind. Tetelito the journeyman was a step down, a significant step down, from Tetelo the star.

"I don't like what I see with most ballplayers today," he says, repeating cant common among old ballplayers. "Mechanics poor. Attitude bad. Money has something to do with it. For the major leaguer, once he has money, it's easy to stop working at the game the way he should. It's easy to rest during the winter instead of playing.

"When we started out, people loved to watch the game but in a way did not like *los peloteros*," he says. "My mother said it would break her heart if I became a ballplayer. Thieves, criminals, she called them. It was not a decent life to lead. Once you were a ballplayer, you had to stay a ballplayer. Her nephew was one of the greatest ever [to play]; I was a professional for a lot of years, but she hated what we did. To be a soldier, a doctor, a lawyer, these were respectable things. But Tetelo and me, outlaws." He shrugs at this.

I ask him if this made it harder to be a ballplayer. He is quick to correct me. "It made us stronger, tougher," he says. "It was romance. We were *peloteros romanticos*—romantic ballplayers. The games were romance. For me, for the players when I played, baseball was like a woman—I love it, I think about it all the time, my hours with it last for ever. But it was like a bad woman. If I had to leave my family behind for the woman I love, if no one would talk to me because of the woman I love, this would make me stronger. Baseball was the woman.

"If we had to play all year, we did. If we had to play two or three times a day, we did. If we had to travel all over to other countries, we did. Money meant something sure—but most of us just thought it was funny, getting paid for the thing we loved.

"Today you hear of players making sacrifices, working on their game. They think sacrifice is to work on the game. In the old days, we made sacrifices, we gave up things, so we could practise and play. To play *beisbol* isn't a sacrifice, it's happiness. That's how we are different."

Did it ever bother him that he couldn't play in the major leagues? "It was never anything I thought about," he says. "It would be like thinking about playing on the moon. Fantasy. Impossible. So why think about it? Black players, Latin players, we could not play in this league that only wants white Americans. Okay, what they want. Fair? I don't care, it's their league, they can do with the league what they want. It's maybe not as good but they don't say it has to be fair."

As we sit and talk, Tetelo starts to regret how some of his words sound, to worry that he might seem bitter. He is happy with the way things have worked out, he says. He wants this to be clear. "The important thing is not where I didn't play," he says. "The important things is that I played for Águilas. I played for the city of Santiago and in front of the Dominican people. I am Águilas for ever, gold and black like the Pittsburgh Pirates. What you don't do in life is never important, I'm proud to have played for Águilas."

At the end of a narrow and steep walkway off the tunnel into the Escogido clubhouse is the dressing room for the ballclubs visiting Los Tigres de Licey. The clubhouses for Licey and Escogido are the quality of the roosts of middling Double A teams, without fancy appointments and comfortable spaciousness, but relatively sanitary with room enough to take a deep breath. The visiting clubhouses, one off the Licey dugout and this off the Escogido bench, are another matter.

The visiting clubhouse on the Escogido side is like a dungeon, and the walk-up is as ominous and haunting as a catacomb. There may be lights, but no one can remember them working. There may be windows, never opened, never letting sun in. Walking up into the bowels of Estadio Quisqueya, I think of all the great players who have walked through these parts. And when reaching the clubhouse I can breathe in that history, for the room overpowers its occupants with the smell of two generations of sweat, urine, and cigarette smoke, among other things. In this room, millionaires and aspirants dress for battle.

Tetelito has not been honoured with a coaching position with Águilas, not given a cushy berth like Pepe Lucas's job with Escogido. With the Santiago ballclub, Tetelito is an all-purpose attendant, overseeing the gofers, sorting among the bats, giving pieces of advice to young ballplayers for the Águilas de Cibao, the Eagles of Santiago.

"When I was a young man, I came to the ballpark to see the Negro League players, Satchel Paige, Josh Gibson, some others. Right then I said, I'm going to be a ballplayer. This is the thing that I have to do. Those Negro players played the game right. They played the game hard. The Dominican people loved them. They played and they entertained the fans. The Negro Leaguers were something strange, Americans who played the game different than we ever saw—Paige with the wind-up, spinning around. When I saw them I decided I have to be a ballplayer. I decided I have to come to the park every day."

Indeed, back in the late '30s American ballplayers from the Negro Leagues, still banned from the lily-white major leagues, were brought to the island by Trujillo in order to prop up Escogido, the floundering team he sponsored. Satchel Paige was the first to come. Cool Papa Bell and Josh Gibson and other luminaries followed. Their amazing talents and their sense of style caused a sensation on the island. Unable to come up with an analogy in American sport, Jorge Bournigal compared the arrival of the Negro Leaguers to Beatlemania. "It was all that people talked about," he said. "The country came to a stop when they played. It was all people would talk about in the streets." It was more than a watershed moment in the history of baseball in the republic; with all its social and political implications— the players' sanction of Trujillo—it was a moment of national history.

"It's still there, still part of our game," Tetelito says. "To play hard but to play with flair. The players come back from America and call the majors 'The Show'. That is not the way in the Dominican. The game at Estadio Cibao and Estadio Quisqueya is 'The Show', but so is the game on the corner with kids playing. To be good and play hard makes you a player, to get fans excited and do things your way makes you a star. To be a star you play the game and celebrate it." There is more than a kernel of truth in what Tetelito Vargas says. Some call it showmanship and theatre, others call it hot-dogging and more profane terms.

The great white American players of that epoch, Joe DiMaggio and Ted Williams among them, played the game like everyone else, but just better than everyone else; that is, their greatness was founded in orthodox play, in solemn and excellent execution of the long-standing fundamentals of the game. If DiMaggio was considered Williams's superior, it was because Joe D. went about his work with stoic etiquette, baseball's honour code.

Fanaticos can still see the influence that the brilliant, unorthodox Negro Leaguers had on the D. R.'s current national heroes. The evidence is in the signatures of the latter-day Dominican stars: the high-leg-kick of Juan Marichal is a retooling of Satchel Paige's exaggerated gyrations; Pasquel Perez's on-the-mound antics, moonwalking after a strike-out and all the rest, recall the vaudeville of the barnstorming clown teams. But the man who is the best example of the Dominican way, of invention outside the mainstream, of absolute individuality instead of conformity, Tony Peña, sits and listens to Tetelito Vargas expound on the subject of Dominican flair.

Peña, then a millionaire catcher with the Cardinals, is dressing in the hallway, which is flooded from recent rains. A rubber mat placed on a frame made of two-by-fours is completely submerged.

With Tony Peña, the influence of the Negro Leaguers can be seen too. For the position of the game most steeped in orthodoxy, catching, Peña devised a thoroughly individual style, radical but effective—he sits, rather than squats, on the ground, with legs splayed. This breaks every rule of baseball orthodoxy. It is also intensely personal; no veteran catcher has tried to adopt his technique, and young catchers have discovered that Peña's game does not provide shortcuts; it is, in fact, more demanding than the traditional way. The role of catcher has long drawn the smart but squat athletes whose work makes them dirty and battered and gnarled. Tony Peña has transformed the role utterly, making it a gymnastic routine in the dirt, making it his own.

"To me this is an old-time ballplayer, Tony Peña," Tetelito Vargas says. "In the major leagues he makes money, real money, not like a lot of others. But every winter he plays here for nothing—he makes the same money as some Dominican kids, a couple of years in the majors and less than an American player from the minors—but he plays. Águilas has the worst travel of all the teams. If he wanted to, Tony Peña could drive his Mercedes to the away games—he could go in a taxi across the country—but he rides the bus. He chooses the life of a ballplayer. He is a friend and a leader and a teacher for the young ballplayers. He is a great man now, but he gives thanks to Águilas and Santiago for helping him when he was a young player. He plays every year. He is a millionaire but in his heart he is a ballplayer like Tetelo and the rest."

Tony Peña is putting on his sanitary whites in the least sanitary conditions in all of baseballdom. He listens to the not-so-faint praise from a man who, for the opportunity of playing for Águilas for three years in the early '50s, has worked for the club for thirty years thereafter. When Vargas has concluded, Peña offers the all-encompassing explanation for his dedication and that of Tetelito. "That's all I wanted to be," he says. "*Pelotero.*"

Roosevelt Comarazamy and I exit the Lucky Seven, flag a taxi, and head across town in Santo Domingo's rush hour. Comarazamy says that he has arranged an appointment with, he claims, the oldest-living star ballplayer in the Dominican, Horacio Martínez, a veteran of the Negro Leagues. Martínez put in a much-varied career in the U.S. while Pepe Lucas was stilling cutting his teeth in the Caribbean. Comarazamy offers one unpromising caveat about the audience. It is unsettling enough to arouse my suspicions about how "arranged" our appointment may be. As we start out in a taxi, he says, straight-faced: "I hope he's still alive."

When we get to the comfortable, one-storey house in a middle-class suburb of Santo Domingo, Roosevelt knocks at the front door and tells one of Martínez's middle-aged sons the nature of our visit. He ushers us into a sitting room where Horacio Martínez, one-time star, sits and shakes and stares at the wall. He is utterly unaware that anyone else is in the room with him. When he played before American audiences, the fans nicknamed him Rabbit for the way he bounded after balls hit to him at shortstop. This day he has the face of a rabbit, twitching nervously, twitching constantly.

"He told us stories about baseball when we were young," the son says, "but he can't talk any more—Parkinson's disease. He's a little senile too maybe. We tell him stories that he used to tell to us."

The son offers to show us pictures of his father in the uniforms of Dominican teams, in the flannels of the New York Cubans and other Negro League teams, the black House of David (a barnstorming clown team in which all the players wore long beards). The photographs are faded and torn at the corners.

There is nothing much that the son can tell us. Roosevelt says that it's a shame there is no Hall of Fame, no museum of Dominican baseball. As his warning at the Lucky Seven suggests, there isn't a directory of former players or a record kept of their passing. It is perhaps revealing of the Latin American culture—that this moment, any moment, is everything; that yesterday is forgotten at midnight and no one can even think about tomorrow. In a nation where old times were hard times, where the past was not even as pleasant as the present, the will to immortalize those who have gone before, that nostalgic longing, does not exist. The history of the game on the island can only extend as far back as men such as Pepe Lucas and Tetelito Vargas. Nearly everything else is, like Horacio Martínez, irretrievably lost.

Unable to speak, unable to feed himself, a prisoner of crippling infirmity, Señor Martínez has only this collection of photographs, a few fragile yellowed clippings and that small eternity, the rest of his life, to contemplate the memories of never-told glories. The children and grandchildren gather around him and relive a few stories that he told them long ago. If it seems that men like Pepe Lucas and Tetelito Vargas are trapped, prisoners of the game that is their lives, then Horacio Martínez plays out his last days in something like solitary confinement. When he dies, he takes with him another link to the Negro Leagues' tradition.

*

The collision between Liriano and the photographer is, in fact, a play of no small consequence. Duncan chops the ball into the dirt in front of home plate and the pitcher, Beard, has difficulty getting the ball over to first. The play is generously scored a single. With Silvestre Campusano at the plate, Duncan steals second on a first pitch called strike. After Campusano grounds out 6–3 and Gilberto Reyes fouls out to the catcher, Wil Tejada, Juan Bell lines a single to left field and drives home Duncan with an insurance run. If Licey's 2–0 lead looked fairly secure, then 3–0 now looks insurmountable. The next batter, Miguel Santana, hits a two-hopper over the bag at third; Luis de los Santos pulls the ball down but has no play at first. Escogido is able to stop the bleeding; Rafael Belliard flies out to Sammy Sosa in right field.

It is now the bottom of the ninth. Pepe Lucas walks to the first-base coaches' box, stopping every couple of steps and waving the photographers off the field. The fans in the red section cheer him. "Pepe, Pepe, Pepe."

He hears their reaction but plays deaf to their exhortations. He then starts in on the umpire at first base. Even as the batter is announced he doesn't let up and the fans continue their chant. Once they called him for curtain calls after home runs. Today they give him mock cheers for tantrums, for the caricature of an angered manager. But his disgust is real. In the dressing room after the game, when the incident is all but forgotten, he will be complaining to Eddie Dennis, the third-base coach, about the umpire.

CHAPTER ELEVEN

The End of the Game

LICEY	000 002 001	3 8 0
ESCOGIDO	000 000 00	0 3 2

As he takes the mound, Juan Guzmán looks like a solid bet for
a shut-out that is eight-ninths complete. When he comes out to
collect three final outs, he will face batters he has overpowered
all evening. Only the most ardent Escogido fan could hold out
hope that his team will have a chance. Escogido has threatened
only once, the man-on-second-none-out situation in the second
inning, but the right-handed Guzmán turned it up, whiffing two
and popping up the other for an escape. For Escogido it has been
a night of a single opportunity weakly squandered. At no other
time has Guzmán conceded so much as a long, loud out.

With the lead-off batter, Nelson Liriano, in the bottom of the
ninth, form holds. Liriano swings at a one-and-one fastball and
lofts a towering pop-up to Licey's first baseman Doug Jennings.
A routine out, one down. Just two outs, six strikes, from shut-out
victory and bragging rights in Santo Domingo.

The next batter is Junior Noboa, the utility infielder. As he
heads to the plate he waves to his wife and three young boys, all

218

with thick thatches of crow-black hair, who watch from the first row behind the Escogido dugout. At the plate, Noboa works the count full. He fouls off two more pitches with defensive swings. With the eighth pitch in this at bat, Guzmán freezes Noboa with a fastball in the black—a bead thrown to the low and outside edge of the strike zone. The umpire, however, submits that the offering is a trifle too low or a smidgen outside. Ball four. Noboa, who would not have made contact with his best Sunday swing, walks to first base, his prayers in this pressure spot answered. For Licey's manager, Ferguson, the walk is not cause for anxiety. Yet.

Junior Felix steps to the plate. On the first pitch Felix lays down a bunt, not a very good one: two sharp bounces, requiring Guzmán to take two steps towards third base. It is not a sacrifice, just Felix's attempt to steal his way to first. It should be an easy out. Guzmán fields the ball cleanly but then makes the smallest hesitation pulling the ball from his glove into his bare hand. All the while, Felix is up the first baseline—not slashing or churning or gritting teeth, but coolly swallowing up ground. When the ball reaches Jennings at first, Felix is already three strides past the bag, decelerating, looking back.

With two batters, neither of whom has laid wood to ball, the game is renewed, lifting the flagging spirits of *los fanaticos de* Los Leones. With the tying run stepping up to the plate, it is a moment of highest tension. The game seemed to be Licey's all night long, but now it is slipping away from them. The exuberance of the Escogido fans, reborn with their club's surge and fuelled by 100-proof rum, contrasts with the angst of the Licey fans along the third-base line.

Joe Ferguson has seen enough. He walks to the mound and then summons Ken Patterson. Guzmán listens to the cheers of the Licey fans and walks to the dugout. The Escogido fans cheer too—they are happy to see the end of Guzmán and the beginning of Patterson, a White Sox farmhand who has struggled lately and, it is rumoured, has a tired arm.

The first batter Patterson faces is Luis de los Santos. Patterson gets in front of the batter one-and-two but then de los Santos flares a ball into shallow centre field. Campusano can only watch it fall in for a single. Noboa reads the flight of the ball well and scores from second. Felix cannot advance past second in deference to Campusano's arm.

LICEY	000 002 001	3 8 0
ESCOGIDO	000 000 00	1 5 2

By now even the most confident Licey fans are apoplectic. Though Los Tigres still lead, the second-guessing begins: why did Ferguson pull Guzmán? After all, he was working on a shut-out and had only given up four hits through eight and a third innings. The radio announcers are working double-time and can be heard above the din two sections away. Geronimo Berroa is the next batter. With the tying run on first base, he steps into the box.

Cut to black—not a slow fade, but a sudden drop of a black curtain. It is night. A moment before, a panorama of baseball. Now a void. The lights have cut out a half-inning early. There are no sights in the gloamin' save the fires behind the outfield walls. The stars and moon are clouded over. There are no sights other than the fires because it is not only Estadio Quisqueya that has plunged into darkness, but, in fact, all of Santo Domingo. Exhaust from traffic and smoke from the garbage fires make the night all the more opaque.

There are only sounds. At first the cry that goes up from the stands is something like a chorus of laughter. Then follow howls of "*coño*" from the punters standing in the betting sections. The vendors try to hunt down the accounts outstanding. The soldiers, the protectors of order, have broken from their repose and are scrambling to secure the clubhouses, the ticket windows, and the stadium offices.

The effect of this blackout is at once paralysing and frightening. Although the rough and desperate barrios of Santo Domingo are not for the faint-hearted or the unarmed at any time—on these meanest streets, denizens pack knives and guns and other killing accessories—during a blackout, all the streets are mean. Santo Domingo becomes like a city during wartime, with soldiers stopping passers-by, with jeeps toting heavy-fire automatic weapons on every corner. Even in Estadio Quisqueya, after the novelty has worn off, darkness brings with it a siege mentality. Through all this nervous time and other such occasions the peace-loving among the patrons must give thanks to the weapons check at the front door.

I sit like most other fans in this section of the stands, with my hands in my pockets. Ramón the usher once advised me during a well-lit night game that I should applaud loud and fast so I can return my hands to my pockets quickly. The pickpockets, he said, don't mind if you're sitting down. They do their best work with stationary targets.

Such a blackout might cause panic, a riotous rush to the exits, among a citizenry spoiled by reliable utilities. The Dominicans, more practised in waiting through such hardships, too experienced to be surprised by them, try to laugh in the black. Those who were fast finishing their *cervezas* and *ron oro* slow down and start sipping their drinks.

Up in the press box, the *periodistas* have found candles and a flashlight and have spilled not so much as an ice cube. So mundane is the blackout that it will not even be mentioned in the morning papers.

After a time—about forty-five minutes, though eternity would seem brief by comparison—one of the bulbs in a bank of dozens lights up in the stanchion above and behind right field. Though no brighter than a firefly, the bulb draws the loudest roar of this night of much loud roaring. The power is returning slowly, uncertainly, like so many things in the Dominican.

As each bulb on this stanchion draws power and begins to glow, at first dimly and then with its usual intensity, the crowd lets out cries of "Whoa. Whoa. Whoa. Whoa. Whoa." It's a rolling cheer, repeated with the rhythm of waves lapping on a shore. When the few bulbs begin to shine, a strange tableau begins to be revealed on the field. It is almost dreamlike in its grainy indistinctness and absurdity. Not only have the *fanaticos* stayed in their seats, but most of the players have remained in their positions: Domingo Michel is sitting down in left field; Gilberto Reyes is standing with hands on hips talking to the ump behind the plate; Belliard, the third baseman, is talking to Eddie Dennis, Escogido's third-base coach. As the lights intensify, Licey's centre fielder, Silvestre Campusano, and its short-tempered shortstop, Juan Bell, are engaged in a game of pepper. Felix, the base runner, plays along; in lieu of his mitt, he uses his helmet to snag the ball. Joining this trio is a youngster, a little barefoot *manicero* who had run out onto the field under cover of darkness. Soon the cheers for the lights are accompanied by cheers for acrobatic plays in this game of pepper, most loudly for those of the young *manicero*. And soon, once this stanchion in right field is fully lit, one bulb on the stanchion in deadaway centre is alight. The process repeats itself. Cheers go up for every bulb. And then to the stanchion in left, the stanchions along the third-base line behind the Licey sections in the stands, the stanchion behind home plate and the neutral territory, and finally the stanchion along the first-base line and behind the Escogido section. The power has returned to the lights sequentially, one lap around the stadium, bringing the players and the game slowly, systematically into view.

The umpires call the managers out to the plate. The directive is clearly stated. If the lights go out again, there will be no waiting; the game will be called immediately. Ferguson is happier with the decision than Regan, but the Escogido manager realizes that he, like the stadium a few minutes ago, is powerless.

Before the game Ken Patterson, a pitcher with a tired arm and a Yanqui tired of the Dominican Republic, said to a teammate that "one day I'm writing a book about my season in the Dominican". Whether or not there would be material enough to warrant such a tome, his position now at this point of crisis has the makings of a short story. He has not been able to throw for forty-five minutes. The game is slipping away from Licey.

Play resumes with Berroa at the plate. The right fielder, who may or may not be a cousin of a prospect at El Complejo Epy, crushes a ball to deadaway centre. From the moment the ball is airborne, it's clear that this will carry the 411 feet to the fence. All that is in question is whether it will clear the high green fence that knocks many prodigous shots down for doubles. The ball reaches, reaches, and then rebounds off the fence just two feet shy of clearing it. Campusano fields the ball on the track, but it is a throw of such distance that Berroa is able to come into third base standing up. The game is tied.

LICEY	000 002 001	3 8 0
ESCOGIDO	000 000 00	3 6 2

The winning run is now ninety feet from the plate. Patterson is distraught. Nobody is warming up in Licey's bullpen. Young Vizcaíno is in the on-deck circle, but Regan calls him back to the dugout. Rufino Linares, the ancient batsmen, will pinch-hit for him.

Ferguson walks to the mound and tells Patterson to walk Linares. Better that any other batter try to beat us. Four pitches later, Linares is on first, the double play in order and Sammy Sosa, the right fielder, is coming to the plate. A sacrifice fly will end the game.

Sosa hits a one-strike pitch, popping it up just twenty feet onto the outfield grass in centre field. Campusano, a busy man in the ninth, fields it, throws to cutoff. Berroa can't advance. Two down. Sasser is the scheduled batter.

Regan again will pinch hit. This time it is Domingo Martínez who steps first to the on-deck circle and then to the plate. Martínez is an overweight first baseman in the Toronto organization who has virtually eaten himself out of a shot at the majors and into a career in the middle minors. He cannot field well enough to be any use in the winter league. With a forty-five-year-old runner on first and a lumbering batter who can scarcely run by a concessionaire, Patterson has reason to hope that neither will leg out a cheap hit.

A ball. A strike, swinging at a fastball. A ball and then another. And then Martínez lines a shot that bounces once into Domingo Michel's glove in left field. Michel holds the ball. Berroa scores. Delirium. After a pause the final entry is made on the scoreboard:

LICEY	000 002 001	3 8 0
ESCOGIDO	000 000 004	4 7 2

The Escogido bench runs on to the field, congratulating Geronimo Berroa, who scored the winning run, and Martínez, who cashed him in. An improbable ending to an improbable evening. Typical.

This is the Dominican game, eventful and chaotic. Will it ever start? is the question at the beginning; Will it never end? is the plaint later that same night. The outcome of the game is as uncertain as the lighting. The game brings together people of peculiar customs and habits. The players are sometimes unpredictable, sometimes unreliable. They are never dull.

Like the American version, the Dominican game brings together men of varying fortunes, not only haves and have-nots, but hads, wanna-haves, and shoulda-hads too. It brings together men desperate to succeed and others bent on wasting their considerable talents. It brings together men of varying fortunes, although their fortunes vary more widely than those involved in the American game. To shed light on the Dominican players is only as difficult as illuminating a single game; that is, it is sometimes all but impossible.

This night is at an end. Pepe Lucas turns his back on the field and walks to the Escogido dugout as a hundred kids run onto the field to mob Martínez and the others. Lucas has no time for such foolishness.

Out above the 411 sign in centre field, violating the custom of the country, the Dominican flag is being hoisted to the top of the flagpole. It must be an Escogido fan who mans the ropes. Even the most patriotic supporter of Licey would let the colours fly no higher than half-mast. And as the children run on to the field, as the fans in red celebrate, and those in blue grieve, as Los Leones exchange high-fives, as Phil Regan heads for a cold shower, the Dominican flag waves in the smoky breeze.

Epilogue

Playoff spots at the end of the 1988–89 season for El Torneo de Beisbol Dominicano weren't decided until the last week of the season. Because of many rain-outs in the last few weeks of the season, rescheduling became a headache. Caimanes del Sur, Maximo Lovaton's near-bankrupt team, played three games against three different teams in the two cities on the last day of the season. Unfortunately for Caimanes and Maximo, the team was eliminated in the second game on that last day, but still had to play the third game because it could have had a bearing on a playoff spot. In the end, Licey was regular-season champion, and Santiago, Estrellas Orientales, and Escogido filled out the other spots in the round-robin. The outcome of the playoffs was as unpredictable as the weather had been all winter. Escogido, zero and seven to open the season, knocked off all-powerful Licey in the final. Phil Regan's Leones fared less well in the Caribbean World Series and did not defend their title in Mazatlán. Zulia of the Venezuelan League won the C.W.S.

For the people around the game between Licey and Escogido that winter, fortunes varied. After the 1988–89 Dominican winter-league season, a few players were blown around by the major-league trade winds. Mariano Duncan was traded from the

Dodgers to the Cincinnati Reds; Sammy Sosa was sent from the Rangers to the White Sox; Domingo Michel won the Triple Crown and later was bought by the Tigers from the Dodgers' minor-league roster. But these were simply coincidental changes when compared to the upheaval and dissent in the Blue Jays organization.

Epy Guerrero, sounded a sour note in the usually harmonious Toronto Blue Jays camp just a few weeks after I talked with him at El Complejo Epy. During spring training, in an article in the *Globe and Mail*, Guerrero talked about leaving the Jays. He accused the ballclub of racism in their handling of its young Dominican prospects. His problems with minor-league director Bobby Mattick were erupting again. Guerrero cited two young prospects in particular: Jimy Kelly, the shortstop who as a thirteen-year-old signed with Guerrero, was being dispatched to A-ball after spending the '88 season with Double A Knoxville; and Junior Felix, the fleet outfielder who seemed to have won a spot on the big-league roster with a stellar training camp, was being sent down to the minors.

After his complaints to the press, Guerrero was called in to meet with his old friend Pat Gillick and the Blue Jays' management. Guerrero then recanted for the public record, denied any dissention, and claimed to have been misquoted.

His complaints in spring training could hardly have been assuaged by developments during the '89 season. Though Felix was promoted to the big-league club and starred for a couple of months before slumping at the end of the season, a good number of Jays' prospects from the Dominican were on their way out of the organization.

Jimy Kelly struggled in A-ball and was dropped from the Jays' forty-man roster; the Mets purchased him in the minor-league draft for $12,500.

Sil Campusano, the erstwhile Best Prospect in the Minor Leagues, the kid who couldn't miss, missed. After an indifferent season in Syracuse, Campusano was left unprotected by Toronto, and the Philadelphia Phillies claimed him in the draft for $50,000; if the Phils want to hold on to Campusano he'll have to remain on their big-league roster for the duration of 1990, or be offered back to the Jays for $25,000. Even at the 50 per cent markdown, Toronto may not buy him back. Campusano's recent form shows that he'd be no bargain. Late in the Dominican winter-league season of '89–'90, Campusano was again playing part time for Licey and barely hitting .100.

Other Dominicans fared little better. José Nuñez was traded to the Chicago Cubs for left-hander Paul Kilgus. Catcher Francisco Cabrera was dispatched to Atlanta in a trade for pitcher Jim Acker.

Nelson Liriano maintained a spot on the big-league roster but divided his time with Manny Lee. Neither one was able to step forward into a full-time role and, as always, both were mentioned in trade talks.

By the start of training camp of 1990, much of the Jays' deep pool of Dominican talent had been drained, though it was not yet dry. Domingo Cedeño had an excellent season in Myrtle Beach. Though the Jays selected Eddie Zosky, a shortstop from Fresno State, with their first-round draft pick, either Zosky or Cedeño will inherit Tony Fernández's job at shortstop a few years from now. Cedeño's stock in the organization remains high. Still, the cases of Kelly and Campusano suggest that Guerrero's theory is true, that the Dominican kids have to be better just to be equal with the Americans. While many American players in their mid-twenties are groomed in the minors for the big leagues, the Jays ran out of patience with Kelly while he was still a teenager, and with Campusano in his early twenties. In fact, it seems that the Dominicans not only have to be better, but better faster.

George Bell has established club records for excellence and outrage. In 1989 he kept pace in both categories. Early in the season, as the Jays struggled, he was suspended for charging the mound against Oakland's Gene Nelson. A few weeks later he struck the last hit in Exhibition Stadium, a dramatic, game-winning home run. Through the press he told fans that if they didn't like him they could kiss "his purple ass". He then went on a tear, a twenty-one-game hitting streak, that by itself virtually lifted the Jays back into the pennant race. At season's end the Jays won the American League East and Bell, with his 104 RBIs, finished fourth in the Most Valuable Player voting. He later stated that on merit he should have been awarded the MVP. But those who cast the ballots, the sportswriters, denied him another medal on his broad chest.

Tito Bell did not fare as well. After being touted as a replacement for Cal Ripken at shortstop in Baltimore, Tito spent most of the season in the minors. He was called up in September, and the man he was supposed to be supplanting, Cal Ripken, was on his way to a third-place finish in the League MVP voting, one spot better than Tito's older brother. By the time Tito took the field against George's team, it was the last Sunday of the season, a meaningless game after the Jays had clinched the pennant. Nevertheless, Tito remains prized by the Orioles, though he wasn't handed the shortstop job in 1990's spring training.

George Bell's friends and neighbours did not have a stellar season. Although Alfredo Griffin did lead Estrellas Orientales into the Dominican winter-league playoffs, he could work no miracles with the Dodgers. For Griffin and many of his teammates, it was a return to earth after their World Series victory. The 1990 season will likely be Griffin's last go-round in the big leagues, at least as a full-time player. Joaquín Andújar was less fortunate. He did not gain the invitation to spring training in '89 that he longed for. But Andújar did pitch for small change in the Senior Baseball League, the thirty-five-and-over circuit in Florida. He fared well enough to earn an invitation to the desperate-for-pitching Expos in the spring of '90, but was let go.

In '89, the Expos took a chance on another long-in-the-tooth Dominican, Dámaso García. When the Expos extended an invitation without guarantees to García, newspapers, including the *Globe and Mail*, inaccurately reported that Dámasito had played with Licey in the winter league. He had only played around with Los Tigres and never even dressed for a game. Yet, miracle of miracles, García not only won a spot on the Expos' Opening Day roster, he hit a homer in his first game with Montreal. Unfortunately, the marriage was never as good as the wedding day. In mid-September, the Expos were out of the pennant race, and sent García home early. But the Yankees signed García in December of '89, and he made the club the following spring.

The year was less eventful for others at that winter-league game between Licey and Escogido.

Ralph Avila, the Dodgers' honcho, must be satisfied with the progress of his young prospects, particularly José Oferman, who tore up Double A ball and seems a year away from the majors.

I saw the Contract God in Florida and he is still rounding up naïve young players and "negotiating" for tomorrow's champions.

There's no word from Julio. He may have made it all the way to New York. And I never found out who bought his glove. Juarino is still doing body work in Punta, and has never returned to El Complejo Epy.

Rico Carty did not follow Andújar to the Senior Baseball League, as he had threatened to do, but he did attend a couple of senior tournaments (at $1,000 a throw) and made his usual appearances at old-timers' games (at a similar rate).

Yesterday's heroes, Silvano Quezada, Pepe Lucas, and Telelito Vargas are still working their respective stations. Finally, one who would be great, Alfredo Arias, hasn't yet won his ticket off the island.

Printed in Canada